# The Rule of Law

For Hilary, as always

# The Rule of Law

## The Common Sense of Global Politics

Christopher May

*Professor of Political Economy, Lancaster University, UK*

**Edward Elgar**
Cheltenham, UK • Northampton, MA, USA

Published by
Edward Elgar Publishing Limited
The Lypiatts
15 Lansdown Road
Cheltenham
Glos GL50 2JA
UK

Edward Elgar Publishing, Inc.
William Pratt House
9 Dewey Court
Northampton
Massachusetts 01060
USA

A catalogue record for this book
is available from the British Library

Library of Congress Control Number: 2013957777

This book is available electronically in the ElgarOnline.com
Social and Political Science Subject Collection, E-ISBN 978 1 78100 895 9

ISBN 978 1 78100 894 2 (cased)

Typeset by Servis Filmsetting Ltd, Stockport, Cheshire
Printed and bound in Great Britain by T.J. International Ltd, Padstow

# Contents

# Preface

No one should start a book with an apology but I feel it is necessary to make one point about this book. As you read the discussions I have set out in the following chapters, you will discover that the rule of law is a very complex issue but if you are looking for an 'answer' I am unable to provide it. Certainly, this is a book about the rule of law, but what I am most interested in is the rule of law as a figure of political speech or commentary. I will discuss the legal issues but this is explicitly not a book of jurisprudence or legal commentary.

My aim is to set out a range of issues linked to the rule of law that have either been underplayed in work on the international (or global) political economy and associated fields, such as global governance, or have been missed entirely through the uncritical use of the term the 'rule of law'. I seek to reveal this shortcoming and hopefully spur others to explore many of the loose ends that appear herein. This book, therefore, maps a field of investigation that I, and perhaps others, will explore in more detail in the next few years. I fully expect that some readers will find things to object to in the following chapters, and I welcome the argument(s) this will spur with and among colleagues, encouraging them to engage with these ideas; I seek to provoke a conversation about the rule of law beyond the realm of legal analysis.

This is to say, this book is an examination of the rule of law, as the common sense of global politics, for those with an interest in the law but little if any formal legal training; it is a book for those who find themselves confronted with the oft-repeated political mantra(s) of the rule of law, and like me have wondered what it might mean and how this discourse seems to have been elevated to a set of commonplaces. Let me also say that although I would regard myself as a political economist of some description, this is a work of interdisciplinary investigation, a work of pluralist (perhaps even post-disciplinary) social analysis. I range widely across various disciplines in the chapters that follow and while I start from a place one might call (critical) political economy, I do not see the scope of this study as limited to the boundaries that might be posited when using this description of an analytical intent; I return to this issue in the methodological interlude.

Given that you may be familiar with my previous work on intellectual property rights (IPRs), let me say (briefly) how that research led me to the issue(s) that I investigate in this book. Much of my work on IPRs focused on how intellectual property was legitimated or justified in contemporary (global) discourse with an attendant interest in the divergence between such political or analytical claims and the social impact of making knowledge into property in the 'real' political economy.[1] Much of this work was concerned with the allocation of benefits and costs and how these were presented by, and to, those involved in the production and use of various forms of information and knowledge, as well of those devising governance structures in which and by which these activities take place. However, it became clear to me that there was an underlying substrata to these claims, narratives and legitimating discourses that I was interested in: key aspects of the political economic realm that I focused on – the World Trade Organization; The World Intellectual Property Organization, for instance – were legally defined institutions working with legal instruments and practices to prosecute an agenda normalizing and expanding the making of property from knowledge.

However, the question of whether the law was the correct mechanism for achieving the results posited as beneficial was seldom if ever discussed in policy debates (although some critics did raise the issue of appropriate mechanisms). It was more often the case that in issue areas such as traditional knowledge both sides of the debate sought to further their priorities through legal instruments. Indeed, it was the support of legal mechanisms to 'protect' traditional knowledge from commoditization into intellectual property, to (re)make traditional knowledge as a specific form of intellectual property that finally led me to wonder more seriously about this underlying (normative) foundation. After some preliminary investigation I came to the conclusion that across the various parties discussing the political economy of IPRs there was little departure from the acceptance, recognition and indeed promotion of the (rule of) law as a mode of resolving difficult political economic conflicts, tensions and divergences of interest. This acceptance was often not articulated but when advocates, policy makers or others did say anything they usually invoked the 'rule of law' as a background narrative of justification or normative anchor. Given that I had spent much of my time looking at IPRs being concerned with such narratives as they were deployed in the political economy of intellectual property, my curiosity was aroused and I have now set out my concerns in this book that you hold in your hands.

---

[1] That work is presented and summarized in May (2010), which represents a review and synthesis of over a decade of reflection and research on the subject of intellectual property.

\*   \*   \*

This book has been in gestation for some years, and I have presented some elements of the work here in various forums over the last five years; many people, who I shamefacedly admit I cannot remember, have offered all sorts of useful advice about sources I might look at, issues I should include and glaring lapses of analytical coherence that I should avoid. I thank all of these people, even if I am unable to name them here. However, I am particularly grateful for the help and advice that the following people have offered during these years: Andrew Baker, Israel Butler, Ed Cohen, Claire Cutler, Morley Frishman, Stephen Gill, Katharina Glaab, Colin Hay, Jan Klabbers, Anna Leander, Suzanne Ost, Morten Ougaard, Sol Picciotto, Peter Rowe, Len Seabrooke, David Seymour, Jason Sharman, Adriana Sinclair, David Sugarman, Teivo Teivainen, Kate Weaver and Antje Wiener. Most helpfully Steven Wheatley of Lancaster Law School very kindly read the entire manuscript after I had completed the first draft and offered some very helpful advice and comments as regards the structure and development of the argument, which helped me immeasurably in my work on the subsequent drafting. Likewise, I am grateful to Stephen Royle who did most of the leg work on *The Economist* editorials and thus saved me a lot of time and effort in the second half of my sabbatical when it looked like I would not get the manuscript finished in time.

While finishing off the first draft of this book I was also lucky enough to read Michael Billig's *How to Write Badly: How to Succeed in the Social Sciences* (Billig 2013) and while working on the subsequent drafts I have tried to follow Billig's advice to be clearer, avoid the overuse of passive '-izations' and ensure that overly technical language does not hide a lack of actual interesting things to say. I hope that the draft has benefitted from Billig's analysis of what is wrong with writing in the social sciences, and if you have not had a look at his book, I thoroughly recommend it as a prompt to self-reflection about one's own writing practices.

Finally, as always I acknowledge the intellectual debt I owe to my father, whose influence remains with me 15 years after his passing. I also would not be able to do what I do without the support and love of my dear wife Hilary Jagger. In the main she is not that interested in the subjects I write about and this allows her to be an oasis of good taste, cultural sensibility and common sense that makes my life balanced, less self-obsessed and focused on matters other than the life of the university and its academic community.

Christopher May, November 2013

# Abbreviations

| | |
|---|---|
| ADB | Asian Development Bank |
| CDF | Comprehensive Development Framework |
| CIDA | Canadian International Development Agency |
| CLEP | Commission on Legal Empowerment of the Poor |
| DSM | dispute settlement mechanism |
| ECJ | European Court of Justice |
| EU | European Union |
| GATT | General Agreement on Tariffs and Trade |
| IBA | International Bar Association |
| ICJ | International Commission of Jurists |
| IDLO | International Development Law Organization |
| IMF | International Monetary Fund |
| IPE | International Political Economy |
| IPRs | intellectual property rights |
| IR | International Relations |
| JAG | Judge Advocate General |
| MDGs | Millennium Development Goals |
| NGO | non-governmental organization |
| OECD | Organisation for Economic Co-operation and Development |
| OPEC | Organization of the Petroleum Exporting Countries |
| SIDA | Swedish International Development Authority |
| UN | United Nations |
| UNMIK | United Nations Interim Administration in Kosovo |
| UNSC | United Nations Security Council |
| UNTAC | United Nations Transitional Authority in Cambodia |
| WDR | *World Development Report* |
| WJP | World Justice Project |
| WTO | World Trade Organization |

# Introduction: the rule of law as the common sense of global politics

The rule of law is humanity's greatest creation, the essential precondition of a civilised, just society. (Schuck 2000, p. 454)

It is difficult to find anyone, whether in government, foundations, corporations or universities, who does not favour encouraging the rule of law in virtually every country and society. (Upham 2004, p. 280)

In an age of images and symbols, elections are easy to capture on film. But how do you televise the rule of law? (Zakaria 2003, p. 156)

The rule of law is often presented as preferable to the rule of men or the rule of force, and as I will argue throughout this book, this has become the common sense of global politics, an unquestioned statement about the world in which we live. To make my starting point clear, it seems to me that common sense includes three elements: norms (preferred practices); ideas (arguments and reasons to support such norms); and rhetoric (discussion of the settled character of such practices).[1] Thus, a common sense notion is a set of practices or actions that are regarded as if not natural, then certainly not requiring extensive or detailed justification. When we push we might encounter statements about why these actions are sensible and require little justification, but common sense is mostly seen as unobjectionable and seldom subject to any extensive critical discussion. The discussion and rhetoric of any common sense takes its practices (and their associated reasons) for granted, often failing to specify them in anything other than a bland and/or allusive manner. I will expand on the role of common sense when I explore 'social imaginaries' in the next chapter, and as I develop the argument throughout the book I hope that what I mean when I say the rule of law is a common sense of global politics will become clear; it is an idea whose alternates seem unwelcome or nonsensical without requiring any detailed discussion of the reason(s) for this preference.

---

[1] I thank Andrew Baker for helping to clarify my idea of common sense and an anonymous publisher's reviewer of the manuscript for suggesting this should be clearly established at the start.

As you would expect, later in this book I will explore in some detail how we might define and understand the rule of law, but here and before going further, it will be useful to at least offer a brief sketch. Adriaan Bedner's recent survey of debates about what constitutes the rule of law helpfully offers a concise scoping of the issue. He suggests that the rule of law is generally seen as serving two clear functions: 'to curb arbitrary and inequitable use of state power' and 'to protect citizens' property and lives from infringements or assaults by fellow citizens' (Bedner 2010, pp. 50, 51). Bedner acknowledges continuing debates about the rule of law, but sorts the elements that are commonly appealed to into three general categories. First, there are 'procedural' elements:

- rule by law; state actions are subject to the law
- law is formalized (clear, certain/fixed; accessible and predictable in application)
- democracy (consent can determine or at least influence legal actions) (Bedner 2010, pp. 56–63).

These procedural elements are complemented by a number of 'substantive' elements:

- law is subordinate to justice
- individual rights and liberties are to be protected
- human rights are respected, as are group rights (Bedner 2010, pp. 63–7).

Finally, he also includes two 'controlling' mechanisms or guardian institutions:

- an independent judiciary
- administrative and other independent bodies are responsible for reviewing legal process (Bedner 2010, pp. 67–9).

Much of this will become increasingly familiar as you read on.

Consequently, debates about the rule of law usually revolve around the relative importance of various of these elements with some commentators arguing that only the procedural aspects are required to assert that the rule of law obtains (a 'thin' view of the rule of law), while others (arguing for the law as a moral value) maintain that without the more substantive aspects no society can be said to enjoy the rule of law (often termed a 'thick' view). There are also debates about which aspects of the law might belong in which category! Some authors, such as Nigel Simmonds (2007), reject these oppositions, insisting that the law is always a moral (or thick) concept because it is never merely descriptive but rather is always an aspiration about the ordering and governing of society (in its distinction from the rule of force or personal fiat). These debates led Jeremy Waldron to suggest that the rule of law is actually an essentially contested concept (Waldron 2002), and consequently, we must understand it not as an absolute that is either present or absent but rather the sort of norm that will vary in degree across all its elements (Waldron 2008, p. 44), requiring nuanced and qualified assessments of some complexity.

There is much more to be said about how we might understand the rule of law and the elements that make up the threshold conditions for an acceptable claim to be made that the rule of law exists in any specific society or community. However, before starting to unpack the rule of law, in this Introduction I will look at the various political discourses that celebrate the rule of law (including a specific discussion of the World Bank's position), as well as the more public discussions in the news media (exemplified by, but not limited to, *The Economist*). The rhetoric of the rule of law encourages a widespread (although unevenly developed) consciousness of its claimed value, and most importantly influences 'modes of thought' by being integrated into individuals' world-view, normalizing the law so that even in extra-legal activity the law is always there as a potential alternative for the resolution of conflict (Berman 2005, pp. 493–5). I have chosen the examples below to illustrate the recitation of the rule of law as a common sense, but they are also intended to begin to show how rhetoric plays a role in (re)producing the dynamic that I examine in subsequent chapters. Unfortunately, conclusively demonstrating the domination of a political discourse that privileges law would require a much more detailed study than this book has space for. Rather, here I will explore some of the contours of the rhetoric of the rule of law, trusting that this will find an echo in your own experience of discussions of (global) politics in the media, and expert and academic commentary as well as elsewhere when global politics is talked about.

It is often observed in the specialist literature that the idea of, and the term, the rule of law has progressively become more widely used in recent decades. As Pietro Costa and Danilo Zolo point out, today the 'expression the "rule of law" is remarkably widespread, not only in political and legal literature but, most notably, in newspapers and political language' (Costa and Zolo 2007, p. ix). Likewise, at the turn of the millennium Adam Bouloukos and Brett Dakin observed: 'In recent years, no discussion of international development or debate over foreign policy has been complete without some mention of the "rule of law"' (Bouloukos and Dakin 2001, p. 145). More recently, Stephen Holmes argued that the rhetoric of the rule of law has been 'successful in globalising that set of ideas, and associating them with certain constructions of the legal, the social and the economic'; it is a 'term of art that saturates contemporary political life and accommodates increasingly broad political desires' (Holmes 2010, pp. 220, 224). Indeed, it is a term freighted with emotion, as Frederick Schauer has observed: 'Insofar as legal systems are perceived to have achieved some measure of success, "the rule of law" becomes synonymous with "the good things about the legal system"' (Schauer 1989, p. 70). However, Waldron notes, it sometimes seems as if it has no more meaning than a manner of cheering 'Hooray for our side' (Waldron 2002, p. 139); it may be little more than a rhetorical flourish. Thus, certainly in debates about governance and government, the rhetoric of the rule of law is common, and may well have been one of the earliest enlightenment values of modernity to be espoused (Sampford 2006, p. 275), but it remains remarkably indeterminate, being frequently evoked on both sides of an argument.

This lack of fixed meaning may actually make the term attractive. As Balakrishnan Rajagopal suggests in his discussion of post-conflict rule of law support programmes, the rule of law is often preferred to a discourse of human rights precisely because it is largely 'empty of content and capable of being interpreted in many diverse, sometimes contradictory ways' (Rajagopal 2008, p. 1359). It may be that the term itself can be regarded as less emotional to invoke than 'human rights' and therefore may serve the interests of those wishing to take a quieter road towards democratization (and liberalization) (Bouloukos and Dakin 2001, p. 158). Thus, generally the rule of law seems to carry with it less problematic intellectual baggage than other developmental terminology and can be presented as non-political in difficult (post-conflict) situations where political order is fragile (or failing).

## THE POPULAR RHETORIC OF THE RULE OF LAW

If the rule of law is now common sense we would expect to find it popping up frequently and widely in discussions of all sorts of global politics. Indeed, Andrew Cortell and James Davis have observed that the 'first sign of an international norm's domestic impact is its appearance in the domestic political discourse' and as it becomes more salient it will be the violation of its strictures that will need to be justified not its observance or adoption (Cortell and Davis 2000, pp. 70–1). This is clearly evident, for example, in the political arguments around the (non-)prosecution of British Aerospace relating to bribery in the al-Yammamah/Saudi Arabia arms contract made by the then UK Attorney General (Lord Goldsmith);

while acknowledging the 'need to maintain the rule of law', he asserted
that it was subordinate to *realpolitik* concerns around 'security, intel-
ligence and diplomatic cooperation' with the Saudis.[2] In response to the
continued non-prosecution, Eric Metcalfe of *Justice* noted that it was
'a sad day for the rule of law when a senior prosecutor bows to threat
from a foreign government and our most senior judges will do nothing
to stop it'.[3] Indeed, much of the political discussion of this case as it
worked its way through the UK courts for two years involved its impact
on the UK's reputation for abiding by the rule of law, not least of all
as non-prosecution broke commitments made when the UK signed the
Organisation for Economic Co-operation and Development's (OECD)
anti-bribery convention.

Leaving the impact the rule of law has on political practice for later,
here I am concerned with the articulation of the rule of law in these
domestic (popular) discussions and debates. In this I agree with Andrew
Loomis's suggestion that it is

> reasonable to assume that the mass public is less cognizant than elites of highly
> sophisticated cause–effect relationships, but more likely to privilege policies
> perceived to be based on principles that coincide with widely accepted societal
> values derived from the national experience. (Loomis 2012, p. 83)

While popular politics may have little engagement with the jurisprudential
debates I discuss later, the more general notion of the importance of the
rule of law has much more salience and political purchase (not least as it
is amenable to quite radical simplification). Moreover, this may relate to
popular conceptions of what constitutes a country's political character
(Loomis 2012, p. 87). Recently Roger Scruton, in discussing the values of
British society, argued that the 'rule of law requires a shared allegiance, by
which people entrust their collective destiny to sovereign institutions that
can speak and decide in their name', emphasising the manner in which
British law was able to articulate *our* values by virtue of the development
of common law *as* the rule of law (Scruton 2013). And interestingly,
Lord Goldsmith, prior to his decision in the al-Yammamah case, himself
observed that the rule of law 'crops up in the [British] press as being something that defines our society . . . [a]nd regimes which engage in abhorrent
practices such as torture are condemned for their failure to respect the
rule of law' (Goldsmith 2006, p. 4). These invocations of the rule of law
often seem to have a multi-layered meaning; something quite clear and

---

[2] 'The BAE affair sends all the wrong signals', *Observer*, 17 December 2006, p. 24.
[3] Quoted in 'Timid justice: BAE and the Saudi arms deal', *The Economist*, 2 August 2008,
   p. 37.

simple for popular appeal, alongside a more legalistic understanding for specialists. Thus, Goldsmith maintains a simple definition for his audience – government to be constrained by law; it is not merely rule *by* law but has some normative content; and universal application – while also pointing to a more complex literature that he is bypassing for ease of argumentation (Goldsmith 2006, pp. 4–8). This is one important key to the rule of law's growing appeal as a global political common sense; its flexibility in use.

The notion of the rule of law certainly has significant popular currency. In the trailer for the film of the stage play *Frost/Nixon*, a quote from the original interview of 19 May 1977 was used, and spoken by the actor playing President Nixon: 'When the President does it, that means that it is not illegal.' Clearly intended to be a shock by virtue of David Frost's in-film response, and where it was placed in the trailer, this suggests how widely the norm of the rule of law (as opposed to the rule of the individual) may be accepted, even by those who would probably find it difficult to describe its more formal dimensions. In a different sort of example, in 2009 Andrew Young (a US clergyman with strong civil rights interests) was quoted as saying, 'Nothing is illegal if one hundred well-placed business-men decide to do it.'[4] A remark that was clearly presented as ironic by the *Financial Times*, again, testifying to the common acceptance of the norm of the rule of law. More explicitly, a distinguished UK senior judge, (the late) Lord Bingham, noted that the rule of law is 'constantly on people's lips' (Bingham 2010, p. vii), although he worried that is not well understood, even as it is deployed in political discussion and debate.[5] Three year's pre-viously, Scott Horton, writing in the US magazine *Harpers*, had set out a critique of the Bush Administration's policy towards Guantanamo detain-ees as a 'war on the rule of law', which he defined utilizing a discussion of British legal history (Horton 2007).

As these four examples begin to suggest, within our (globalized) politi-cal discourse the importance of abiding by the rule of law has significant appeal, with the norm widely discussed in a range of places. In another example, in Joseph Stiglitz's recent intervention into debates about inequality, he spends some pages focusing on the rule of law primar-ily as regards access to justice, although he appears to see no need to define or explore the term more generally (Stiglitz 2013, pp. 234–58). A more detailed account runs through much of Niall Ferguson's revision-ist celebration of the British Empire (a book and TV series). Here, the British concern with law and the introduction of common law procedures and practices is presented as having had a significant developmental

---

[4] Andrew Young, 'Wit and wisdom', *FT Magazine*, 6 June 2009, p. 13.
[5] See my discussion of the book in May (2011).

pay-off for post-colonial states lucky enough to have been part of the Empire; indeed he concludes that 'we should not underestimate the benefits conferred by British law and administration' (Ferguson 2003, p. 361). Moreover, he argues that due to the increasing liberal character of imperial policy the 'rule of law had to take precedence, regardless of skin colour' (Ferguson 2003, p. 195), and as such the imposition of this norm led to the establishment of legal systems that would subsequently be advantageous to societies in the post-imperial period. This presentation of the rule of law's centrality was expanded eight years later in his account of *Civilisation* where (in a triumph of anachronism) the rule of law is presented as one of the 'killer aps' for the achievement of a modern civilized society (Ferguson 2011). Likewise, in Samuel Huntington's widely cited and discussed *Clash of Civilisations* the rule of law is listed as one of the key distinguishing characteristics of Western society (Huntington 2002, p. 70), a significant change from the position he had adopted earlier (discussed in the next section). These books have been widely discussed in the media, with their authors approached for comment pieces and TV or radio appearances, and as such the rule of law as popular rhetoric has been reinforced through use.

In another widely discussed recent volume, *Why Nations Fail*, Daron Acemoglu and James Robinson similarly suggest that the rule of law is a key component in the political virtuous circle they see supporting economic development. Focusing on political institutions and the incidence of inequality, the authors regard the rule of law as an integral part of the progressive establishment of a pluralist polity that can support the innovation and enterprise that supported (and supports) successful economic development (Acemoglu and Robinson 2012, pp. 302–34, *passim*). They see the rule of law as a norm that by virtue of its own logic may serve the needs of the wealthy, but thereby also protects and supports the rights of the general populace.[6] However, the norm is underspecified in this account, with its contours sketched in around only one (albeit important) element; equality in law. The authors indicate that the rule of law is more than just procedure, and identify equality of treatment as the manner in which it differs from the rule *by* law (where laws can be applied to different groups differently), but their treatment of the rule of law overall remains underdeveloped.

That there are now popular academic books that stress the rule of law as a key component in economic development is indicative of the manner in which in the past 20 years the discussion of the rule of law has migrated from the limited and narrow legal specialist publications, where for years

---

[6] A parallel to E.P. Thompson, to whom I return later.

the ins and outs of its definition had been explored, to a situation where the rule of law is a commonly deployed political term, increasingly requiring little explanation when used. This reached its apogee (perhaps) in the UK Constitutional Reform Act 2005 that explained (in full) in its first Article that: 'This Act does not adversely affect, (a) the existing constitutional principle of the rule of law'.[7] This left the work of defining it to others, with no indication of whether further detail was absent because it was not required, as everyone would know what was meant, or that in the drafting an insoluble dispute about meaning had arisen. It certainly worried Lord Bingham, who's last book (Bingham 2010) was intended to set out an acceptable basis for understanding the term. This lack of a firm definition was also noted in the press, with Martin Kettle of the *Guardian* asking: 'What does the rule of law actually mean? If we cannot say what the phrase means then it is not much use as a governing principle' (Kettle 2006) before setting out Bingham's conclusions. Bingham's book was (later) published by Allen Lane, a mass market publisher, and garnered significant attention across the media.

Nor should we forget that law and its practices have become a key element in popular culture: US TV series such as *Perry Mason, Boston Legal, Law & Order, The Good Wife, Ally McBeal* and *LA Law*[8] as well as UK series like *Rumpole of the Bailey, North Square, Silk, Judge John Deed* and *Kavanagh QC* have all aired on primetime TV and have no doubt contributed to the familiarity many have with legal terminology and even legal debates. Indeed, in her presidential address to the Law and Society Association in Glasgow in 1996, Susan Silbey suggested that through such programmes the 'practices and ideals of the law, the history and the fictions, become part of the engagement between social movements and corporate capital in diverse corners of the globe' (Silbey 1997, p. 221). If one might doubt the legal impact of TV programmes, Phillipe Sands has identified the role that the Fox TV series *24* played in contributing to the belief that torture was both effective and (legally) acceptable at Guantanamo Bay prison camp. As he makes clear in a number of places in *Torture Team* both military personnel and government legal advisers were enthusiastic watchers of *24* and explicitly referred to it in their discussions with Sands about procedures of interrogation at Guantanamo. This is not to claim a direct causal link but, as Sands suggests, it (de)sensitized various

---

[7] Available at http://www.legislation.gov.uk/ukpga/2005/4/contents (accessed 13 May 2013).

[8] For the top 25 legal TV series as voted for by the American Bar Association see http://www.abajournal.com/magazine/article/the_25_greatest_legal_tv_shows/ (accessed 4 February 2013).

individuals to the illegitimacy of torture (Sands 2008, pp. 73–4, 87–9, 272), indicating some influence over their views of the (rule of) law.

The result of all this talk of the rule of law has led anthropologists John and Jean Comaroff to observe that it 'is not unusual any more to hear the Euro-language of jurisprudence in the Amazon or Aboriginal Australia. Or among the poor of Mumbai, Madagascar, Cape Town and Trench Town' (Comaroff and Comaroff 2009, p. 34). In their overview of anthropological studies of governance they find numerous and widely spread examples of the shift of politics into the law, and the use of the idea(s) of the rule of law as a language through which the poor now often articulate their political demands. For instance, in upheavals around the judiciary in Pakistan, Abdullah Freed Khan has noted that across the country in interviews with farmers, workers and others mobilizing behind the popular lawyers' movement, the idea of the value of the rule of law had considerable popular currency (Khan 2010). This is also reflected in the reception of the work of Hernando de Soto and the Commission for the Legal Empowerment of the Poor, discussed in Chapter 5; de Soto's work has been much debated and again has expanded the recognition of the idea of the rule of law in the analysis of development and economic inequality. And, as I mentioned in the Preface, much of the discussion of how to protect traditional knowledge now encompasses legal solutions despite many indigenous communities' lack of legal structures and practices that could be compatible with (what we would now call) the rule of law.

It seems likely that the discourse of the rule of law has become so common partly due to its expanding use in the press. Writing in the *Wall Street Journal* at the turn of the millennium, the columnist Paul Johnson suggested that the 'most important political development of the second millennium was the firm establishment, first in one or two countries, then in many, of the rule of law' (Johnson 1999). Focusing in the first instance on equality before the law and everyone being subject to it, Johnson offers a potted history of the rule of law that dates its first 'emergence' around the eleventh and twelfth centuries before plotting a course that, while recognizing crucial British developments, accords greatest value to the constitutional innovations of the American revolution. For some, this tradition has been forgotten. Discussing the Parliamentary Debate about the fate of Abu Qatada, Peter Oborne lamented, under the title 'The rule of law in Britain is diminished by the furore over efforts to deport Abu Qatada to Jordan', that the MPs seemed to have forgotten the UK's long legal history and sought to extra-legally deport a man who has committed no crime in the UK (however unpleasant one might regard him to be). He complained that:

It has been very clear for a long time that something has gone wrong with British justice. A succession of Home Secretaries have targeted, at different times, each of the central principles that underlie the national system of law: trial by jury, habeas corpus, free speech, as well as the abiding tenet that there should be a strict separation of powers between the judiciary and the executive. (Oborne 2012)

The latter (partial) list will appear again as the book proceeds, as these are well-rehearsed elements of the norm of the rule of law.

Elsewhere, in light of the continuing revelations of illegal practices at international banks, before and during the financial crisis that broke in 2008, some have called for the return of the rule of law to the financial sector. For instance, Democratic Senator Ted Kaufman argued in the *New York Times* in 2010 that there was a need to 'return the rule of law to Wall Street, which has been seriously eroded by the deregulatory mindset that captured our regulatory agencies over the past 30 years' (Kaufman 2010). However, the appeal to the rule of law is not limited to the (global) political economy; its normative remit spreads much further. In summer 2011, after a controversy regarding the conduct of an English cricketer, James Lawton of the *Independent* entitled his discussion of the day's troubles: 'Rule of law is trampled on to protect "spirit of the game"' (Lawton 2011). The discussion didn't invoke the norm in any detail, but clearly assumed that the rule of law itself (including the 'laws' of cricket) is an important value to be upheld. More normally the appeal to the rule of law is focused on the political realm, whether (in the UK) it was controversy over Archbishop Williams's comments on Sharia law (leading to critics invoking the rule of law against such legal pluralism) or complaints about the UK government's suspected complicity in the illegal rendition of terrorist suspects for interrogation. From discussions of the reach of News International's control of the press to the role of Twitter in libel cases, from the death of UK nationals in foreign countries (such as the investigation of the murder of Neil Heywood in China in 2012) to discussions of corporate power, it is seldom long before someone refers to the rule of law as the standard against which behaviour and practices should be judged.

Unfortunately, a full and extensive survey of this media coverage would be unwieldy to conduct here and so I will focus on one exemplary publication; here I look at *The Economist* as an illustration of the widely read news media discourse around the rule of law.

## *THE ECONOMIST* AND THE RHETORIC OF THE RULE OF LAW

It seems likely that the news media helps to shape and influence discourses through repeated use of particular terms and tropes over a longish period. This influence is not a single cause of shifts in political ideas, but in important ways can affect the 'mood music' of political debates. *The Economist* is one of the few magazines that can make a reasonable claim to be a global publication; it is not part of the 'popular press' but has consistently positioned itself as the journal of record for the global business elite (Starr 2004, p. 377, 2008). Martha Starr concludes her detailed analysis of the magazine's coverage of globalization by arguing that its analysis

> alleviates anxieties about uncertainty and change by tracing out a familiar trajectory along which readers can orient themselves . . . *The Economist*'s coverage not only fulfils readers' expectations of being provided with high-quality analysis and information but it also supplies *a vision of the world and tools for identity construction and self-understanding* to factions of dominant groups seeking to define their strategies and positions in the changing global configuration. (Starr 2004, p. 395, emphasis added)

Indeed, she has argued that *The Economist* seeks to develop for its readers an authoritative view of the globalized economy (Starr 2008, p. 35). This authority is developed by presenting opponents and critics of neoliberal economics as misinformed or misunderstanding the evidence; here *The Economist*'s self-avowed focus on an analytical method is vital, rendering opposing argument as 'subjective' or 'particular' and thus to be discounted (Starr 2008, p. 49). Thus, in presenting the rule of law as a vital component to the contemporary global political economy, *The Economist* has contributed to, and reflected, the move to recognize it as underpinning progress and development. In the last 20 years the magazine has slowly normalized its treatment of the rule of law to the point that in the second decade of the new millennium there is little need to offer any ancillary remarks to convey the meaning; the editors just assume you know what they mean when they write the 'rule of law'; they expect readers to have become acclimatized to the rule of law. However, it was not always like that.

Because I am most interested in changes in how *The Economist* itself has presented the rule of law I am only going to discuss the 'op ed' pieces that precede the main news sections of the magazine, as it is here that the magazine's editorial views are set out explicitly and unapologetically. I have chosen to focus on *The Economist*'s articulation of the rule of law for

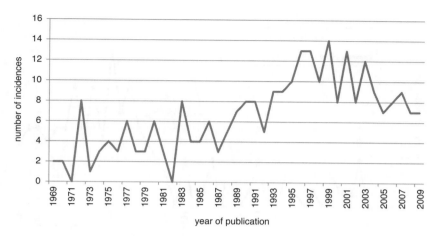

*Figure I.1    The rule of law in* The Economist: *combined incidence of term and norm elements*

20 years either side of 1989 (the end of the Cold War), not least as it seems to be the case that more generally the contemporary interest in the rule of law can be increasingly detected from the beginning of the 1990s, and I wanted to see if this was also indicated by the magazine's editorials. I will discuss both the incidence of explicit uses of the term in editorials and the uses of elements that one might regard as part of the rule of law norm (as drawn from the discussion in Chapter 2), even if these are not explicitly coded (in editorials) as the 'rule of law' (Figures I.1 and I.2).[9]

The first thing that is clear from the chart of combined mentions of the norm and its components is that there is a clear step change around the end of the Cold War. As far as the use of the term itself, the peak year is actually 1999 with ten editorials that year explicitly mentioning the rule of law, with the use of the elements (rather than the term) actually peaking four years earlier with seven editorials appealing to various rule of law norms (without explicitly using the term). Across the period the trend is clearly upwards with only two years containing no editorials mentioning the rule of law (or its elements); 1971 and 1982. The rule of law may not be central to the concerns of *The Economist* but we can nevertheless easily detect an expansion of its interest across these 40 years. Space precludes a detailed analysis of the content of 40 years of editorials (at five a week,

---

[9] The data analysis on which the following account is based was produced by Stephen Royle (my research assistant) and to whom I extend my thanks.

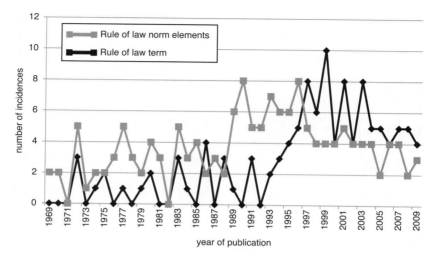

*Figure I.2    The rule of law in* The Economist: *incidence of term and incidence of norm elements*

over the period this amounts to 10,000 editorials), but it will be useful to have a look at a few snapshots of how the magazine has treated the rule of law over the years.

At the beginning of this 40-year period *The Economist* seemed relatively uninterested in the rule of law: in 1969 only two editorials mentioned anything related to the norm, and in both cases these were issues related to the need to enforce contract law.[10] Within the period examined, 1972 sees the first mentions of the term itself, although until 1985 it never features more than twice a year and in nearly half of these intervening years is not mentioned in an editorial at all. Perhaps unsurprisingly, many of the invocations of the rule of law and/or its normative elements in the early 1970s are related to questions linked to the manner in which unions are exercising their power and influence (and occasionally this theme is revived, for instance, in a 1983 editorial by which time the Thatcher government was changing union laws in the UK quite dramatically).[11] Later in the decade, the magazine's concern shifts to foreign affairs (crucially the rule of law in India and China) as well as the use of judicial review as a response to

[10] *The Economist*, 'Half a step onward', 4 January 1969, p. 5; 'In place of government', 21 June 1969, p. 5.

[11] See, for instance, *The Economist*, 'Stand or deliver', 6 May 1972, pp. 13–14; 'Rule of what?', 29 July 1972, pp. 11–13; 'So who does rule?', 11 May 1974, p. 13; 'Not for spiking', 3 December 1983, pp. 14–15.

a perceived decline in legality by the UK Labour government. The focus remains political, however, rather than making any extended link to economic development (as would develop later).[12] In the early 1980s the concern for the rule of law abroad remains, but an issue that continues to be of considerable salience starts to be discussed: the relationship between terrorism and the rule of law. Here, the defence of liberalism is only possible if the rule of law is extended to its enemies as well; extra-judicial solutions merely undermine the legitimacy of the state (and therefore help the terrorists).[13] Thus, importantly in these first 20 years, the notion of the rule of law as a necessary component of economic development plays almost no part in the occasional discussions of the rule of law. Until the end of the 1980s, *The Economist* maintains an almost exclusively political and legal perspective on the rule of law and its related normative elements when it occasionally raises the issue, even when discussing issues that would later be related to economic development such as contract law or anti-corruption regulations.

In the 1990s, however, it is possible to identify a shift both in the frequency of discussions of the rule of law and their focus. The first mention in an editorial (during the sample period) of the rule of law as part of economic development is in a discussion of the legal underpinnings (primarily property rights) required to enhance the prosperity of ethnic minorities, in 1990.[14] A year later, an editorial entitled 'A prospect of growth' explicitly maintains that law and order (and by implication the rule of law) is required for economic development.[15] Now a slowly growing number of mentions of the rule of law in political and legal terms is joined by editorials that link the rule of law with economic development (around the same time the World Bank was making a similar move, as will be discussed below). By 1994, editorials are starting to make the link much more explicit and the rule of law is presented as a multidimensional norm, including political, legal/procedural and economic aspects.[16] Most obviously, the editorials during the 1990s increasingly set out the need for

---

[12] See, for instance, *The Economist*, 'Think of a constitution', 16 August 1975, p. 12; 'Brave new India', 3 January 1976, p. 9; 'Unnecessary privilege', 23 October 1976, p. 14; 'All honourable men', 21 May 1977, pp. 12–13; 'Baby over the balcony', 16 July 1977, pp. 11–12; 'Rule by no law?', 11 February 1978, pp. 9–10; 'The best place for Bhutto', 10 June 1978, p. 15; 'China grows up', 29 September 1979, pp. 13–14.

[13] See, for instance, *The Economist*, 'Into terrorist hands', 9 February 1980, p. 18; 'Listen, friends of Ireland', 9 May 1981, pp. 11–12; 'A bridge to Ireland', 23 May 1981, pp. 11–13; 'Law against terror', 19 February 1983, pp. 18–20; 'Is justice political?', 11 August 1984, pp. 14–15; see also 'The Irish Question', 17 April 1993, p. 16.

[14] *The Economist*, 'Black entrepreneurs please', 7 April 1990, pp. 16–19.

[15] *The Economist*, 'A prospect of growth', 13 July 1991, pp. 15–16.

[16] *The Economist*, 'Democracy works best', 27 July 1994, pp. 11–12.

reform in other countries to facilitate their economic development and (re)integration into the international economic system; that is, for *The Economist* the rule of law has now become a key element of the global political economy.[17] By the end of the decade, *The Economist* had started to set out a much fuller and wide-ranging account of the rule of law as a major element in economic prosperity and growth.

In the first decade of the new millennium, the focus of *The Economist*'s attention was increasingly international with editorials focusing on individual countries that lacked the rule of law (or where it was being challenged), such as Argentina, China and Russia, while also consolidating a more economics-related approach.[18] This was perhaps best exemplified by a couple of articles that while not editorials set out the position that the magazine had now adopted. In March 2008, *The Economist* dedicated an entire three-page 'briefing' to 'Economics and the rule of law', which intended to demonstrate that the rule of law was not only an issue for politics and/or law.[19] The briefing suggests that the importance of the rule of law was prompted by the 'crumbling' of the Washington Consensus in light of its failure to produce the expected results and the search for what was missing. Citing a number of the scholars whose work I discuss later (such as Brian Tamanaha, Thomas Carothers and Michael Trebilcock), for perhaps the only time *The Economist* dedicates several paragraphs to the discussion of competing meanings of the rule of law to conclude that this is a discussion/debate that will never be finally resolved into a con-

---

[17] *The Economist*, 'A prospect of growth', 13 July 1991, pp. 15–16; 'All or nothing', 25 September 1993, pp. 15–16; 'Patten's next stand', 2 July 1994, p. 16; 'Whose justice for the Hutus?', 30 July 1994, pp. 18–19; 'Democracy works best', 27 July 1994, p. 19; 'Right to punish China', 11 February 1995, pp. 15–16; 'Can it keep the peace?', 21 October 1995, pp. 18–19; 'The republic of Oz?', 24 February 1996, p. 17; 'Changing China', 23 March 1996, p. 16; 'The quality of Korean mercy', 31 August 1996, p. 14; 'Polls to nowhere', 23 November 1996, pp. 20–2; 'After Deng', 22 February 1997, p. 15; 'Iran's new face', 2 August 1997, pp. 13–14; 'Confronting the past', 1 November 1997, p. 16; 'Clinton embraces Africa', 21 March 1998, pp. 17–18; 'Malaysia's incomplete democracy', 20 March 1999, pp. 19–20; 'Indonesia's next president', 16 October 1999, pp. 22–4.

[18] *The Economist*, 'Ex-dictators are not immune', 28 November 1998, pp. 15–16; 'Nigeria falls apart again?', 4 March 2000, pp. 22–3; 'Peru's fight for democracy', 15 April 2000, p. 19; 'Africa's elusive dawn', 24 February 2001, pp. 17–18; 'Who will condemn China?', 24 March 2001, p. 23; 'Putin's Russia', 31 March 2001, pp. 16–18; 'Fit to run Italy?', 28 April 2001, pp. 17–18; 'Out with the old, in with the old', 9 November 2002, pp. 15–16; 'Out of Patagonia', 24 May 2003, pp. 12–13; 'Still taking on the world', 3 July 2004, pp. 11–12; 'Next steps in Colombia', 12 February 2005, p. 13; 'How to make China even richer', 25 March 2006, p. 9; 'Thou shalt not steal', 27 May 2006, p. 12; 'Unintended consequences', 15 July 2006, p. 12; 'China's next revolution', 10 March 2007, p. 11; 'Stand up for your rights', 24 March 2007, p. 12; 'A chance to change course', 20 June 2009, pp. 12–13; 'Opportunity missed', 19 September 2009, pp. 14–15; 'A good example', 24 October 2009, p. 20.

[19] *The Economist*, 'Briefing: economics and the rule of law', 15 March 2008, pp. 95–7.

sensual position. The briefing does, however, argue that (for economists especially) the rule of law is becoming increasingly central to discussions of growth and development. Two months later, in their 'Special report on EU enlargement' again there was a detailed discussion of the rule of law, this time focusing on the rule of law as a mechanism for reducing corruption in transition states.[20] However, this extensive coverage in the main part of the magazine did not translate into any necessary expansion of the coverage of the rule of law in editorials, with 2008 down somewhat from the peak in the late 1990s.

What I have attempted to establish (albeit in a rather summary form) is that the end of the Cold War was a pivot point for the rule of law in *The Economist*. Prior to the end of the 1980s, its editorials were overwhelmingly focused (when occasionally mentioning the rule of law or its elements) on the political and legal aspects of the norm. However, after 1989, while this focus remained, the notion that the rule of law might be a crucial part of economic development, and that it was something that was lacking in states that sought to (re)integrate themselves with the global political economy, caused editorials to be more internationally focused as regards the benefits of the rule of law, and to also increasingly emphasize the economic benefits of acceding to the norms' strictures. Nowadays when the rule of law appears in *The Economist*'s editorials it is seldom contextualized or defined, seen as being obviously of value and non-controversial, just common sense. This is by no means the only media or intellectual forum in which these shifts might be detected, but *The Economist* is a useful barometer of international elite views, while also acting to (re)produce these perspectives among those seeking to join the developed global political economy.

## PROFESSIONAL/SPECIALIST INVOCATIONS OF THE RULE OF LAW

Moving into more specialized discussions, I will now explore what David Kennedy has referred to as the 'policy vernacular' of the rule of law (Kennedy 2001), as opposed to the popular rhetoric that I started with. These two sets of discussions are not unconnected, and both have contributed to the rule of law becoming the common sense of global politics. Expert ideas are only likely to be widely influential when they are seen as describing instruments rather than (political) goals (Lindvall 2009), as

---

[20] *The Economist*, 'Trust me: the theory and the practice of the rule of law', in 'A special report on EU enlargement', 31 May 2008, pp. 14–15.

may be inferred from the above discussion of the popular rhetoric, and hence one of the key developments in the rise of the rule of law norm has been its depoliticization; its (post-colonial?) move to being rendered as a technique (albeit the most fundamental) of governance. The link between the state and the rule of law has been diluted through a greater emphasis on the depoliticized function of governance as opposed to government, as I discuss below.

It is also worth noting that the understanding of the term can vary between cultures or political systems, not least because there is no differentiation in the English word 'law' between the concepts, distinguished elsewhere by different words: 'law as legislative will and Law (capitalized) as right reason' (Fletcher 1996, p. 35). Indeed, George Fletcher suggests that English commentary on law has often cultivated an ambiguity between what Germans would call *Gesetz* – the law as laid down, its formal rules – and *Recht*, which encompasses some claim to an ethical value (Fletcher 1996, p. 13). Likewise, the French distinguish *loi* and *droit*, the Dutch between *wet* and *recht*, and the Finns between *laki* and *oikeus*, to give three further (but still European) examples.[21] Because of such linguistic differences the Council of Europe, as promoter of European democratic ideals, sought in its Resolution 1594 (2007) to banish translation issues from an authoritative depiction of the rule of law, noting that although the European Union, the Organization for Security and Co-operation in Europe and their member states were all committed to the rule of law there was little common understanding of the norm. They therefore sought to build on the case law of the European Court of Human Rights to stress that

> the terms 'rule of law' and pre-eminence du droit are substantive legal concepts which are synonymous, and which should be considered as such in all English and French language versions of documents issued by the Assembly as well as in the member states in their official translations.[22]

The resolution goes on to clearly state that the rule of law cannot merely be formal law(s); there are European values focused on human rights that, even if not necessarily specifically articulated in law, nonetheless should be regarded as part of the rule of law itself. This distinction between the formal and the substantive views of the rule of law is discussed at length in Chapter 2.

Conversely, looking back a little, less than 20 years ago, Paul Cammack in a highly critical account of *Capitalism and Democracy in the Third*

---

[21] I am grateful to Jan Klabbers for this point and examples.
[22] See Council of Europe, Resolution 1594 (2007), available at http://assembly.coe.int/ASP/Doc/XrefViewHTML.asp?FileID=17613&Language=EN (accessed 17 May 2013).

*World* (Cammack 1997) made no mention of the rule of law, hardly referring to law or legal structures at all; although occasionally mentioning the protection of property rights, he never contextualizes this in a wider analysis of the role of law in capitalism or democratization. Then this would have hardly been noteworthy, but now would seem to be missing a key element of the debates about which he was concerned. It is the debates that have changed, however. Similarly, in *Capitalism vs. Capitalism*, Michel Albert's much cited discussion of the clash between the Anglo-American and German/Japanese models of capitalism (Albert 1993), the role of lawyers and litigation is presented as a cost on business, but the rule of law (explicitly) or the legal structures required by capitalist market economies are not discussed. Again, Samuel Huntington's well-known (and often cited) discussion of democratization, *The Third Wave* (Huntington 1991), occasionally elliptically mentions legal practices and issues, but has no detailed account of any links between democracy and the rule of law (although he mentions in passing that the Helsinki Final Act in 1989 linked them) (Huntington 1991, p. 89). In a long list of variables underpinning democracy, near the bottom (23rd in a list of 27) he includes 'traditions of respect for law and individual rights' (Huntington 1991, p. 38), which might be a proxy for the rule of law. However, while dispensing all manner of advice to would-be democratizers of the 'third wave', Huntington remains ambivalent and largely silent on the role of the (rule of) law; an omission that would hardly pass unremarked today but which in his more recent work he has not repeated. Thus it is perhaps unsurprising that in the mid 1980s Mark Kelman found only 20 books in the Stanford Law Library that focused on the rule of law and half of those were appealing for an international rule of law as a way to promote peaceful coexistence (Kelman 1987, p. 292). A search only on my own bookshelves would now produce at least three times that many!

This is not to say, however, that debates about the rule of law were necessarily absent from discussions of international politics before the end of the Cold War. In the late 1950s Abbé Jean Boulier criticized the International Commission of Jurists' (ICJ) position (and work) on the rule of law in an argument that would be familiar to many on the left today. He argued that the ICJ was hopelessly compromised by its depiction of the capitalist rule of law, which included no space for a more pluralist definition that would allow non-capitalist states to enjoy the benefit of being part of a wider society that valued the rule of law (Boulier 1958). In his view the ICJ, despite protestations of neutrality, was prosecuting a liberal project, and thus continuing the Cold War by other means. The ICJ's position would also not be unfamiliar today (and indeed is often referred to by those claiming a historical trajectory for the norm); for the

ICJ, the rule of law embraced a 'broader conception of justice than the mere application of legal rules whatever they happen to be in any particular state at any given time' (ICJ 1966, p. 2). Across a number of meetings, the ICJ's members sought to elaborate their view of the rule of law, and defend their conception against critics like Boulier, presenting the rule of law as 'dynamic' by recognizing (at conventions held in Africa, Asia and South America) how the rule of law was actually adopted and recognized in a wide variety of states (with the exception of totalitarian states) (ICJ 1965, pp. 14–17).[23] While of limited general political visibility, the work of the ICJ seems likely to have contributed to the early elaborations of the rule of law norm that pre-dated its more recent ubiquity.

At least until the 1960s these sorts of discussions were highly specialized and were seldom conducted outside closed events and remained confined to limited circulation publications (Marsh 1961). In the final quarter of the twentieth century and into the new millennium this relative obscurity has been transformed by the rise of the rule of law as a key and explicit component in (global) political order. As Paul Kahn has suggested, by the turn of the millennium, the

> West had taken a decisive turn towards the rule of law as the single source of political order. A modern constitution imagines no political situation or action to which the law does not apply: it can imagine nothing that cannot be evaluated as a matter of law. (Kahn 2011, p. 54)

In this view political rhetoric now reaches most often towards the law for responses; invocations of the rule of law allow actions and situations to be swiftly judged and clearly communicated.

David Trubek argues that the rule of law is an increasingly deployed rhetoric because it represents the common ground between the contemporary political 'projects' of democracy (democratization) and of markets (or neoliberalization). In both cases the rule of law represents a set of institutions that can be depoliticized and presented as a technical response to shortcomings of society without the ideological baggage that would come with more explicit demands for democracy and liberalization (Trubek 2006, pp. 84–5). Thus, as David Kennedy puts it:

> There is something mesmerizing about the idea that a formal rule of law could somehow substitute for struggle over [political and economic] issues and choices – or could replace contestable arguments about the consequences

---

[23] An account of the competing colloquia (one in Chicago, one in Warsaw) in the late 1950s that sought to find a consensual definition (and substantive content) for the rule of law can be found in Marsh (1961, pp. 230–40).

of different distributions with the apparent neutrality of legal best practice. (Kennedy 2006, p. 144)

The rhetoric of the rule of law may be popular just as much for what it obscures as for what it says about any particular political evaluation. For instance, the Princeton Project's self-avowedly bipartisan report, *Forging a World of Liberty Under Law*, suggested that to enhance support across the political spectrum, one of the new (and narrower) foci of US foreign policy should be 'strengthening the rule of law, personal freedoms and democratic governance' (Princeton Project 2006, p. 59). The report emphasizes in a number of places that the rule of law is a crucial part of the structure of liberal democracy that the USA should seek to promote (Princeton Project 2006, pp. 29, 59); however, it does little to fix the normative meaning of the term in use other than to repeatedly link it to the protection of liberty and the provision of 'accountable government, basic civil rights and civil liberties' (Princeton Project 2006, p. 39), leaving the rule of law as a surprisingly underspecified aspiration for interventions, which seemingly requires no detailed justification.

As this indicates, the rule of law is often bundled together with other values of the (so-called) 'international community' when they are expressed by its (self-proclaimed) leaders: democracy, human rights and the contribution of markets to development (Barnett and Duvall 2005, p. 6). However, not all commentators agree that these values are so closely linked. Fareed Zakaria (at the time the editor of Newsweek International) argued at length that while the rule of law is certainly a crucial liberal value, not least of all in its role of protecting liberty, it is less clear that it is necessarily co-terminus with democracy (Zakaria 2003). Here the rule of law can protect against the excesses of democracy and its dangers. In another well-known intervention, Hernando de Soto promotes the rule of law as a method for freeing the poor from the constraints that stop them capitalizing on their creativity and entrepreneurship (which I discuss in Chapter 5); this is a story that policy makers frequently welcome. In his analysis the rule of law presents a way of fostering localized development without having to go against the strictures of the multilateral aid agencies and institutions (de Soto 2000). Helpfully, de Soto's prescriptions are fully compatible with the recommendations of the World Bank and others.

The contemporary strength of the norm of the rule of law articulated and promoted by key international agencies also encourages states to adopt this language or terminology (even if their actions may fall short); to celebrate being a state that does not accept the rule of law no longer seems to make sense. As Shirley Scott and Olivia Ambler observe:

> States often demonstrate their acceptance of the ideology of international law
> by referring in their rhetoric to the 'rule of law'. . . [but this] ideology of inter-
> national law is integral to the international distribution of power, and hence the
> rhetorical emphasis that the US has for many decades placed on the importance
> of the rule of law has served not only to strengthen international law but [also]
> to reinforce a source of legitimacy on which the US has frequently drawn.
> (Scott and Ambler 2007, pp. 72, 74)

The rhetoric may serve different states' governments differently, with some using it to demonstrate an interest and willingness to be seen as part of the 'international community' while more powerful states (most obviously the USA) use the rule of law as a method to legitimate their position.

Additionally, it is possible that the expansion of the rhetoric of the rule of law is a response to perceived illegality (and its costs) in the now globalized political economy. If 'deviant globalization' is as widespread as some commentators believe (see, for instance, Gilman et al. 2011) and criminal activities are integral to the flows and structures of the global political economy (Friman 2009), then one response would be for governments to ratchet up the calls for the rule of law globally. This would especially be the case as black markets and illegal activity, centred on morally suspect services and products (drugs and the sex trade), are frequently an adjunct to 'legitimate' globalization. Of course, in one sense it is the rule of law that produces the criminal activity by establishing the distinction legal/illegal, but its rhetorical use also leaves aside political discussions about the value or otherwise of prohibition or the question of what encourages such activity, to focus on issues of security and stability. Here, the rhetoric of the (lack of) rule of law becomes a way of summarizing problems in the international system that stem from the ability of criminal actors and organizations to enjoy sanctuary from which they can operate across the global system.

The use of the rhetoric of the rule of law to identify the 'lawless' has been an abiding theme of US political development: repeatedly 'lawless others' have been subjected to domination and/or violence in the service of the greater civilizing project of manifest destiny. Natsu Taylor Saito argues that recent instances of US self-exemption from the rule of law are merely the contemporary (re)iterations of a one-sided view of the rule of law (Saito 2010). The rule of law for others but not us, as it were! Conversely, in an extended critique of Jack Goldsmith and Eric Posner's criticisms of the efficacy of international law, Michael Scharf has argued that when one actually examines the opinions/advice of the US State Department of Legal Advisors (and the impact of this advice on US foreign policy) one sees a much higher level of recognition of the legitimacy of international law than would be expected by critics (Scharf 2009). Thus, following Louis Henkin's famous assertion (Henkin 1979) it does seem that most of the time most states (including the USA) do abide by their international legal obligations, allowing them to argue that the rule of law does obtain in the international system. The culture of the acceptance of the rule of law is constantly being promulgated and supported in the global political system, making explicit rejection difficult (in diplomatic terms at least). One of the main but by no means only organization that works hard to promote the rule of law is the World Bank.

## THE RULE OF LAW AT THE WORLD BANK

The World Bank is one of the most important (and influential) producers of knowledge about development in the world today. It is not just the extent of its lending that makes the Bank influential; as Catherine Weaver suggests, 'what it *says* about development shapes other multilateral, bilateral, and national governmental strategies and defines the *conventional wisdom* on global development' (Weaver 2008, p. 10, second emphasis added). For Weaver, the 'power the World Bank enjoys in shaping global ideas about development theory and practice is arguably un-replicated by any other development agency, think-tank or university' (Weaver 2008, p. 73). Bank President James Wolfensohn made research a central element in the Bank's activities in the mid 1990s, and certainly since then the production and dissemination of authoritative knowledge has been significant (van Waeyenberge and Fine 2011). Therefore, the Bank's 'discovery' of rule of law reform marked an important shift towards the rule of law becoming a common sense of global politics. Linked to the move to consider 'governance' as within the Bank's remit, the rule of law was depicted as a depoliticized technology. The timing of this move is hardly inconsequential: at the end of the Cold War and the collapse of the communist bloc, the World Bank in the early 1990s was seeking a different set of justifications for its policy prescriptions and aid interventions; governance and the rule of law fitted this need rather well.[24]

In the late 1980s (and into the 1990s) Ibrahim Shihata (then the Bank's General Counsel) made a strong case that to further its developmental aims, the Bank needed to attend to the manner in which states were governed to ensure that the aid provided was used effectively and efficiently (Shihata 1991a). Responding to increasing internal pressure for governance to be taken seriously (Weaver 2010, p. 58), Shihata carefully

---

[24] Guilhot (2005, pp. 188–221) offers an extended history of the manner in which the World Bank's involvement and interest in human rights evolved over its history; see also Weaver (2008).

reconsidered the Bank's statutes and mandated mission, allowing him to introduce 'good governance' as an area that required attention, and which had previously been undersupported with some negative impact on the efficacy of Bank programmes in recipient countries. Shihata's move was successful due to the clear failure of developmental policies (particularly) in Africa where state structures were unable to support (or facilitate) the sorts of policies the Bank favoured (Guilhot 2005, p. 213; Krever 2011, pp. 299–301). Alongside increasing engagement with non-governmental organizations focused on human rights, these practical failures opened up a space for an approach that stressed the need for good governance for development policies to be successfully initiated and sustained.

However, the depoliticized character of Shihata's discussion of governance and the rule of law also reflected the ideological terrain of research within the Bank that remained dominated by (neo)classical economists who were resistant to anything that resembled political theory. This prompted Shihata to focus on the law as an enabler of market-based development (Weaver 2008, p. 107); the rule of law was conceived as a limitation on the ability of the state to 'interfere' in the private sector, rather than a more positive (and political) perception of the rule of law as underpinning social development (in terms I will introduce later, Shihata's is a thinner reading of the rule of law). The difficulty of articulating this position is that such a depiction of the rule of law, intended to establish its non-political character (and thus its universality), is historically specific; it is how the (rule of) law has been conceived of in liberal capitalist societies (Krever 2011, pp. 317–18; Tshuma 1999, p. 85). Laws that were not 'market friendly', or more specifically that did (or do) not support standard capitalist economic relations, are not regarded as 'good' laws nor central to the rule of law.

Shihata's rhetoric on the role of law in development (which would quite quickly become orthodoxy at the Bank) is essentially circular: a good law (or legal system) is one that promotes development (as defined by the Bank), while the success of the developmental process (as supported by the Bank) is demonstrated by the existence of a rule of law that fosters and supports development (Pahija 2011, p. 198). Once the Bank was able to (re)focus on 'good' governance as a key determinant of developmental success, and given that (almost) any form of governance will involve the rule of law, the justification for (potentially) wide-ranging intervention in the politico-legislative system of recipient states was in place, provided it was supporting economic development. As Sundhya Pahija puts it:

> The absence of a positivistic system of law justifies intervention to further development as a process, but development as an end-point justifies the privileged

place of positive law in the first place. *And if a society demonstrates reluctance to embrace such a legal system, then that reluctance become further justification for the necessity for intervention.* (Pahija 2011, pp. 198–9, emphasis added)

Thus, by shifting the Bank's concerns towards good governance, Shihata (and those within the Bank promoting this approach) achieved a significant move towards more strident intervention in recipient states' political systems. However, for these interventions to continue as part of the Bank's activities, the 'myth' that these were only intended to address economic and/or technical problems had to be maintained (Weaver 2010, p. 62). This required strong (ideological) maintenance of the 'technical' presentation of the rule of law.

Once the World Bank articulated (repeatedly) the relationship between the rule of law and economic development, beginning in the late 1980s/early 1990s, then even organizations that broadly kept clear of 'political' concerns could involve themselves in the promotion of the rule of law 'as developmental technology' by referring to the Bank's position (Pahija 2011, p. 185), and, as noted above, around this time *The Economist* also shifted its treatment of the rule of law (quite possibly influenced by materials from the Bank). In Nicholas Stern's history of the first 50 years of the Bank's intellectual role in global politics, it is notable that the notion of the rule of law is largely absent, and in data from 1991 on the staff profile of the bank, those with legal training are a vanishingly small proportion of the staff employed at that time (Stern and Ferreira 1997, p. 586, *passim*). However, this was changing almost at the same time that Stern was compiling this history. As one commentator puts it, the Bank's lack of interest in the law was replaced at this time by the view that the rule of law is 'a magic wand that promises to resolve virtually every conceivable economic and social problem' (Faundez 2005, p. 568), although this may have been sustained by the lack of lawyers on the staff who might have had a more nuanced view of the possibilities of law.

Michael Goldman has concluded that 'Bank knowledge is a tactical technology whose power should not be underestimated, whatever one's interpretation of its truth value' (Goldman 2005, p. 135). He quotes a Bank-contracted environmental technician: 'You and I may say that our *World Development Reports* are BS [bullshit]. But I go to Sri Lanka and officials there quote from the latest report word for word. That's music to our ears' (Goldman 2005, p. 145). Therefore, it will be useful to briefly examine a couple of crucial *World Development Reports* (WDRs) and to see how the rule of law appears on the website of the World Bank, these being two important aspects of the organization's public face.

The WDRs are a key carrier of the World Bank's position(s) and are an important conduit through which the view of the rule of law established by Shihata was disseminated to the (global) policy community. One is particularly important in this regard: the 1998 WDR – *From Plan to Market*. Space precludes an extensive treatment of the manner in which each successive WDR has accepted and built on the conclusions of *From Plan to Market* but, for instance, in following year's report, *The State in a Changing World*, the Bank allows that states have generally expanded their share of gross domestic product (GDP) and seeks to ensure that they are doing what the Bank's analysts believe is of value. The first item on the list entitled 'First job of states: getting the fundamentals right' is: 'Establishing a foundation of law' (World Bank 1997, p. 4). This focus on law is limited throughout the report to a concern for the sanctity of property rights, the predictability of market rules and the need to limit corruption (none of which might be objectionable, but as the subsequent chapters will show is a relatively limited view of the rule of law).

This limited focus may indicate that the writers of the 1997 report expected their readers to have read and digested the previous year's report, which contained an entire chapter on the rule of law. Largely focusing on the post-communist transitional states (but also drawing more general conclusions), *From Plan to Market* acknowledges that many countries are conducting forms of legal reform but emphasizes that the effects have been uneven (World Bank 1996, p. 13). Interestingly, before reaching the chapter on the rule of law the reader is introduced to the importance of property rights (World Bank 1996, pp. 48–9), here emphasizing the prioritization of legal structures that the following year's WDR would also exhibit, and stressing the establishment of assigned property rights to the strategy of privatization in transition economies. In the next major section of the report on the consolidation of change(s) in societies that are in transit between their communist past and their new future, which will be more fully engaged with the global capitalist economy, the 'legal institutions of the rule of law' are the first element discussed, at some length.

Chapter 5 of *From Plan to Market* focuses on 'developing the rule of law' and stresses that this can only be achieved by both the top-down legislative development of 'good' laws, alongside the 'bottom-up demand' for the rule of law (World Bank 1996, p. 87). However, as the chapter progresses to specifics, the forms of law that are focused on move from those that might (plausibly) be meeting a widespread demand (property) to those for which the demand is likely to be coming from a focused business community (both domestic and foreign); company and investment law (World Bank 1996, pp. 90–1) and competition law (World Bank 1996, p. 92). The latter is summarized as the dismantling of monopolies (often specified as state-owned) to allow new competitive market entrants. The rest of the chapter then moves to focus (again) on issues of some wider salience such as the reduction of corruption and the defeat of organized crime (World Bank 1996, pp. 95–6). These are brought together as ways of increasing the level of trust in the state and enhancing its credibility to the 'business community', and of delivering constraints on the (abuse) of state power. Most crucially, while issues of democratization's link to the rule of law are included, the thrust of the discussion is about the ability of the rule of law to both help foster development and for development to enhance/expand the 'demand' for the rule of law itself (World Bank 1996, pp. 97, 144). In the following WDRs the rule of law is more taken for granted as underlying condition development rather than something that again has to be set out. In *Building Institutions for Markets* (World Bank 2002), for instance, there are a number of aspects of the rule of law discussed (such as reform of the judiciary and the regulations of markets) but the overall need for the rule of law is taken as a given throughout the volume.

The World Bank also seeks to influence states' governments (and policy makers) through other means. I look at the programmes supporting rule of law development in Chapters 4 and 5, but it is worth also noting that the Bank's website represents a major depository of materials intended to support the Bank's reading of the rule of law. Two clicks away from the home page, under 'topics': 'Law, Justice and Development', the following statement appears at the top of the main page: 'The rule of law is a principle of fundamental importance to the World Bank. It lies at the heart of what the Bank is, what it does, and what it aspires to accomplish.'[25] There are also a number of resources on the various elements of the website, with a large number of reports under the 'projects and operations' segment where the rule of law has its own section. Although far too numerous to consider here, the extent of the World Bank's operations can be gauged from the over 800 project reports that are available under 'rule of law'. Most interestingly and following a decade of the Comprehensive Development Framework (CDF), the rule of law is now so well embedded that it is much less stridently pushed as now 'good governance' (and thereby the rule of law) has been mainstreamed. The move from an earlier structural adjustment, through a period of governance (during the 1990s) to the CDF in the new millennium (Santos 2006, pp. 267–8) has therefore involved the move from the rule of law as technology requiring separate justification and stipulation to the position now (as common sense) where

---

[25] See http://web.worldbank.org/WBSITE/EXTERNAL/TOPICS/EXTLAWJUSTICE/0,, menuPK:445640~pagePK:149018~piPK:149093~theSitePK:445634,00.html (accessed 29 April 2013).

it is embedded in the World Bank's more comprehensive approach to development and requires no separate justification.

Because the rule of law is (still) understood by the Bank as a depoliticized developmental technology, albeit embedded within a more general approach to socio-economic development, any requirement for knowledge of the local legal systems of recipient countries is downplayed and undervalued. Indeed, Weaver quotes a staff member lamenting that as regards governance, the Bank lacked a 'real working theory of the state' (Weaver 2008, p. 93), making it clearly difficult to engage with discussions about the particular (and local) political developments behind the 'mechanisms' of governance. Thus, a common criticism of World Bank and other rule of law programmes has been the ignorance of local circumstances and their impact on the introduction (or expansion) of the rule of law (Tamanaha 2011). Although by no means limited to the World Bank, Julio Faundez's more general criticism certainly seems to apply to Bank programmes:

> The blend of legal formalism and instrumentalism is a convenient methodological shortcut as it enables [legal support] practitioners to offer legal advice without having to go through the tedious, difficult and often unrewarding task of understanding the societies they purport to help. (Faundez 2005, p. 574)

I will return to the issue of local culture and the rule of law in Chapters 4 and 5 but here merely note that this is hardly a surprising outcome from the presentation and discussion of the rule of law as a (universal) depoliticized technology.

Although the World Bank's adoption of the rule of law as an anchoring concept is important, the Bank in one sense was late to the field, following in the footsteps of the law and development movement of the 1960s and 1970s. For some commentators this suggests that the Bank's influence is therefore overstated (Hammergren 2010). Moreover, within the Bank the understanding of the rule of law is hardly monolithic; rather like a duck on a calm pond, while externally it presents a commitment to the rule of law, beneath the surface different parts of the Bank (such as the Legal Department or the Public Sector Unit) seem to deploy varying understandings of its character (and crucial elements) and be in continued discussion about its role (Santos 2006). Nevertheless, what is notable is that while the law and development movement struggled to expand its reasoning beyond the specialist context in which it worked, the Bank seems to have contributed to a much wider recognition of the rule of law's role in (global) society, even if this has not produced anything approaching consensus on its 'necessary' character.

Finally, while there is a considerable literature that discusses and analyses the rule of law, it is far from clear that there is much substantive connection between the Bank's and other specialist depictions and the invocation of the rule of law in the more popular discussions that I discussed above. They all may share the term, but the understanding of what the rule of law entails is often different, and in the popular rhetoric vague and underdeveloped; often meaning little more than law is important to governance (Brooks 2003, p. 2283). However, the recitation of the shared terminology has allowed it to become widely deployed (if less well understood) precisely because different groups all seem (at least) to be discussing the same the thing. This is not to say that these discourses are completely unconnected but rather that while the term flows pretty freely between various groups its meaning is less well travelled, leading to quite wide variances in how the rule of law is understood, even as it is widely appealed to.

\* \* \*

This chapter has been intended to illustrate Lord Bingham's claim that the rule of law is 'constantly on people's lips' in the political classes and more widely, but this is not necessarily to claim that the rule of law is uncontroversial or a settled concept. Many states may claim they are subject to the rule of law but often these claims can be peeled away to reveal practices that hardly accord with all the elements that might plausibly be drawn from the definitional debates that I will set out in Chapter 2. Nevertheless, what I suggest we do see is an extensive and widespread invocation of the rule of law as a political norm, without any necessary consensus on what the substantive content of this norm would be beyond some pretty basic procedural practices. In Chapter 3 I will examine some arguments about the norm's carriers and its agents of (re)production as well as the timing of the 'legalization' of global politics, but what I have sought to establish here is that the rule of law is much discussed, even if its articulation is often accompanied by little detailed specification of what it might actually entail.

# 1. The rule of law as a social imaginary

> The rule of law does not promise results so much as it promises an approach, a process, a practice of reason-giving, a set of argumentative conventions. (Torke 2001, p. 1450)

> Studying the law we become part of it. The consequence is that our deepest cultural commitment – the commitment to the rule of law – remains one of the least explored elements of our common life. (Kahn 1999, p. 2)

> Such a high degree of consensus on the virtues of the rule of law is possible because of relative vagueness as to its meaning. (Chesterman 2008a, p. 3)

As I hope I have demonstrated in the Introduction, the idea of the rule of law is often appealed to in discussions of, and deliberations about, politics. Now I want to suggest that one useful way of understanding the contemporary resonance of the rule of law is to regard it is a 'social imaginary'. Charles Taylor's idea of the 'social imaginary' stems from his focus on the 'way ordinary people "imagine" their social surroundings' carried in 'images, stories and legends'; he focuses on ideas that are shared by 'large groups of people, if not the whole of society'; and on those ideas that represent a 'common understanding that makes possible common practices and a widely shared sense of legitimacy' (Taylor 2004, p. 23); a social imaginary is a particular form of common sense. Taylor sees a social imaginary as complex while

> incorporat[ing] a sense of the normal expectations we have of each other, the kind of common understanding that enables us to carry out the collective practices that make up our social life . . . [and] some sense of how we all fit together in carrying out this common practice. Such understanding is both factual and normative; that is, we have a sense of how things usually go, but this is interwoven with an idea of how they ought to go, of what missteps would invalidate the process. (Taylor 2004, p. 24)

Moreover, this includes a clear recognition of ideal cases from which judgements can then be made as regards the fit between the imaginary and the practice. Beyond this set of ideals 'stands some notion of a moral or metaphysical order, in the context of which the norms and ideals make sense'. Thus, the social imaginary is a 'wider grasp of our whole predicament;

how we stand to each other, how we got to where we are, how we relate to other groups and so on'. We need to understand our practice for it to make sense to us and for us to act, but this wider set of ideas has no necessary limits for Taylor. Thus, it 'can never be adequately expressed in the form of explicit doctrines because of its unlimited and indefinite nature' (Taylor 2004, p. 25). It is fluid and under-defined in a formal sense but nevertheless shared as a story of how we are, alongside a clear idea about 'what makes these norms realizable' (Taylor 2007, p. 175). Already it seems to me that this has some applicability to the idea of the rule of law, whatever debates there are about its meaning in jurisprudence and elsewhere.

The practices and understandings encompassed by such a social imaginary do not relate to each other in a unidirectional manner; 'If understanding makes the practice possible, it is also true that it is the practice that largely carries the understanding.' That is to say: 'At any given time we can speak of the "repertory" of collective actions at the disposal of a given group of society. These are the common actions that they know how to undertake' (Taylor 2004, p. 25). This common understanding does not require theorization in the first instance; it is what we know we need to do to be part of society. Therefore, the

> understanding of what we're doing right now (without which we couldn't be doing *this* action) makes the sense it does because of our grasp on the wider predicament: how we continuously stand or have stood in relation to others and to power. This in turn, opens out wider perspectives on where we stand in space and time: our relations to other nations and peoples . . . and also where we stand in our history, in the narrative of our becoming. (Taylor 2004, p. 27)

New theories may penetrate this generalized notion of the possible, and eventually, as it is more widely recognized (or accepted) and adopted, so the social imaginary's new element 'begins to define the contours of their world and can eventually come to count as the taken-for-granted shape of things, too obvious to mention' (Taylor 2004, p. 29). However, Taylor also warns that the recognition of a new social imaginary should not be taken to indicate that it has completely replaced forgoing understandings (rather it will continue to interact with these previous understandings), and although it may also seem to have become self-evident, the job of analysis and engagement is to unpick this obviousness to reveal the history and construction of the social imaginary as currently manifest (Taylor 2007, pp. 168, 169). Its development must be therefore regarded as dynamic *and* social.

For Taylor, anticipating Margaret Archer's approach to the development of ideas in society, which I explore in the methodological interlude that follows this chapter, the relationship between the practices that embody the social imaginary and the prior theory or theories that have in some way informed this practice (before being rendered schematic through general social use) is a dialectical relationship (Taylor 2007, p. 177). This means that, like Archer, Taylor refuses to identify either structure (the social imaginary) or agency (social practice) as the final determining factor in social relations. Indeed, Archer argues that focusing on agency alone and offering a 'bottom-up' causal explanation would make 'no allowances for inherited structures, their resistance to change, the influence they exert on attitudes to change, and crucially. . ., the delineation of agents capable of seeking change' (Archer 1995, p. 250). At the (posited) beginning of any particular history of a social imaginary there will be structural elements carried forward from preceding ways of being, reflecting previous expectations of acceptable practice.

This emphasizes that agents do not have completely free rein; again linking Archer and Taylor, it seems sensible to accept that any voluntary actions are going to be 'trammelled by past structural and cultural constraints and by the current politics of the possible' (Archer 1982, p. 470). Historically extant social imaginaries are themselves the products of previous clashes of social forces, previous interactions of ideas, material capabilities and institutions as I will elaborate in the methodological interlude. Agents' actions may be the immediate cause of specific moments of solidification, but they also remain embedded in larger structures, including material causes, state institutions and the structure of global capitalism that both constrain and empower as Taylor's own discussion of the wider context of social imaginaries indicates (Taylor 2004, 2007). However, as Archer also stresses, '*all* structural influences . . . *are mediated to people by shaping the situation in which they find themselves*' (Archer 1995, p. 196, emphasis in original). In a parallel analysis, towards what they term an interactional analysis of international law, Jutta Brunnée and Stephen Toope make a similar point:

> [L]egal structures constrain social action, but they also enable action, and in turn are affected and potentially altered by the friction of social action against the parameters of the legal structure . . . Stability may be aided by explicit articulation of a norm in a text, but it is ultimately dependent upon the underlying shared understanding and a continuous practice of legality. (Brunnée and Toope 2011, p. 112)

The key issue is therefore the difference between the inherited imaginary/ imaginaries (playing out in institutionalized practices) and the continuing (or changing) interests of specific agents. As I will set out when considering Archer's insights into agency and ideational change, where there is a mismatch between the structurally available benefits and the politicized interests of marginalized agents, this may be translated into tensions and strains in the system.

For now, the more important question is: is the rule of law a social imaginary? In Taylor's depiction, the social imaginary is all about a sense of the normal expectations and common understandings that enable the collective practices that make up our social life. The rule of law has at its centre an expectation about how rules and governance should proceed (or be practised) and indeed expectations as regards practice are central to the norm. Moreover, Taylor's suggestion that a social imaginary presents us with a sense of how we all fit together in carrying out this common practice again parallels the rule of law's establishment of the manner in which individuals can expect to work together constrained by specific laws. A social imaginary's provision of a repertory of practices is evident when it offers a limited range of actions that are acceptable, in that they demonstrate the law is being followed and its practices are to a large extent easily known. If a social imaginary is both factual and normative, providing both a sense of how things usually are and an idea of how they ought to be (what missteps would undermine such practice), the rule of law again would seem to be a social imaginary in its descriptive and normative treatments of what it is to be practising or working within the law, and what would be regarded as illegal (by virtue of the process of adjudication). In Taylor's argument a social imaginary involves a clear recognition of ideal cases from which judgements can then be made as regards the fit between imaginary and the practice; the rule of law structures exactly these sorts of judgements, not least of all in the debates about how such rule of law 'standards' might be operationalized.

In Taylor's treatment the imaginary is underdefined but nevertheless is a shared story of how we are, alongside a clear idea about how we might realize such a world. Certainly the rule of law as a norm is underdefined as the contested discussions around its meaning that I discuss later will demonstrate, but equally in its presentation of a set of consensual procedures seems able to offer a guide to how a minimal claim about the rule of law might be assembled. The development of the rule of law (as an idea) is itself dynamic and subject to the sorts of (social) forces of change that Taylor's account seems to encompass. Thus, Taylor's analysis allows an account to be developed both of how the rule of law as a social imaginary may have replaced other understandings of the mechanisms of global politics and why debates continue even if the basic idea of the rule of law seems to have become a global common sense.

Taylor's analysis of the social imaginary prompted Manfred Steger (2008) to examine the rise of the global imaginary and the practices by which this developed and has been contested. In one sense, what I will be doing in this book is developing one small aspect of the most recent global imaginary that Steger discusses as the 'morphology of market globalism' (Steger 2008, pp. 170–212). We might also understand the rise of the rule of law as a social imaginary to be (possibly) associated with the political development of the idea of a 'world community' typified by the rise of human rights as a mode of understanding a post-national human community of interest. For such a norm to develop it needs to be able to lay claim to the notion of a view above and beyond the plurality of human communities (Bartelson 2009, p. 181, *passim*) and as such if human rights remain contested in this regard it may be the case that the rule of law has been able to fill that role. In these two aspects of the global imaginary (the market and human rights) one other element of Taylor's description of the social imaginary comes into focus; the idea of the social imaginary as part of the background presumptions of the social is reflected by the rule of law being commonly seen (whatever the debates about its meaning and scope) as a key element of how we have chosen (as a human race) to govern ourselves. The rule of law is able to offer a globalized frame of reference for action inasmuch as it guides (relatively easily) the general travel of judgements about the politically acceptable and the unacceptable.

If the rule of law is a social imaginary, its normative appeal seems likely to be linked to its political value for communities and societies more widely than merely the members of any (global) political elite. This is likely because, as E.P. Thompson famously argued, the rule of law not only limits the actions of the ruled but constrains rulers as well: the law 'may disguise the true realities of power, but at the same time . . . may curb that power and check its intrusions' (Thompson 1975, p. 265). Indeed, Thompson himself was keen to emphasize that due to the inhibitions it put upon power, the 'rule of law' was an 'unqualified human good' (Thompson 1975, p. 266), even while clearly identifying the injustice of particular laws. This reveals two assumptions that may be central to many casual appeals to the rule of law: firstly, that the most significant forms of power are (or can be) concentrated in government, which is then governed by, and governs through, the rule of law; secondly, that the rule of law itself can constrain and limit subjectively articulated power over individuals when such actions do not conform to the (objective) strictures of the law (Unger 1976, pp. 178–9). Of course, Thompson is aware that the law may not be able to fulfil all these hopes: there are forms of social power that are articulated outside the purview of the law and that it cannot constrain; the hoped-for objectivity can never be achieved because the rule of law must by definition be the rule of people through interpretation and adjudication – the police, lawyers and judges; and modern democratic states' governments as legislators can never be separate from the

interaction of conflicting social interests. Nevertheless, Thompson's point
is that whatever the compromises and shortcomings of the rule of law, it
can deliver a better approximation of social justice than the absence of law
is likely to achieve; Thompson's ends here are hardly (politically) eccentric
or trivial (Krygier 2004, p. 257). However, Thompson adopts a relatively
'thin' (using a term that will be explained in Chapter 2) or procedural view
of the law, requiring that all are treated equally under its rule. Certainly,
unjust laws must be challenged, but the rule of law is better than its
absence; it is a necessary but not sufficient condition for a just society in
Thompson's view.[1]

As Karl Klare once pointed out (while offering qualified support
for Thompson's position), '[t]o treat law as mere sham is to dishonour
centuries of struggle in which the poor and oppressed attempted to fill
the law with humane content, to hold the law to its own pretensions to
justice' (Klare 1979, p. 133). While any analysis needs to engage with
specific forms of law, it must also recognize the value of its more general
normative and political claims, and Thompson was keen to emphasize
that it is impossible to imagine a developed and complex market society
without law (Thompson 1975, p. 260), and this of course is the power of
its normative production in modern society. He goes on to argue there
is an 'imbrication' (overlapping) of law and productive relations, which
means that legal institutions and the capitalist market economy are always
interconnected and impossible to completely separate. At the same time
that laws structure productive relations (most obviously, but by no means
exclusively, through property rights and legalized commodification),
such law also changes in reaction to shifts in political economic relations
mediated through the legal apparatus. In this analysis, the imbrication of
law and productive relations is 'endorsed by norms' although such norms
are always subject to conflict and need to be constantly (re)produced
(Thompson 1975, p. 261). The structures of the law and the social relations
of capitalist economic activity are not related in a unidirectional manner
but rather are intertwined in a simultaneous layering, each one affecting
the other. Relating this to the general appreciation of the social milieu,
in the words of Phillip Corrigan and Derek Sayer, the law 'works on and
with wider moral classifications to "encourage" some ways of seeing (and
being) and outlaw others . . . [and] rules least noticeably yet most directly
through its forms: through the ways in which it "encourages" us to present
and represent ourselves' (Corrigan and Sayer 1981, pp. 40–1). It shapes
and influences societies' practices at the same time that it reflects both

---

[1] For an extensive discussion of Thompson's position on the rule of law, as well as a discussion of three important critiques, see Cole (2001).

the deliberations over these practices and decisions on their individual applicability.

This approach to the rule of law, when worked through at the global level, has promoted analyses that identify a move to a form of global constitutionalism (which I discuss at some length in Chapter 6). Those who see this as a positive move regard the work of various international organizations (primarily, but not limited to, the World Trade Organization) as establishing a constitution for the global system, which while focused on certain issue areas is starting to establish a process by which a rule of law can develop its own character rather than being beholden to states and their (international) interests. For critics, this development is not so much the development of the rule of law as a governance mechanism parallel to that which has been developed in liberal states and which is subject to democratic deliberation, but is rather the imposition of a specific set of norms and rules that favour particular actors and foster a particular neoliberal structure to the global system. In this critique, the constitutionalization of the global system is actually neoliberalization; the rule of law on which such a shift is predicated is not a neutral technology but an extension and continuation of imperialistic domination by other means (Gill 2003; Mattei and Nader 2008). However, whatever one's view of global constitutionalism, the rule of law is not only required but has to have been established by some means; the rule of law does not support such developments 'naturally' and without its own political history.

Therefore, and responding to the arguments John Hobson has recently made about the endemic Eurocentrism of International Theory (Hobson 2012), I see the rule of law not only as a Western/European value to which non-Europeans respond/adapt but as a response itself to the manner in which global politics has developed during the last decades. There is a much longer legal and political history to which attention might be paid, but even in my shorter/narrower historical focus it is important to avoid obscuring the non-Western political pressures that have shaped and influenced the development of the rule of law in global politics. That is to say, we must not see an analysis of the rule of law merely being a product of US domination of the global system. Thus, the sort of approach offered by Anne-Marie Burley is partial and would need to be added to; at the beginning of the 1990s she argued that multilateralism is the

> form to be expected from a set of international regimes established by a liberal state with a strong tradition of seeing the world in its own image and a missionary drive to make it so . . . taking responsibility for the world meant regulating abroad as at home, in form as well as substance; more importantly, however, a mindset that could transfer the American administrative revolution to the world by formulating every problem in terms of a need for centralized intervention

and every solution in terms of a regulatory institution was a mindset that itself
was shaped by the liberal conception of the rule of law. (Burley 1993, p. 145)

While this still has some potential analytical purchase on the development
of the rule of law as global common sense, here I want to suggest a more
dialectical process behind the rule of law's conceptual hegemony. In a
theme that will be returned to in a number of ways in the course of the
argument, we might say (in the words of Rajeev Dhavan) that it is best
to see law as struggle (Dhavan 1994): a struggle for meaning, a struggle
for legitimacy and perhaps most obviously as a struggle to obtain and
sustain justice. The parties to these struggles are varied and there are great
inequalities of power but the norm of the rule of law is often both the
subject of and the terrain over which these struggles take place. As E.P.
Thompson once suggested: 'The greatest of all legal fictions is that the law
itself evolves, from case to case, by its own impartial logic, true only to its
own integrity, unswayed by expedient considerations' (Thompson 1975,
p. 250). Rather, the rule of law can also be seen as the realm over which
debates, deliberations and disputes over the appropriate balance of public
and private power (in any given situation) may range (see, for instance,
Friedmann 1971). The rule of law, although often presented as neutral, is
deployed politically, but by both sides to different proposed ends.

As this suggests, one key aspect of this book is how we understand
the 'normativity' of the law; how we understand the way law shapes and
guides social actions by creating social obligations of one sort or another.
Sylvie Delacroix has formulated the social position of law as follows:

> [T]he normative dimension of the law cannot ever be taken as a 'given' estab-
> lished once and for all, provided the officials' minimal commitment condition is
> verified. Understood dynamically, law's normativity may be said to be brought
> about every day. Each time an individual is led to assess law's normative claims
> in the light of morality's demands, each time a judge is led to re-articulate what
> we want law for: these cases contribute to shaping the 'fabric' enabling law's
> normativity. (Delacroix 2009, p. 130)

Law's normative function is dynamic and constantly in a process of
becoming through its interaction with the society that it is intended to
govern. For Delacroix, the key to understanding normativity is appreciat-
ing any specific actors' commitment to the norm and how this is enacted,
as well as the obligations it may entail. Systemic normativity is enacted
through the actions and practices of those so 'guided'.

Moreover, this is not to be regarded merely as an instrumental relationship between norm and acting social individual (or corporate actor) but
rather as the result of a dialectical relationship between the law (and its

procedures) and common perceptions or prescriptions of the rule of law (Houtzager 2001, p. 11). Everyday socio-legal practices both (re)produce perceptions of the rule of law and also may shift the actual obligations this entails over time. Thus, in the international realm, as Brunnée and Toope suggest,

> law is created, maintained or destroyed through day-to-day interactions of communities of legal practice. Legal obligation cannot be reduced to the exist-ence of fixed rules; it is made real in the continuing practice of communities that reason with and communicate through norms. Although the stock of shared understandings may be relatively limited in international society, law making is possible ... To be meaningful, international law may need to track what little common ground there is, even if that ground is confined to a shared sense that future interactions should be *legal*, rather than purely social or political interactions. (Brunnée and Toope 2011, p. 131, emphasis in original)

This shared sense is, of course, the acceptance of the rule of law as a common sense, as a social imaginary, (re)produced through the practice of interactions between communities utilizing the rule of law as a common (background) norm.

Law's normativity, however, is understood quite differently by econo-mists and legal analysts; the former see the law as a set of incentives that are intended in some manner to support the (re-)emergence of equilibrium in social relations, while the latter see normativity as part of a structure of socialized obligation and (often) reciprocal agreement that the rule of law delivers social value (Kornhauser 1999). Rather than seeking to choose between these two understandings, I work on the basis that they are com-plementary aspects of the rule of law, which while potentially balanced differently in any specific case are both always present when seeking to fully appreciate how the rule of law works as a normative force in social relations. Another way of expressing this is to follow Robert Cover and stress that

> law is neither to be wholly identified with the understanding of the present state of affairs nor with the imagined alternatives. It *is* the bridge – committed social behaviour which constitutes the way a group of people will attempt to get from here to there. (Cover 1995, p. 176, emphasis in the original)

The rule of law, then, is how societies are shaped by their views about the good life as refracted through governing practice(s), partly a statement of social obligation, partly a structure of incentives (albeit mostly negative). When there are conflicts between reasons for acting (or not acting) the legal is the final arbiter of a decision (even if in any particular considera-tion this is not made explicit). The 'political' problem of the rule of law is that either consciously or inadvertently across (global) politics, actors have a tendency to elevate their political values to those of more neutral (but potentially enforceable) legal norms that are then intended to 'trump' other reasons for other actions and practices (Spaak 2005, p. 400). Thus, as the rule of law norm has 'emerged' as a key element of global politics, so it has acted to (partly) depoliticize conduct and conflicts.

## THE SOCIAL IMAGINARY OF THE RULE OF LAW AND GLOBAL POLITICS

Let's pause a minute and test whether the rule of law is part of your common sense (a social imaginary you recognize); try for a minute to think whether you would like to live in a world that was not governed by law(s). As Paul Kahn puts it, this is almost the 'equivalent of imagining a world without gravity' (Kahn 1999, p. 4). Although, to be fair, if you are a (political) anarchist, then you will likely believe a world without laws is possible,[2] but for everyone else I contend that even if you are unfamiliar with the details of the legal system, you are likely in general terms to favour the rule of law. We might then ask whether the expansion of the rhetoric of the rule of law indicates the strength of the norm or that the rule of law is subject to increasing challenge. If the latter, the articulation of the common sense is inversely proportional to its acceptance; the rule of law is not celebrated because it has finally been established but because it is often challenged, or does not command uncritical allegiance.

Therefore, one of the chief reasons for writing this book is a belated response to David Kennedy's observations (made over a decade ago) that:

> Those most enthusiastic about the rule of law as a development strategy treat it as a recipe or ready-made rather as a terrain for contestation and strategy . . . From a lawyer's point of view, these ideas about law expect the legal order to perform feats we know it rarely can accomplish and expect law to remain neutral in ways we know it cannot. (Kennedy 2004, p. 157)

Indeed, as he goes on to argue, depoliticization is rife:

> The idea that building the 'rule of law' might *itself* be a development strategy encourages the hope that choosing law *in general* could substitute for all the perplexing political and economic choices which have been at the centre of development policy making for half a century . . . The campaign to promote the

---

[2] But also see Taiwo (1999) for an argument for why some Marxists might also disagree with Thompson's (quasi) Marxist appeal to the rule of law.

rule of law as a development path has encouraged policy makers to forgo pragmatic analysis of the choices they make in building a legal regime – or to think
that the choices embedded in the particular regime they graft onto a developing
society represent the only possible alternative. (Kennedy 2004, p. 151, emphasis
in original)

The rule of law is not as simple as the discourse popularly promulgated
would imply, even though much expert commentary has come to accept
(and set out) these complications and variability. Kennedy's remarks have
a wider salience than merely the realm of development and legal capacity
building or technical assistance (although this is an important area that I
will examine later), but rather indicate something about the utilization of
the idea of the rule of law more widely.

The rule of law has become a common sense discourse (a social imaginary) meant to both describe the global system but also act as a guide for
what ought to be happening. It has joined human rights and democracy
to become part of what Amachai Magen has called the 'virtuous trilogy'
upon which legitimate international order is now regarded as resting
(Magen 2009, p. 53). As David Sugarman and Ronnie Warrington have
pointed out:

> Law is an influential story: it is one of the privileged ways through which society
> presents and defines the world to itself . . . Law is more than a structure of
> restraint, setting the boundaries within which individuals pursue their self inter-
> est. It is one of the major processes by which the dominant representations of
> society are created and justified. Law, is therefore, one of the major languages
> through which ideas are expressed. (Sugarman and Warrington 1995, p. 126)

Thus, when the rule of law is invoked it suggests that what is at stake is
not merely the existence of law, but something more; we seem to be invited
to evaluate the legitimacy of a system of laws in a specific circumstance.
That is to say, the rule of law is about more than the laws themselves; it is
concerned with the (social) values that are expressed through those laws,
and whether these values are legitimately furthered or promoted through
a legal system (Humphreys 2010, p. 5). Evaluations of the rule of law
have become central to the manner in which judgements are made about
which states, or political groups and organizations, are friends and which
are enemies. Those identified as following or working through the rule of
law are to be regarded as acting acceptably, and those identified as falling
short are regarded as problematic societies, failed states or enemies (Adler
and Bernstein 2005, pp. 309–10). The rule of law is not merely a value
that is applied to domestic states, but is also presented as an aspiration
for the international realm. Indeed, the articulation of the (global) social
imaginary of the rule of law is clearly evident at the United Nations (UN).

At the end of the Cold War (and in response to the general presumption that this was a historical threshold) the UN launched the Decade of International Law (1990–99) (UN Resolution 44/23, 17 November 1989).[3] Unlike other UN 'decades', for women or biodiversity, this decade was rather low key with little associated publicity and as such it is difficult to establish a direct causal link between this UN decade, states' actions and the expansion of the rhetoric (Suter 2004, p. 352). A year after the end of the decade, the UN's Millennium Declaration stressed the need to strengthen the rule of law three times; firstly, under Peace, Security and Disarmament, the declaration noted a need 'To strengthen respect for the rule of law in international as in national affairs and, in particular, to ensure compliance by Member States with the decisions of the International Court of Justice, in compliance with the Charter of the United Nations, in cases to which they are parties.' Secondly, under Human Rights, Democracy and Good Governance, the text declared, the UN 'will spare no effort to promote democracy and strengthen the rule of law, as well as respect for all internationally recognized human rights and fundamental freedoms, including the right to development'. Finally, under Strengthening the UN, the document suggests a need to 'strengthen the International Court of Justice, in order to ensure justice and the rule of law in international affairs'.[4] That said, while recognized as an enabling mechanism, the subsequent Millennium Development Goals (MDGs) did not explicitly include a rule of law-related goal.[5] If this was due to those focused on the rule of law failing to make the case for their inclusion, subsequently the rule of law has continued rising up the political agenda, which suggests that in the post-2015 reconfiguration of the UN's strategic developmental goals, the rule of law will likely be much more central.

Indeed, since the 2005 UN World Summit (celebrating 60 years of the UN) when the rule of law was identified as one of the four key areas that demanded greater attention by the UN and its associated organizations, supporting the rule of law (most often in post-conflict societies) has become a major element in the work of the UN (Bull 2008, p. 5, *passim*). More recently, on 24 September 2012 the UN General Assembly held a 'high-level meeting' on the rule of law, bringing heads of state and governments

---

[3] The text of the resolution is available at http://www.un.org/documents/ga/res/44/a44r023.htm (accessed 8 May 2013).

[4] All quotes from the Millennium Declaration at http://www.un.org/millennium/declaration/ares552e.htm (accessed 9 May 2013).

[5] The MDGs are: Eradicate Extreme Hunger and Poverty; Achieve Universal Primary Education; Promote Gender Equality and Empower Women; Reduce Child Mortality; Improve Maternal Health; Combat HIV/AIDS, Malaria and Other Diseases; Ensure Environmental Sustainability; Develop a Global Partnership for Development.

together with the General Assembly to 'reaffirm our commitment to the rule of law and its fundamental importance for political dialogue and cooperation among all states' (UNGA 2012, p. 1). The resulting document goes on to assert the link between the rule of law and human rights, development, an independent judiciary, and equal access to justice as well as a number of other elements usually regarded as being central to an evaluation that the rule of law obtains in any specific instance. By linking the national and international rule of law the document reflects a shift in the focus of the 'international community'; the UN Decade of International Law was focused on the rule of law between states, but this has been developed (through the processes that this book focuses on) to produce a linked political concern with the rule of law within states (Bouloukos and Dakin 2001, p. 147; Pahija 2011, pp. 172–253). The ascendance to the role of (global) societal value spans domestic and international/global concerns about governance.

Reflecting this support for the rule of law the UN website now has a dedicated section (under international law) on the United Nations and the Rule of Law, which starts with the following paragraph:

> Promoting the rule of law at the national and international levels is at the heart of the United Nations' mission. Establishing respect for the rule of law is fundamental to achieving a durable peace in the aftermath of conflict, to the effective protection of human rights, and to sustained economic progress and development. The principle that everyone – from the individual right up to the State itself – is accountable to laws that are publicly promulgated, equally enforced and independently adjudicated, is a fundamental concept which drives much of the United Nations work.[6]

The page then goes on to briefly expand on how the rule of law is 'embedded' in the UN's activities, noting that '[o]ver 40 UN entities are engaged in rule of law issues and the Organization is conducting rule of law operations and programming in over 110 countries in all regions of the globe'. The page offers links to key documents and statements, but in the top right hand corner also has a large box that links to the dedicated UN Rule of Law website and documentary repository.[7] The dedicated website offers a wealth of materials, documents and reports on UN activities related to the rule of law as well as more thematic policy documents and other resources including training and practitioner networks. The range of resources on offer demonstrates that the rule of law is a major element in the discourse of governance that is mobilized by the UN through its work

[6] http://www.un.org/en/ruleoflaw/index.shtml (accessed 1 May 2013).
[7] http://www.unrol.org/ (accessed 1 May 2013).

and complements the extensive material available on the World Bank's website. However, the structures of the UN and its charter, as well as the particular character of the international realm, have meant that (as I will discuss later) the UN Security Council (UNSC) is both (potential) champion of the rule of law but (problematically) hardly constrained by rule of law considerations in the final instance.[8]

Sometimes the norm of the rule of law can act to obscure differences between (national) versions of legal practice and can present them as part of the established, legitimate and achieved (global) political settlement. Jurisprudential discussions of the rule of law are consequently often of less importance to the norm than a purely legal analysis might assume. In this sense, I am interested in the norm of the rule of law in a similar manner to which Jason Sharman is interested in the manner in which the rhetoric around tax havens operates to establish various regulatory norms (Sharman 2006). One of the key parallels between our projects is that like the term 'tax haven', the rule of law is a site of contest(s) about meaning. However, the negative evaluation encapsulated by the term tax haven has significant impact on states' reputation as regards their ability to secure inflows of foreign investment. Conversely, the term rule of law is a badge of modernity, political legitimacy and acceptable political behaviour. To some extent my perspective here is a mirror image of Sharman's given that I am interested in the normative and positive reputational impact of claims to be governed by the rule of law.

In Sharman's study of the campaign by the OECD against (so-called) tax havens, he argues that the use of rhetoric and the political norms so 'performed' can lead to certain political actions becoming difficult if not impossible. This parallels my concerns as it is this notion of rhetorical power as deployed when the rule of law is raised in political debate that I am interested in. Sharman concludes that:

> The potential for the powerful to be entrapped by the stratagems of the weak, the slipperiness of meaning and language, and the unpredictability of policy effects mean that the control of dominant actors is never unchallengeable and their projects rarely go to plan. But international political economy is still most commonly a matter of the strong regulating as they will and the weak suffering as they must. The interplay of rhetoric and reputation may just as readily entrench inequalities as undermine them. (Sharman 2006, p. 161)

In Sharman's study the 'weak' were able to mobilize the OECD's norms to defend themselves against some political interventions (over

---

[8] See Chesterman (2008a) for an interesting set of recommendations intended to allow the UNSC to more fully shackle itself to rule of law norms and standards of practice.

non-intervention/sovereignty and the OECD's role as adjudicator not legislator, for instance); in the analysis of the rule of law I develop herein, what is most important in understanding the rhetoric is the widespread use of the normative claim, even though it is often 'honoured in the breach'. Understanding the rule of law and its rhetoric nevertheless taps into the same issues Sharman examines: the role of reputation as a relational quality and the role of rhetoric (rather than necessary action) in the attempt to maintain a reputation in the global political economy. This is especially relevant to the OECD as at the fourth World Justice Forum (in 2013) their head of statistics and indicators announced that the OECD now would be using the World Justice Project's Rule of Law index, which I discuss briefly later, as its authoritative indicator.[9]

There is also a considerable amount of commentary on the rule of law (to which I will return) that suggests that the rule of law is a form of conveyor belt for liberalization; that introducing the rule of law into the economic sphere will foster a form of spill-over into other areas of society and thereby act as a prompt to liberalization, although, as often this link seems to be more a matter of faith than hard evidence (Silverstein 2003), it again stresses that the rule of law is a social imaginary. Brian Tamanaha has described this position as:

> A mutually reinforcing circle exists, according to this faith, in which the rule of law begets democracy, which begets social welfare capitalism, which begets liberal rights, which begets women's rights. The causal arrows presumably go in all directions, each supporting the other, with the rule of law bearing substantial weight and responsibility for the whole. (Tamanaha 2011, p. 233)

He goes on to suggest that the difficulty is that while the rule of law is often treated by its (developmental) proponents as a general purpose technology, actually it is part of a mutually supporting set of institutions and practices that do not necessarily obtain whenever the rule of law is introduced as a political solution (Tamanaha 2011, pp. 235, 237). The actors that seek to deploy the law-as-technology are an important part of the analysis I develop later, not least of all as one of the key changes that seems to me to lie behind the expansion of the rhetoric of the rule of law (and its celebration) is the increasing professionalization of much of global politics, which has normalized the notion of the rule of law into a fundamental value of global politics; the common sense of global politics or its social imaginary.

---

[9] Zsuzsanna Lonti, presentation, World Justice Forum IV, Den Haag, Netherlands, 9 July 2013.

\* \* \*

I have now set out the main themes that I will be exploring in this book, and in the following methodological interlude I will say something about how I will approach these themes; that is to say, I will discuss how I do political economy. Once I have introduced my method, I then set out the range of ideas about legality that have patterned the jurisprudential discussion of the rule of law, before then (in Chapter 3) seeking to identify the agents through whom the (re)production of the rule of law as a common sense (the process of legalization) takes place. In the following two chapters (4 and 5) I examine how this plays out on the ground in two areas that have been the focus for much activity and commentary related to the rule of law: firstly, in post-conflict states where programmes seek to build (legal) capacities to reintroduce social order; then following a discussion of the rule of law as a developmental 'technology' I explore in a more general sense the link between the rule of law and the capitalist system of economics (and its links to economic development). I then refocus (in Chapter 6) on the idea of a global constitution (based, as it must be, on the rule of law), before in the last main chapter exploring two modes of challenge to the rule of law, one internal – civil disobedience – and one external or structural – the extent of legal pluralism – which in some senses undermines claims for a universalized rule of law in any substantive sense. The book concludes with some final reflections on the rule of law.

# A methodological interlude: how I do (global) political economy

My approach to International Political Economy (IPE) draws on a number of sources and is greatly indebted to the work of Susan Strange and Margaret Archer. I have laid out this approach in detail before and here repeat some of that discussion and elaborate particularly pertinent aspects that are directly relevant to the analysis set out in this book.[1] Although the discussion here reveals how I have developed my ideas, I do not believe an appreciation of my argument is dependent on looking under the bonnet (so to speak), and so if theoretical issues are of little interest to you, there is no necessity to work through this interlude; you can easily just pick up the argument in Chapter 2.

I start from the position that the rules that are the substance of social institutions are not natural, but are the products of social relations, expressed as knowledge about social reality, and knowledge of possibilities or constraints. These rules are reproduced by use; they may shift as new pressures are brought to bear on a social institution as a whole (or in part), but at any time the rules appear fixed; they appear as the structures of society. Thus, although the generation of knowledge produces institutions that appear as structures, it also allows for shifts as rules react to changes in the social relations within an institution's realm of influence. The operation of forms of power over such knowledge generation is crucial to understanding how certain narratives or rhetoric are used to establish the rule of law as the common sense of global politics and, as will become clear as you read on, I therefore see the rule of law as a dynamic norm that is constantly in a dialectical process of becoming.[2]

Susan Strange suggested that knowledge as a source of power in the

---

[1] Here I would also like to (once again) acknowledge the work of Susan Sell. Our jointly authored book on the history of intellectual property was the first place that this approach was articulated (broadly) in this manner and I would not have been able to develop my account of my method without the early and extensive aid that co-authorship offered.

[2] This might also be regarded as a position that rejects the reification of the rule of law (see, for instance, Gabel 1980; Kramer 1991, pp. 205–69); I have discussed my own position on reification (as related to intellectual property) elsewhere (see May 2006) and here have not sought to develop this particular direction of analysis, although I regard it as a perfectly plausible position to take.

international political economy is seldom accorded sufficient weight in analyses. It may be hard to analyse because what is believed, what is known (perceived as understood or 'given') and the channels by which these beliefs, ideas and knowledge are communicated or confined are not easily quantifiable. This lack of materiality and measurability, she argued, led to misrecognition of the importance of knowledge, but is also a result of the way the power of (and within) the knowledge structure manifests itself. As power derived from knowledge is often based on acquiescence, authority may flow from a socialized belief system, or from the status conferred by possession of knowledge (Strange 1988, pp. 115–18). There is seldom a clear power relation based on the utilization of material resources in the distribution and use of knowledge-derived power, and this led Strange to develop the idea of a knowledge structure.

Strange identified three sorts of change that should be accorded some importance within the analysis of this knowledge structure: changes in the provision and control of information and communication systems; changes in the use of language and non-verbal channels of communication; and changes in belief systems (Strange 1988, p. 116). The first group of changes is concerned with the control of the conduits of information and knowledge; the ability to constrict or alternatively facilitate the flow of knowledge around the global system. The second is concerned with the issue of the representation of knowledge and information. Issues of education and the ability to utilize information are crucial here; access is only part of the problem – there is a requirement for intellectual tools and practical, technical training as well. The third area of change is more fundamental and includes socialized systems of knowledge of which I will be arguing the rule of law is one significant element.

The key to this approach for thinking about power in the international political economy, power that is mediated through a knowledge structure, is that for Strange this structure is only one of four structures that act on each other. The other three structures that complete her overall characterization of structural power are: security; production; and finance (Strange 1988). However, the distinction between the knowledge and other structures starts to break down when a form of knowledge (here the rule of law) constructs, patterns and influences the practices in the other structures. This erodes the formal distinction between Strange's structures, seen as ontologically separate spheres of activity. However, her taxonomy of structures is not meant to identify hermetically sealed realms; quite the opposite: they are interpenetrated, and coexistent within a coterminous realm of political economy (Strange 1988, pp. 24–8). Indeed, they are meant as an aid for identifying lacunae in political economic analyses rather than a closed account of the field itself, and are an invitation to a pluralist epistemology, one that does not necessarily promote one form of evidence, information or form of data above another.

It is within the interactions of all four structures that specific 'bargains' between authority and market as a mechanism of control will be struck. In any particular case there is an (albeit temporary) settlement, produced by the mobilization of power, between the use of political authority to pattern the distribution of benefits and the use of a market mechanism. This settlement is never absolute; there is always an element of both mechanisms but the bargain made in a particular instance will allocate either authority or market as the lead distributional device. To adopt Strange's analysis of power, a mechanism of interaction between the structures that results in this settlement must be identified, and it is to this question I now turn.

## STRUCTURAL INTERACTION AND CHANGE

The central question that any analysis utilizing the idea of the knowledge structure needs to address is: how does knowledge interact with and affect the other structures? For Strange, it is the control of information and know-how that enables structural power to set the agendas in the other dimensions – security, finance and production. Broadly conceived, these other structures respectively set the agendas: in the realm of social welfare (stretching from local law and order, including national security, to the threat of war in the international system); in the realm of provision of credit and the economics of fiscal relations between state and non-state actors; and in the realm of productive relations, that is to say, the distribution of benefits and profits from industrial and economic activities. One of the main purposes of this sort of power is the transfer of risk from the powerful to the relatively powerless to further the retention of benefit by certain groups at the expense of others (May 1996). So, for Strange, structural power is agenda-setting power: the power to circumscribe choice in such a way that the limitation of choice is not perceived as such by the actors in social relations (Lukes 2005). This ability to set agendas also acts to obscure the particular political economic interests that certain rules and limitations on social action may serve. To carry this to its apparent logical conclusion is to place the knowledge structure in a foundational role: if the manipulation of knowledge is how agendas are set, and agenda setting is a central role of structural power (in that it shapes outcomes by ruling some as impossible and others as feasible), then knowledge issues must shape structures. This would require the knowledge structure to act as the primary structure; the foundation of the other structures.

However, Strange's position was always that the four structures interact, with none being necessarily prior in any particular situation. Therefore, to understand how structural power over knowledge reproduces social institutions the links and exchanges between materiality and knowledge (between the world and how we conceive of it) are of central importance. Thus, while it is analytically acceptable that knowledge or information can be a direct influence on specific actions, this is not the only aspect of its influence. The ability to establish warrant for truth claims enables power to define the social agenda of possibilities, within which resistance and opposition are mobilized. It sets the limits within which acceptable social practices can take place. Therefore, a critical IPE needs to reveal those social forces that support particular settlements and suggest alternatives that may be currently portrayed as implausible by the dominant set of institutional rules. If knowledge plays an important role in the agenda-setting processes of structural power, then the knowledge structure is itself subject to this agenda-setting process. The social institutions that set the agenda of social relations are themselves subject to structural power flowing from the knowledge structure *and* the other three material-focused structures; that is to say, material factors will impact on knowledge. Specifically, the manner in which the normative agenda of the rule of law is (dynamically) developed is not external to an account of the global political economy but rather remains a key aspect of the manner in which (Strange's notion of) structural power is both (re)produced and articulated.

## TRIANGULATION AND THE RULE OF LAW

Following work that I have developed with Susan Sell (May and Sell 2005), here I elaborate and develop further the approach we used to examine the political economic history of intellectual property. The 'triangulation' approach that I deploy draws its inspiration from the triangular interactions that Robert Cox identifies between material capabilities, institutions and ideas (Cox 1996, p. 98) and this works well as an analysis of specific aspects of Strange's general depiction of the structures of power in the global system. Cox's three ideal typical forces are a heuristic device for the examination of more specific complex realities (Cox 1996, p. 100), and produce an analysis that suggests that the ascendance of the rule of law has been a product of the interaction between three forms of social force:

- ideas: the political (and social) conception of the role of law (the norm of the rule of law);

- material capabilities: the resources used to (re)produce systems of law;
- institutions: the (global) political institutions that have 'normalized' the rule of law.

This allows institutions to be located in relation to their own history and the material capabilities they are linked with, as well as an account of the ideational developments they represent, which underpins a clearer depiction of the modes of interaction between Strange's overarching structures. Crucially, such an approach locates these social forces in the workings of the (historically specific) capitalist system (Cox 1996, p. 101). Recognizing the work of social forces in establishing the rule of law firmly locates such analysis within the contemporary political economy, not in some idealized world of legal relations, separate from the working of the global system.

Cox has highlighted the relationship between discourses and institutions insofar as institutions are perceived as legitimated. The weak will acquiesce when the strong, seeing their mission as hegemonic, are willing to make concessions to secure acquiescence and, crucially, if the strong can 'express this leadership in terms of universal or general interests, rather than just as serving their own particular interests' (Cox 1996, p. 99). Likewise, Quentin Skinner has emphasized the role of ideas and norms in politics, and perhaps most importantly how the rhetoric converges at the same time conflicts over practice remain. As he argues, when political actors seek to

> legitimise their conduct, they are committed to showing that it can be described in such a way that those who currently disapprove of it can be bought to see that they ought to withhold their disapproval after all. To achieve this end, they have no option but to show that at least some of the terms used by their ideological opponents to describe what they admire can be applied to include and thus to legitimate their own seemingly questionable behaviour. (Skinner 2002, p. 150)

But this can also involve

> [m]anipulating the criteria for applying an existing set of commendatory terms. The aim in this case is to insist, with as much plausibility as can be mustered, that in spite of contrary appearances a number of favourable terms can be applied to your own apparently questionable behaviour. (Skinner 2002, p. 153)

Moreover Skinner believes that

> [p]eople generally possess strong motives for seeking to legitimise any conduct liable to appear questionable. One implication is that they will generally find it

necessary to claim their actions were in fact motivated by some accepted principle. A further implication is that, even if they were not motivated by any such principle, they will find themselves committed to behaving in such a way that their actions *remain compatible* with the claim that their professed principles genuinely motivated them. (Skinner 2002, p. 155, emphasis in original)

And this suggests that we can agree that to 'study the principles [political actors] invoked will thus be to study one of the key determinants of their behaviour' as even if they are acting in bad faith there is a clear link between the articulated principles and norms used to justify their actions and those actions. This is because, they 'cannot hope to stretch the application of existing terms indefinitely; so they can only hope to legitimise, and hence to perform, a correspondingly restricted range of actions' (Skinner 2002, p. 156).

However, it may also be the case that the rhetoric (in this case, of the rule of law) acts to coerce political actors by denying them rhetorical resources by which to establish a plausible rebuttal to a negative evaluation of actions/stances (Krebs and Jackson 2007, p. 42). As Ian Stewart once commented about the rule of law: 'such expressions are triggers to exclude from discussions anything that is contrary to certain preferred statements, so that those that are preferred appear to lie beyond discussion, and hence have a suprahuman existence' (Stewart 2007, p. 4). However, for this coercion to have some purchase the political realm in which claim and evaluation are deployed must (at least potentially) be public, and the rhetoric not so flexible and permissive that a plausible claim be made by either side (Krebs and Jackson 2007, p. 57). On one level, at least some commentators would argue that this is exactly the difficulty with the 'rule of law' but I will return to this issue in subsequent chapters. Nevertheless, what remains of interest is why the rule of law *now*?

This question of why certain outcomes have come to pass is a central concern for a 'critical theory'. In Cox's formulation, such critical theory

> does not take institutions and social power relations for granted but calls them into question by concerning itself with their origins and how and whether they might be in the process of change ... Critical theory allows for a normative choice in favour of a social and political order different from the prevailing order, but it limits the range of choice to alternative orders which are feasible transformations of the existing world. (Cox 1996, pp. 88–90)

However, this is much more than merely the need to 'add history and stir'. What is required is sensitivity to the interaction of structures and agents within a continuing history of hegemony (and its reproduction). While I do not trace back the long history of the rule of law, subsequent chapters explore even its relatively recent history as a common sense of global politics as dynamic and still developing.

In this approach to political economy, the gaps between ideas and material conditions hold the key to understanding change. Margaret Archer offers an excellent way of conceptualizing the relationship between ideas and material conditions including institutions (that is to say, between Cox's social forces), not least of all because she refuses the temptation to identify either structure or agency as the final determining factor in social relations.[3] As I have already mentioned, Archer argues that focusing on agency alone and offering a 'bottom-up' causal explanation would make 'no allowances for inherited structures, their resistance to change, the influence they exert on attitudes to change, and crucially . . ., the delineation of agents capable of seeking change' (Archer 1995, p. 250). At the beginning of any particular sequence of history there are structures carried forward, reflecting previous political economic settlements, here regarding the manner in which the rule of law might be understood in a particular (historical) situation. But at the same time there are agents who are disadvantaged as well as those who manage to capture the benefits of the system at that particular juncture.

This is not to argue that agents have a completely free rein; they are constrained to some degree by the structures in which they find themselves, by the 'accumulated facts' (Onuma 2012) that result from prior (idea-driven) actions, but equally their actions are not finally determined by the structures. In other words, as Archer points out: 'voluntarism has an important place . . . but is ever trammelled by past structural and cultural constraints and by the current politics of the possible' (Archer 1982, p. 470). Historically extant structures are themselves the products of previous clashes of social forces, previous interactions of ideas, material capabilities and institutions. Agents' actions may be the immediate cause of specific moments of settlement, but they also remain embedded in larger structures, including material causes, state institutions and the structure of global capitalism, that both constrain and empower. Indeed, structural change itself can alter agents' interests if such change renders existing institutions less useful and agents begin to be harmed by a continuation of the status quo. Archer stresses that '*all* structural influences . . . *are mediated*

---

[3] In subsequent work Archer has focused increasingly closely on the question of individual reflexivity (Archer 2007, 2012). While this is clearly an important aspect of the social processes that she models (and which I discuss below), here I am more interested in the process as a way of indentifying the role of the rule of law as common sense than in explaining individual's actions, although this would be an interesting subject for a series of empirical or biographical investigations (of the sort Archer conducts) within the actor-groups I will deal with in subsequent chapters.

*to people by shaping the situation in which they find themselves'* (Archer 1995, p. 196, emphasis in original). The issue is the difference between the inherited structures (playing out in institutionalized settlements) and the continuing (or changing) interests of specific agents.

Put simply, structure and accumulated facts condition but do not determine agency. The power of agency lies in its 'capacities for articulating shared interests, organizing for collective action, generating social movements and exercising corporate influence in decision-making' (Archer 1995, pp. 259–60). This leads Archer to identify two types of agency: primary and corporate agency. Primary agents have neither organized nor articulated their interests and seldom participate strategically in shaping or reshaping structure. By contrast, corporate agents are 'those who are aware of what they want, can articulate it to themselves and others, and have organized in order to get it; [only they] can engage in concerted action to re-shape or retain the structural or cultural features in question' (Archer 1995, p. 258). In this sense, affected primary agents must develop collective, 'corporate' forms, to engage effectively in the political process of structural change or defence. Corporate agents 'pack more punch in defining and re-defining structural forms, and are key links in delimiting whether systemic fault lines (incompatibilities) will be split open . . . or will be contained' (Archer 1995, p. 191). In order to be successful, agents need some form of organization and the ability to articulate their interests. They need 'technical' expertise, political power and access to resources, including the very institutions they may wish to change. Agents may become dissatisfied with the status quo, recognizing that the structural incongruities threaten to reduce benefits and power, but unless they are able to organize a collective response they will be unable effectively to challenge more formalized groupings.

Following Archer: where there is a mismatch between the structurally available benefits and the politicized interests of marginalized agents, this may be translated into tensions and strains in the system, which are

> experienced as practical exigencies by agents whose interests are vested in the impeded institutions . . . Their situations are moulded in critical respects by operational obstructions which translate into practical problems, frustrating those upon whose day-to-day situations they impinge, and confronting them with a series of exigencies which hinder the achievement or satisfaction of their vested institutional interests. (Archer 1995, p. 215)

In these confrontations the shift in ideas about the structural settlement starts to become more apparent. While the beneficiaries will attempt to maintain the universality of the systems of justification of the status quo, the challengers will seek to identify the emerging practical (real) gaps in the institutional reflection of the dominant ideas of the current settlement.

Triangulation suggests that this process may be spurred by changes in the manner by which law is supported by political resources (of one kind or another), alerting the disadvantaged to new possibilities; shifts in the ideas about the rule of law emerging in society more generally; or by developments in legal institutions that are regarded as attempts to further advance the benefits of a particular group. These structural incongruities present distinctive 'situational logics which predispose agents towards specific courses of action for the promotion of their interests' (Archer 1995, p. 216). Archer calls this a 'contingent incompatibility' in which reproduction, or a continuation of the status quo, hinders the achievement of specific agents' aims. To claim that structural incongruity 'conditions oppositional action is merely to argue that such corporate agents are in a situation whose logic is to *eliminate* practices which are hostile to achieving their vested interests' (Archer 1995, p. 331, emphasis in original). The aggrieved seek to eliminate hostile practices.

In this perspective on change in the global system, structural incongruities may spur action, but discursive strategies can also constrain change or render it coherent and legitimate, not least of all as actors struggle to bring their actions and claims into line with each other (Skinner 2002). Or, as Archer puts it:

> The interaction of a variety of material interest groups, each of which has become articulate in its own defence and capable of detecting self-interest in the claims of others, is enough to preclude any drift back to unquestioned structural [settlements] . . . The groups have mobilized, ideas have helped them to do it, and assertion will not fade away because the material interests it seeks to advance do not evaporate. (Archer 1995, p. 322)

This indicates why arguments for the status quo, or even its further structural strengthening, need to be constantly rearticulated and defended in the political arena not least of all by the assertion of something as common sense (here, the rule of law). As disparities between perceived 'reality' (both technological and political) and the narrative of the previous (institutionalized) settlement become wider, so the pressure for change grows and the defence becomes more fervent.[4]

---

[4] In Mark Bevir and R.A.W Rhodes's similarly focused analytical approach these are referred to as 'dilemmas' (Bevir and Rhodes 2010). For an extended discussion of how Bevir develops the analysis of how dilemmas shape changes in agents' ideas and beliefs see Bevir (1999, pp. 221–64).

## STRUCTURAL POWER

Having explored the manner in which agency and structure might interact
in the realm of political economy, there remains the issue of how this
informs an analysis of the interaction within Strange's multi-structure
model. Deploying an analysis of the knowledge structure, it is necessary
to understand not only how aspects of 'recognized reality' inform 'knowledge' but also how the knowledge structure informs what is recognized in
other structures. This needs to go beyond (but without dispensing with)
the conception of a knowledge structure affecting the other structures
through the utilization of information, and establish the mechanisms (or
processes) that allow the knowledge structure to mediate the interaction
between the other structures. The role of the knowledge structure is central
to the interactions between other structures but does not exclusively
determine the outcomes.

The key role of the knowledge structure is the attempt to keep potential
issues out of politics altogether: structural power controls (or more accurately, seeks to control) the agenda to obscure and hide conflict. Though
potential conflicts (and contradictions) will still exist, they may never
be actualized. As Steven Lukes has pointed out there may be a '*latent*
conflict, which consists of a contradiction between the interests of those
exercising power and the *real* interests of those they exclude' (Lukes 2005,
p. 28, emphasis in original). This involves a counter-factual argument: a
particular settlement is recognized and it is suggested that this settlement is
obscuring aspects of potential social conflict (that is to say, expected conflicts are not manifest) and thus the absence is explained by the operation
of structural power.

This positing of absent (though analytically expected) conflict suggests
that the prevailing authority or power, through intervention in institutional practices, aims to define problems and by doing so, the choices of
solution. By controlling the agenda, the decision-making process may
be presented as fair and equitable because unpalatable or unacceptable
solutions never reach the agenda for consideration; they are ruled nonsensical or 'uninformed'. In this way, language can be crucial: illogical,
'extreme', idealistic, outdated, opinionated, 'political' alternatives may all
be stigmatized and below them there is a sub-strata of positions that are
irrational or 'stupid'; moreover, such judgements may be implied by political discourse rather than necessarily made explicit. The agendas that are
formed are not just explicit lists from which social actions are chosen, but
the implicit (sometimes hardly conscious) choices among perceived alternatives made by social actors; their world-views (their social imaginaries;
their common sense). The formation of agendas through the 'prism' of the

knowledge structure informs the choices (and the perception of available choices) made in the other structural dimensions of the global political economy. But the power relations within the other structures (and the changes therein) also feed into the process of contradiction and elaboration of alternatives, establishing what is 'possible' given specific material resources.

The recognition of legitimate alternatives can be constricted by power relations. Expectations about the results of social actions are needed to make decisions as to their possibility or viability, but the recognition of what can be done at a particular juncture is subject to knowledge structural agenda formation. This agenda of possible alternatives is itself related to the pattern of power resources elsewhere (in the security, production or finance structures). Thus, materially existing (and therefore possible) options cannot be marginalized indefinitely. The contradiction between the existence of the resources to produce particular outcomes and the representation of their non-existence will lead to pressures for change at the level of social relations, as Archer contends. The conflicts within material social relations – the competition for scarce resources, for security, for the limited provision of credit and so forth – feed into the continual (re)construction of agendas within the knowledge structure. Where these conflicts may imply different settlements from those that currently shape outcomes, resistance to such change is possible through the knowledge structure's shaping of expectations and the reinforcement of institutional rules. But where legitimized alternatives do not satisfactorily reflect changes in social forces, it is unlikely that resistance to change through the knowledge structure can prevail forever. In other words, changes in the patterns of power in the production, financial and security structures will shape the agendas in the knowledge structure as time goes on.

Through the recognition of contradictions and complementarities within the interactions of the actors in the global political economy, power within all the structures is constantly being both challenged and reinforced. Material resources appear in different guises in different structures, and trans-structural resource use leads to changes in agenda setting in the knowledge structure as the potential for new resources to impact on particular structures is either resisted or utilized. The historic ability to set or police agendas may be challenged by those enjoying some emerging material resource advantage in a particular structure. Through changes in agenda setting, there may be attempts to reconfigure conflicts to lend more weight to different resources. The 'history' of threats itself may be rewritten in an attempt to reinforce an agenda that reflects the current availability of material resources. Therefore, in the complex social relations of the global political economy the different structures of power interact through agenda setting. The power within each structure – security, production, knowledge, finance – is the product of its interaction with the other three by virtue of the resources needed to maintain a legitimated agenda-setting ability. And while this might imply some priority for the knowledge structure, this is not the case. The structures cannot be finally separated or prioritized; each needs resources only available in other structures. Power is produced through combinations of ideational and material resources.[5]

## FOCUSING ON IDEAS IN (INTERNATIONAL) POLITICAL ECONOMY

Having discussed my approach to IPE with its focus on the role of norms and agents, and knowledge (in a general sense), here I will finish by relating my work to some other work looking at the role of (economic) ideas. The study of ideas by political economists has been gaining ground for some years, and there is clearly a significant overlap with the approach I have detailed above. Vivien Schmidt has gathered a range of approaches that 'take ideas and discourse seriously' and rendered them/us as 'discursive institutionalists' (Schmidt 2010, p. 2). She summarizes the approach in a table (part of which I reproduce) and which seems to me to be a reasonable characterization of my method as elaborated above, as well as indicating how my work links with the 'ideational turn' in IPE.

Schmidt presents this discursive institutionalism as shown in Table M.1.

Overall such approaches to political economy, like the analysis being developed in this book, take ideas seriously as causes of social action and practices, while being clear that these ideas cannot merely be read off from the structures of the political economy; ideas are not merely determined by material conditions.

Setting out the aim of such work, Colin Hay has therefore recently suggested that analysis must not remain grounded in an overly materialist understanding of the manner in which (political) interests are formed. Rather,

> if actors can misperceive or fail to recognize their materially given or 'genuine' interests, and it is their perceptions of such interests rather than those interests

---

[5] Although expressed and developed rather differently I see clear parallels between my own approach to IPE and that of Rodney Bruce Hall (2008); in the main our influences and analytical elements are quite different but we seem to end up with a relatively similar approach to IPE. Likewise, although from a different disciplinary focus, there are considerable parallels (in intent, if not necessarily in methodology) between this approach and that of 'moral economy' as a critical approach to political economy (see Sayer 2000, 2007).

*Table M.1    Discursive institutionalism: key elements*

| | |
|---|---|
| Object of explanation: | Ideas and discourse of sentient agents |
| Logic of explanation: | Communication |
| Definition of institutions: | Meaning structures and constructs |
| Approach to change: | Dynamic – change (and continuity) through ideas and discursive interaction |
| Explanation of change: | Endogenous process through background ideational and foreground discursive abilities |
| Recent innovations to explain change: | Endogenous construction through reframing, recasting, collective memories and narratives through epistemic communities, advocacy coalitions, communicative action, deliberative democracy |

*Source:*    Schmidt (2010, p. 5).

themselves that informs, guides and motivates their action, then the context that they inhabit is no longer an obvious guide to their behaviour . . . [and thus] to the extent that ideas might exert an independent influence on outcomes, the analogy between natural and social/political systems breaks down, and hence the appropriateness of naturalism as an epistemological guide to political science diminishes. (Hay 2011, pp. 73–4)

However, as Hay then goes on to observe, given this potential (at least partial) disconnect between the ideational and the 'real',

one might be forgiven for expecting similarly located actors to reach widely divergent perceptions of their own self-interest. Yet what is remarkable is that, by and large, they do not. That is, of course, conventionally taken as a confirmation of the extent to which material interests are, for similarly located actors, essentially shared. *Yet it is surely rather more plausible to see such similarities in perceived interests as a reflection of the prevalence, at any given point in time of conventions for the evaluations of one's interests.* (Hay 2011, p. 76, emphasis added)

Unsurprisingly, what I am arguing is that it is exactly this form of conventional perception of interests (around social regulation) that is encompassed by the rule of law.

Adopting a perspective similar to Hay's suggests that what becomes crucial is not to explain how the rule of law represents the interests of specific classes or groups in the political economy but to explain how and why particular subjects (or groups of subjects) 'came to conceive (or, more accurately, to reconceive) of their interests in such terms' (Hay 2011,

p. 80). This suggests a focus on the 'social and political processes in and through which interests are identified, constructed and rendered' (Hay 2011, p. 81). Moreover as Mark Blyth has pointed out, ideas related to the economy are especially conducive to collective impact; as the market is the sum of individuals' actions, and perceptions shape actions, if most believe the economy to work in a certain way and shape their actions accordingly, then the character of the economy is likely to follow such perceptions (Blyth 2002, pp. 41–4). However, as Archer's approach emphasizes, this is not merely a one-way causal chain; ideas certainly help shape actions and practices, but as importantly for analysis, practises and agents, particular actions impact on the manner in which ideas are (re)produced and (re) formed. Thus, an analysis of the ideational in political economy cannot help but be dialectical if it is to capture the role of ideas but refuses to finally accord either ideas or materiality any general determinacy. This parallels John Campbell's suggestion that discussions in politics that seek to foreground ideas can avoid the temptations of a casual idealism by ensuring to maintain a strong account of the link between ideational and material factors, interests or issues (Campbell 2002). It is this requirement for a fully developed appreciation of such interactions that holds my method close to Archer's perspective.

Generally, one of the main concerns of political economic approaches to ideas has been the relationship between putative (or supposed) universal ideas, values or norms and the local conditions in which they play out in a globalized system. Perhaps the most obvious area where the issue of ideas and global context meet in the contemporary realm of the rule of law is in the often perceived tensions between the rule of law's universalism and local customs' norms, or traditional laws. Norm diffusion (or more actively promotion) can only take place in these circumstances through a process of extended negotiation between the universalized idea and its localized recipients, whose own perceptions and ideational commitments will result in a localized settlement that while recognizably still with the normative 'family' (here of the rule of law) may also diverge in important aspects (Acharya 2004). Local interests linked to the material relations of the particular society or polity interact with external ideas, values and norms that more globally engaged interests have adopted or wish to promote for their own benefit. This interaction between perceptions of interests and material society in the realm of the political economy influences social dynamics. In Mark Blyth's view this means that '[e]conomic ideas can create the basis of a mutual identity between differently located economic and political agents. In short, they can build bridges across class and consumption categories through the redefinition of agents' interests' (Blyth 1997, p. 246). Thus, in the case that I am concerned with here, the rule of law becomes a key normative driver, where negative results for specific agents become individual issues not systemic ones.

That said, it is also important to recognize that just because ideas are regarded as important does not mean that they are necessarily singular or fixed. In the case of the rule of law this is especially the case, as will become clear during the subsequent discussion. One of the central elements of the approach to ideas that I work with is that analysis must not merely be concerned with the role socially constructed ideas play in political economy but as importantly must account for their continued (re)construction (Hudson and Martin 2010, p. 111). Ideas cannot be treated as essences held static for analytical purposes; political ideas are protean in that they are not only unfixed, they are always in political flux. What then is of interest is the processes, practices and actions by which the struggle to fix ideas takes place and is confronted by social forces and material circumstances that undermine ideational settlement.

However, while I start from the position that ideational consolidation and contestation are never completely achieved nor finalized, it is likely that certain ideas benefit from network effects, in that once certain influential or powerful groups begin to articulate a particular idea (or norm), even as it also shapes their own actions, so those with whom they are connected politically will need to at the very least also share discursive elements and amend their practices in line with these ideas if they are to avoid conflicts (Pierson 2004, pp. 39–40). As these ideas become reinforced through this interaction, so the network of agreement will expand as other actors also engaged with those who have initially articulated the particular idea and its associated actions or practices. As Schmidt very clearly and helpfully concludes:

> Without discourse, understood as the exchange of ideas, it is very difficult to explain how ideas go from individual thought to collective action. We don't after all know what people are thinking or why they act the way they do until they say it. And we don't for the most part engage in collective action or in collective (re)thinking of our actions without the articulation, discussion, deliberation and legitimatization of our ideas about our actions. (Schmidt 2010, p. 15)

It is the role of the norm of the rule of law in these interchanges and how it has become so normalized to be a common sense that is my focus.

Of course, not all ideas are equal and those whose supporters are best resourced are more likely to prosper and spread (Pierson 2004, p. 75). Moreover, to take a particular legal example, as Paul Pierson notes (glossing research into legal change):

Once particular social environments have been judicialized, other actors involved in these domains face powerful incentives to adapt. Judicial procedures become a key part of the rules of the game . . . Repeated employment of judicial procedures over an extended period of time is likely to generate profound change in norms. (Pierson 2004, p. 159)

The strength of the norm of the rule of law ensures that it is unlikely (if not actually formally impossible) for such trends to be effectively reversed; once adopted and normalized the manner in which the idea of the rule of law brooks no alternative (no non-legal alternative, that is) ensures that it continues to find actors seeking to benefit from the enjoyment of its (normative) scope for their actions and practices.

This, most certainly, is not to argue that there is one clearly accepted definition of the idea of the rule of law. Rather, as Jeremy Waldron has pointed out, the 'formal ideas are not always what ordinary people, newspaper editors and politicians have in mind when they clamour for the rule of law' (Waldron 2011, p. 4). Nevertheless, it remains a popular and appealing phrase (and idea) because it responds to two powerful contemporary aspects of political and intellectual opinion: the desire for universal truths that can be articulated across our increasingly globalized world society; and to the growing mistrust of politics itself (Upham 2004, p. 280). The rule of law can be presented as a universal value that at the same time seems to be reassuringly technical (non-political) in its application. These perceived advantages may actually be chimerical, as will be developed in subsequent chapters, but are nonetheless powerful for that. Moreover, for ideas to be powerful or influential, as well as legitimate, in politics they need to be relatively widely known and while not necessarily fully understood at least acknowledged as meaningful and applicable. Ideas that shape actions are also reinforced by the 'accumulated facts' (Onuma 2012, p. 173) of their articulation into practice; and it is these practices I will now start to focus on.

# 2. Defining the rule of law, between thick and thin conceptions

> No one in the international community is quite sure what the term 'rule of law' actually means. (Bouloukos and Dakin 2001, p. 145)

> [The] 'Rule of Law' is almost never carefully defined as a concept; users of the expression allude to meanings they assume to be clear and objective but that are not so. (Mattei and Nader 2008, p. 10)

> [O]ne fundamental problem with measuring the success of rule of law reform initiatives is that the parties assessing them may have something quite different in mind to those implementing them. (Ringer 2007, p. 182)

There are extensive debates about what the rule of law might be and I do not intend to try to assert a single authoritative definition, not least as this has evaded experts in jurisprudence and legal philosophers of greater intellect than me. Rather, I seek to establish the range of elements that are (relatively) frequently identified in ruminations on the rule of law, and that inform the sorts of practices and behaviours that those who appeal to the rule of law might think they (and/or others) are likely to be held to. Political language can only be stretched so far, and by asserting their acceptance of the rule of law political actors must in some way recognize its legitimacy (or at least specific elements of it), even if this remains a cynical political manoeuvre.[1] If the rule of law norm is used to evaluate others' political systems or practices, it is the elements discussed below that are usually used (in various weightings) as evaluative criteria. As Ian Johnstone puts it: '[o]nce governments rhetorically accept a legal norm, they begin to argue about its interpretation and application to the particular case at hand rather than the validity of the law itself' (Johnstone 2010, p. 181); it is this rhetorical repertoire that I explore below.

There are many ways of setting out these debates. I could have presented them chronologically with (perhaps) an argument about origins of the norm (May 2012) or conversely I might have distinguished between

---

[1] See the discussion of Quentin Skinner in the methodological interlude that precedes this chapter.

particular traditions of jurisprudence – positive and natural law traditions. Many contemporary discussions of the rule of law start with Albert
Venn Dicey and his famous depiction of the rule of law in *Introduction to
the Study of the Law of the Constitution* (Dicey 1915 [1982], pp. 107–273).
Here, the rule of law is an integral part of the British Constitution, and
encompasses the acceptance of the absolute supremacy of the law, the
requirement that all be treated as equal by the law and the central importance of the British 'legal spirit'. Dicey has been criticized for 'merely
enshrining his own political philosophy under the guise of the rule of
law' (Cosgrove 1980, p. 83), but while he certainly seems to have coined
the phrase the 'rule of law', his treatment, although influential, is (for my
concerns here) a little too embedded in a focused discussion of the history
of the British Constitution to help us quickly delineate the norm.

Given his continued prominence in the social sciences we might also
begin with Max Weber's account of the rule of law; here, law (or more
precisely 'legality') is one of the three central modes by which authority
(or domination) is legitimated (Weber 1970, pp. 78–9). The use of law is
prompted at least partly by the ability of lawyers to establish the social
authority of their practices due to their proclaimed ability to analyse and
interpret the dominant mode of modern politics: the spoken or written
word (Weber 1970, pp. 95, 217). (I return to the role of lawyers in the next
chapter.) Weber's account sees the rule of law as contributing to the rationalization of contemporary capitalist society, but (in a dialectical relationship) also reflecting such rationalization. There is a causal link between
the development of (the rule of) law and the development of modern
capitalism (linked to the calculable character of rational law), but at different times Weber wavers about the strength of determination he wishes
to accord to the relationship (Feldman 1991, pp. 222–3). While law and
society are linked dialectically, most often for Weber influence is stronger
from law to society (and specifically towards the forms of economic relations) than in the other direction. Although not standing outside of social
relations, the rule of law maintains certain formal elements and practices
that are relatively unaffected by socio-economic transformations, indicating that while law may have influenced the development of capitalism, the
law itself as a (quasi) rational system pre-dates it.[2]

Reflecting on Weber's treatment of legal history, Harold Berman
and Charles Reid suggest that the four forms of law Weber proposes –
traditional law; charismatic law; formal-rational law (based on consistency

---

[2] The main source for Weber's depiction of law is the long Chapter VIII, 'Sociology of law',
in Weber (1978, pp. 641–900), where the themes alluded to in this and the next paragraph
are set out and explored in some (historical) detail.

of rules); and substantively rational law (based on fairness and equity) – are not necessarily ideal types that can be found individually (or sequentially) in the history of law, but are elements that have been (re)combined in the Western legal tradition in various ways at various times (Berman and Reid 2000). Moreover, Weber criticizes formal-rational law on the basis that while operating through rational processes, it fails to accord any weight to extra-legal questions, such as the ability of the wealthy to gain advantage through the ability to hire expert practitioners to plead their cause. In the terms I use in this chapter, only when social irrationality is defeated by a 'thicker' reading of the law can the rule of law properly be said to obtain (Feldman 1991, pp. 226–9; Weber 1970, pp. 219–21). Weber does not present a progressive teleology, but rather indicates (empirically) that the rule of law may often entail a conflict and struggle between supporters of a thick and thin reading of its normative content or character (although he does not use such terms).

However, rather than take this historical jurisprudential route, I have chosen to organize the discussion around a continuum of meaning from the thinnest definition(s) or lowest threshold for a judgement that the rule of law obtains, to much more substantive views that raise the threshold of when we can say the rule of law exists. Moving along the continuum from thin to thick depictions of the norm, the definition of the rule of law becomes more exacting, or challenging as a goal. This may remove the history from these debates, but it is the range of meanings deployed that I want to capture here, although clearly the way the norm has developed is of some importance for my perspective and plays a part in the subsequent analysis.

Not only are there debates about the content and requirements of the norm of the rule of law, there are also disagreements about what it is meant to achieve (Krygier 2006; Ringer 2007; Waldron 2002, p. 159). Defining the rule of law is not easy partly because the term itself contains an immediate ambiguity inasmuch as it implies both rule (as direction, control: ruling) and rules as guides for actions (rules as parameters) (Schauer 1991, pp. 167–9). It is this secondary meaning that raises difficulties: what parameters does the rule of law set on behaviour? Does it merely require explicit rule following, or is ruling by law indicative of a certain form of rule in itself?[3] We need to make this sort of distinction because, as many have pointed out, citing the examples of Nazi Germany, India during the

---

[3] There is a famous (in legal circles) debate between Herbert Hart and Lon Fuller (conducted in the pages of the *Harvard Law Review*) on the morality (or otherwise) of the law, which is parallel to my concerns here, but space precludes a detailed account of its specific contours; see Lacey (2008) for a good guide to its content and context.

Emergency or Apartheid in South Africa, there may be circumstances where the rule of law brings about unjust outcomes (Dhagamwar 1998, pp. 122–32; Dworkin 1985, pp. 12–13; Dyzenhaus 2007). Therefore, when considering the rule of law we often also judge the content of the law itself and the manner in which the law interacts with the society that it purports to govern or regulate. Following many other writers, I refer to these as a 'thick' view of the rule of law encompassing a wider set of legal norms such as equity and justice, and a more process and institution-focused 'thin' rule of law that seeks only to specify method rather than content.[4]

These contrasting depictions are both ideal typical; thick and thin conceptions of the rule of law are separated by a continuum between nodal points, along which definitions may move in one direction or another, rather than being two clearly distinguishable modes of thought! Although it is an interesting issue, I do not seek here to answer the perfectly legitimate jurisprudential question: how thick does a rule of law conception need to be, to be regarded as at the thick end of the continuum? In the end this is a political judgement, not a well-defined benchmark. It is also worth stressing that even the thinner (or procedural) notion of the rule of law is normative as it supports a view about good and proper modes of procedure that cannot be said to be natural or non-social. Thus, the rule of law's thick–thin continuum is a range of normative positions and while tendencies or relative positions can be identified it is unlikely that we would find anyone expressing the ideal typical end points themselves.

Finally, due to its complexity the rule of law is a norm, ideal or value to which any legal system may aspire, but may only reach unevenly (some elements may be nearer the norm that others) (Sampford 2006, pp. 59, 62). It is not a single standard against which legal systems can be easily measured, but rather a politicized process of evaluation. Indeed, Richard Fallon argues that practically any judgement about the rule of law in a particular case is likely to be about whether it is good enough to qualify and it's unlikely that all commentators will necessarily agree that any particular legal system fully realizes the rule of law (Fallon 1997, p. 38). Debates are often couched in terms of 'departures' from the rule of law or the 'weakening' of the rule of law, or particular actions

---

[4] A small sampling of analysts who have worked with this bifurcation includes: Bassu (2008), HiiL (2007), Hutchinson and Monahan (1987), Magen (2009), Møller and Skaaning (2012), Ngugi (2005), Peerenboom (2002), Ringer (2007), Sampford (2006), Thompson (2012) and Trebilcock and Daniels (2008). Although also see Rose (2004), who refers to the difference as between the 'narrow view' and the 'more lofty', Craig (1997) (and others), who prefer 'formal' and 'substantive', Fallon (1997), who sets out four (complementary) ways of understanding the norm or (in his words) 'ideal' and Kleinfeld (2006), who divided approaches between those focused on ends and those focused on institutions.

'undermining' it (Waldron 2008, pp. 44–5). This lack of precision can cause significant problems in the evaluation of capacity building and legal/technical assistance programmes of the sort I will be exploring later; with no clear criteria for success, any programme's worth becomes a subject of political assertion rather than judgement based on data or unambiguous evidence. It is not clear whether we should ascribe this difficulty to political cowardice on behalf of the rule of law's supporters (Staton 2010) or whether, as the discussion below (perhaps) implies, it is too complex an issue for a settled consensus on more than very basic procedural issues to emerge.

## THE RULE OF LAW CONTINUUM

For Brian Tamanaha, the rule of law is a historically shifting norm: at the turn of the millennium a thin, instrumental or procedural rule of law norm was dominant, while earlier in history (and most obviously prior to the Enlightenment) a thicker, more substantive understanding of the rule of law was the dominant norm, albeit under different terminology (Tamanaha 2001, pp. 104–6). A decade later, the thinner view is not necessarily as dominant in the divergent discussions of (global) politics, but recognition of this continuum suggests that any claim that the content of the rule of law norm is largely self-evident or obvious is misplaced.

Francis Fukuyama sees the distinction I explore here as spatial; generally, Americans view the rule of law as procedural and as such it cannot encompass social objectives (although clearly views within the USA differ widely), while Europeans are happier to accept a thicker rule of law with social policy ends introduced through adjudication (Fukuyama 2004, pp. 156–7). Conversely, for Boaventura de Sousa Santos, thinner approaches reflect the 'streamlining of the emancipatory potential of the rule of law and the conversion of the latter into just one more technique of regulation' (de Sousa Santos 2002, p. 341); the thicker approach to the rule of law has now become a central aspect of the counter-hegemonic resistance that confronts contemporary neoliberal (globalized) capitalism (de Sousa Santos 2002, pp. 278–311, 445–6). Others have suggested that the thicker conception represents a normative trajectory observable over the last 50 years, by which good governance, democracy and human rights have found their way into the core definition (Bouloukos and Dakin 2001, p. 147). Without an agreed definition (and thus a telos or agreed end point) the rule of law could, however, subsequently be moved away from these specific values (Kahn 1999, pp. 106–7); there is no clear narrative of progress in the rule of law. A thicker rule of law position is not only a wider analytical treatment of legality; it is a political tool that is increasingly deployed in (global) politics.

The thicker conception of the rule of law prompts a wider analysis of the effects of law, moving beyond a concern with formal regulation and pro-cedural matters, towards an expanded conception of the manner in which law contributes to the constitution of society and its practices, relations and structures. This leads Paul Kahn to argue that the

> rule of law is a social practice: it is a way of being in the world. To live under the rule of law is to maintain a set of beliefs about the self and community, time and space, authority and representation. It is to understand the actions of others and the possible actions of the self as expressions of these beliefs. Without these beliefs, the rule of law appears as just another form of coercive governmental authority. (Kahn 1999, p. 36)

Thus, as critique, a thick conception of the rule of law claims that thin depictions remove any concrete notion of the good society from the evaluation of accordance with the rule of law (Kratochwil 2009, p. 196), as we must consider the content of the law itself and the manner in which the law interacts with the society that it purports to govern or regulate. Indeed, critics of the thin conception argue that what it misses is that the very establishment of the rule of law is a process of norm creation, and not merely the instigation of a set of procedures (Brooks 2003, p. 2285). This distinguishes between a claim for the rule of law that merely seeks to identify a society that deploys legal procedures to regulate and shape behaviour, and a society where the rule of law itself precludes and forbids certain (ab)uses of political power. Those proposing a thin depiction of the rule of law argue that unfortunately there is nothing to guarantee that the extra-legal norms recognized in this manner will be progressive or liberal, and thus evaluations around the rule of law should be confined to just practice and leave the social outcomes for the political realm, seen as clearly separate from the legal realm.

## THE THIN RULE OF LAW

As his work is frequently cited, I start with Joseph Raz's attempt to establish the essential character of the rule of law. Raz counter-poses the rule of law or government with the rule of men, but immediately notes that this distinction is impossible to maintain, as social organizations are made up of individuals (Raz 1979a, p. 212); whatever the law's claims as regards its technical prac-tice, human deliberation and interpretation are always present.

At its most basic, law 'must be capable of guiding the behaviour of its subjects' (Raz 1979a, p. 214); that is to say, it must not be secret nor physically impossible to follow and must be available for scrutiny so that such legal 'guidance' can be assessed and followed. Raz then goes on to produce a set of principles that underpin the rule of law.

1. All laws should be prospective, open and clear; laws cannot be retroactive,[5] nor should they be difficult to understand, ambiguous or imprecise.
2. Law should be relatively stable, because it frequently guides future and planned actions. While there is always a need for new laws to be enacted and old laws to be reformed, this should be kept to a necessary minimum to allow guidance of social behaviour to be coherent.
3. The making of particular laws (particularly legal orders) should be guided by open, stable, clear and general rules. The rule of law must encompass a framework for its own development and amendment.
4. The independence of the judiciary must be guaranteed. If the law is to be predictable and stable, then adjudication must be guided by legal principles, not extra-legal political influence.
5. The principles of natural justice must be observed including a fair hearing, absence of bias and open processes.
6. The courts should have review powers over the implementation of other principles to ensure that conformity to the general rule of law is maintained.
7. The courts should be easily accessible; there should not be impediments of cost or time, because otherwise it is difficult for people to be sure of the guidance offered by the law.
8. The discretion of the crime-preventing agencies should not be allowed to pervert the law. The rule of law should not appear arbitrary nor driven by extra-legal considerations of its agencies (Raz 1979a, pp. 214–18).

Raz himself admits this is a partial and incomplete list, but stresses even these aspects of the rule of law can only be judged in relation to the key requirement that the law is able to offer guidance as regards social activity and practice.[6]

---

[5] Although see Charles Sampford's book-long reflection on the issue of retrospection in law (Sampford 2006).

[6] Lon Fuller's perhaps equally famous list of eight elements of the rule of law is: generality; publicly available; no retroactivity; clarity of exposition; no contradictions; no impossible prescriptions; stability; consistency in application (Fuller 1969). See Marmor (2004) for an argument that Fuller's list is not as thin a conception of the rule of law as might be initially presumed.

Interestingly, Raz sees the rule of law as an essentially negative value: 'conformity to [the rule of law] does not cause good except through avoiding evil and the evil which is avoided is evil which could only have been caused by the law itself' (Raz 1979a, p. 224). If law is the arbiter of good and evil, then 'evil' is merely a function of the place where this line is drawn! However, this essentially 'empty' conception (Tamanaha 2004, p. 95) implies that the rule of law, without the content that the thicker norm gives it, remains a tool that can be used by arbitrary power to harm individuals or groups within its jurisdiction. Thus, the rule of law both opens the possibility of arbitrary rule and through a subsequent (but for Raz, clearly separate) legal ideology forestalls this development, unless, that is, the rule of law is present but the normative (legal) ideology is not. This view has been subject to some criticism, not least of all from Jeremy Waldron, who has argued:

> Raz is wrong about this. The Rule of Law is an ideal designed to correct the dangers of abuse that arise in general when political power is exercised, not dangers of abuse that arise from law in particular. Indeed, the Rule of Law aims to correct abuses of power by insisting on a particular mode of the exercise of political power: governance through law. (Waldron 2008, p. 11)

Raz would be unlikely to disagree if one could fix upon a definition of 'abuse' that both he and Waldron might agree on; hence the difficulty – abuse of power is often in the eye of the (political) beholder.

What this negative view also suggests to Raz is that the rule of law is merely one (political) virtue among a number of others. In a pluralistic society, there can be no single defining set of social norms that directly map onto the rule of law and hence there is no single (thick) rule of law norm, leaving only the thin rule of law able to claim something approaching a universal applicability (Raz 1994, pp. 370–8). He concludes that

> conformity to the rule of law is not itself the ultimate goal. The subservient role of the doctrine [of the rule of law] shows both its power and its limitations. On the one hand, if the pursuit of certain goals is entirely incompatible with the rule of law, then these goals should not be pursued by legal means. But on the other hand one should be wary of disqualifying the legal pursuit of major social goals in the name of the rule of law. After all, the rule of law is meant to enable the law to promote social good, and should not be lightly used to show that it should not do so. Sacrificing too many social goals on the altar of the rule of law may make the law barren and empty. (Raz 1979a, p. 229)

Therefore, Raz starts from an 'empty' or minimalist position on the rule of law to stress that merely arguing that something should be maintained or done because it conforms to the rule of law is to say relatively little when it comes to social actions. The claims identified with the thicker rule of law lie elsewhere in the political process and by including them alongside the procedures of the rule of law the evaluative question is compromised and corrupted. A similarly thin view led Robert Summers to suggest: 'not only is the presence of the rule of law not a guarantee that the resulting legal state of affairs is good, *overall, its absence (at least in some of its institutional forms)* is not, as such, necessarily bad' (Summers 1993, p. 140, emphasis in original). By reducing the normative heft of the rule of law, its political role is thereby narrowed and many political criticisms thereby side-stepped.

Reflecting this view, Friedrich Hayek, while accepting that the rule of law has some substantive content, limited this content to the protection of liberty and freedom.[7] Hayek sees the rule of law as presenting facilitative legal arrangements but the notion of 'command' must be minimized if the rule of law is to be maintained. For Hayek, 'it is more important that there should be a rule applied always without exceptions, than what the rule is' if the rule of law is to be maintained (Hayek 1944 [1993], p. 59). That said, Hayek still requires the law to maintain equal treatment of all: the rule of law

> implies limits to the scope of legislation: it restricts it to the kind of rules known as formal law, and excludes legislation either directly aimed at particular people, or at enabling anybody to use the coercive power of the state for the purpose of such discrimination. It means, not that everything is regulated by law, but, on the contrary, that the coercive power of the state can only be used in cases defined in advance by the law and in such a way that it can be foreseen how it will be used. (Hayek 1944 [1993], p. 62)

Glossing Hayek's position, three key attributes underpin the rule of law: generality, equality and certainty (Tamanaha 2004, p. 66). Moreover, in Hayek's view it 'is not a means to any purpose, but merely a condition for the successful pursuit of most purposes' (Hayek 1973, p. 113). The law is a multipurpose human (social) technology second only to language in its lack of a specificity of purpose. Nevertheless, while retaining an essentially thin conception, Hayek also seeks to move a little towards a more substantive understanding of the rule of law to ensure that it is not used to produce unjust outcomes, inasmuch as justice is served by equal treatment. At the centre of Hayek's understanding of the rule of law is an unresolved tension, however: on one side, Hayek, the libertarian, wishes to reduce the state's coercive power over the individual; on the other, he

---

[7] See also Michael Oakeshott's depiction of the rule of law as a mode of human association, where law 'is not concerned with the merits of different interests' (Oakeshott 1983, p. 141).

also wishes to recognize that some state services (supported through the tax system) are worthwhile and legitimate even if they violate the basic principles of generality and equality (Westmoreland 1998). His position is interesting (as regards the mapping of the rule of law conceptual continuum) because it illustrates how difficult it can be to maintain a thin rule of law position that seeks to exclude substantive content.

Thin conceptions of the rule of law reduce law to its positive legal characteristics, and given that this then suggests that the source of law is the legitimate agency of government, it becomes difficult to conceive of how such a system can also hold the government (or state more generally) to account, as they are also its progenitors. Governments tend to reserve to themselves the power to decide what the limits to the rule of law are, and when other values (most obviously, national security) should be privileged. For instance, it is no surprise that the Deputy Prime Minister of Singapore, speaking in 2007, was keen to stress that the rule of law must not be viewed in the abstract:

> It must be [viewed] within a certain socio-political and historical context . . . It is not possible to have a universal prescription when applying the Rule of Law. These issues have to be determined according to the social, cultural and political values of each society. . . There is a core set of principles undergirding the Rule of Law that should exist in every society. These include an independent judiciary, the right not to be arbitrarily arrested and, when arrested there will be the conduct of a fair trial, conduct of free and fair elections so that the people can change the government of the day; the right to personal safety and security. (Jayakumar 2009, pp. 143, 145)

Although this is not the thinnest depiction of the norm one might be able to imagine, it does give a flavour of how some societies (or more accurately their governments) would want to reserve considerable latitude as regards the substantive elements of the rule of law to themselves. For supporters of the thin depiction, crucially this allows states with considerable political differences to still agree to uphold a basic set of legal values.

To summarize: a thin reading of the rule of law sees it as a generalized (largely non-political) yardstick for gauging social organization, and thus when Stefan Voigt recently tried to establish a method for measuring the attainment of the rule of law, he ended up with a list of elements (separation of powers; judicial review; judicial independence; judicial accountability; prosecutorial independence; fair trials; basic human rights), which while including some thicker elements (most obviously human rights), largely was concerned with the effectiveness of legal procedure rather than their content (Voigt 2012). For many commentators, these thin conceptions reduce law to its positive legal characteristics, leaving the problem of how to hold government or the state to account; Voigt and others would likely counter that this is taken care of by a stress on independence. Indeed, there remain clear political advantages at the thin end of the continuum, unencumbered as it is by substantive content. Potentially, there can be pretty wide agreement about what the rule of law, so defined, entails; its lack of substantive content reduces the potential to offend those with differing cultural (and political) histories or traditions; and it allows states with considerably different political systems to share knowledge of the law's procedures and to learn from each other without finding it necessary to share views about the ends of the rule of law (HiiL 2007, p. 18; Neate 2009, p. 7). Whether this silence about substantive ends is possible or plausible is where thicker conceptions of the rule of law depart from thinner ones.

## THE THICK RULE OF LAW

In its contemporary form, the more substantive characterization or thicker conception of the rule of law may reflect the development of the welfare state and the associated expansion of rights that might be thereby recognized and protected (Barber 2004, p. 483), alongside moves towards the development of the (international) law of human rights in the second half of the twentieth century. The ICJ, Delhi Congress, over 50 years ago produced one of the clearest early examples of the thicker position. The ICJ argued that once it has been accepted that the rule of law is about building a free society, and such a society must be 'primarily concerned with the rights of the individual', then it follows that:

> a lawyer who accepts the ideal of a free society as the basis of his conception of the Rule of Law cannot ignore that aspect of men's dignity and worth which finds expression in a demand for a minimum standard of material well-being in addition to the bare maintenance of political freedoms within a framework of law and order. (ICJ 1959, p. 193)

This implies the inclusion of a relatively wide conception of justice (both political and economic) in the rule of law, and includes values such as democracy and welfare. In itself such an expansion of the norm may lead to tensions between rights, hence Raz and others' resistance to such a thicker reading of the rule of law. Indeed, the ICJ made plain in the mid 1960s that this extension was exactly what it (collectively) had in mind, including in its definition of the rule of law a wide range of issues, from freedom of religious observance to a right to education, from a right to privacy to the freedom of the press and including a range of economic rights (ICJ 1966).

The ICJ constructed a complex and multifaceted network of elements that would indicate a state had adopted and supported the rule of law.

However, critics of the thicker reading of the norm are concerned that neither historically nor analytically is it the case that any substantive elements of the rule of law would necessarily be positive, progressive or just; the ICJ's collection of elements is seen merely as the recitation of a particular political position (as in Abbé Boulier's criticism of the ICJ mentioned earlier). Although the thicker view of the rule of law is usually perceived by its promoters as including progressive positive values, their critics argue that they are either ignoring or discounting the possibility that other unacceptable values may be advanced and claimed to be consistent with the rule of law. Defenders of the thin reading see promoters of the thicker conception as compromising the rule of law by seeking to accomplish things that have not been possible by different means (Zywicki 2003). For those who prefer the thin definition, the rule of law must not be contaminated by such political goals.

Conversely, if the law is itself subject to argument, interpretation and rhetoric (MacCormick 2005), then to limit the rule of law merely to the formal rules obscures the operation(s) of the law in action, and what actually happens when judicial authorities make judgements. This (normative) difficulty is now often resolved by linking the rule of law to other already legitimated sets of international norms. Thus, Hans Corell (past Under-Secretary-General for legal affairs at the UN, and its Legal Counsel) has asserted that the rule of law 'must be adopted with full respect for applicable international standards in the field of human rights' (Corell 2001, p. 263); the rule of law norm explicitly includes the full range of international legal undertakings and (at least implicitly) customary international law (Corell 2001, p. 269). Similarly, David Dyzenhaus, focusing on the rule of law in a state of emergency, argues for a substantive norm that appeals to these principles of international human rights law as a way of understanding the manner in which judges try to resolve the tension between the rule of law and the executive's claimed requirements of national security (Dyzenhaus 2006). (This was also the approach adopted by the late Lord Bingham, which I discuss below.) If additionally we recognize that the debates that have advanced and consolidated the contemporary conception of human rights have included interlocutors from non-European societies, then the depiction of human rights as merely an imperialistic imposition can to some extent be pre-empted (An-Na'im 1999, pp. 152–3; Twining 2009). This may enhance a claim that linking the rule of law to human rights supports a depiction of the norm that moves beyond the thinnest end of its continuum of meaning but can retain a claim to universality.

This type of approach underpins Terry Nardin's point that the thin depiction of the norm often

> means little more than that the positive laws of a given community are obeyed and enforced, no matter what the form or substance of those laws. By this standard there is no discernible distinction between the rule of law and just plain law. The solution to this difficulty is to add as much moral content as is needed to make that distinction, but to avoid stuffing the expression with substantive values. (Nardin 2008, p. 396)

Using Nardin's metaphor, the norm might be seen as moving along its continuum as more moral content is stuffed in by commentators seeking to distinguish mere procedure from legality. Here, Jørgen Møller and Svend-Erik Skaaning's depiction of this normative range is illustrative of how Nardin's approach might play out analytically, where the rule of law continuum runs from the top (thin) to the bottom (thick) of the column 'concepts' (Table 2.1).

Of course, there might be considerable argument about the terminology on the left hand side, and the thresholds on the right (Waldron 2008, p. 45), but this additive process (or stuffing!) for moving along/across the continuum seems to reflect common understandings of the differences between conceptualizations of the rule of law.

This certainly responds to the observation that the thinnest characterizations of the rule of law miss something about how most people would regard the law's contribution to a well-ordered society (Marmor 2010, p. 668). However, for some critics a rule of law grounded in liberalism is merely the rule of the values propounded by certain powerful groups (and thereby merely seen as a set of arguable premises). Ugo Mattei and Laura Nader (2008), for instance, develop the position that the (pretended)

*Table 2.1   Typology of rule of law definitions*

| Concepts | Defining attributes |
| --- | --- |
| Rule by law | Power exercised via positive law |
| Formal legality | + general, public, prospective, certain and equally applied |
| Safeguarded rule by law | + control (checks and balances) |
| Liberal rule of law | + negative content (liberal rights) |
| Democratic rule of law | + consent (lawgivers chosen by competitive elections) |
| Social democratic rule of law | + positive content (social rights) |

*Source:*   Møller and Skaaning (2012, p. 145).

universality of the rule of law, by excluding much that is local/regional and established under different legal norms, is undermined by the actual imposition of a Westernized rule of law that seeks to structure societies to enhance and facilitate the plunder of their local resources. In jurisprudential discussions this sort of argument has prompted a range of positions on the lack of formal determinacy in law (Solum 1999) as well as a discussion of the question of pluralism in law, to which I return in Chapter 7. The thicker the rule of law is, the more difficult it is to read off potential judicial decisions from the formal content of the law, as they are guided by extra-legal concerns, and thus the law's ability to guide social actions is compromised, leading to its claim to be the rule of law, in Raz's terms, being undermined.

Although it is unlikely any formalist would argue that adjudication can be completely dispensed with, any recognition of indeterminacy (or flexibility in decisions) opens up the question about the role of norms, values and the political position of the adjudicating authority, the judge in a court of law. It is a relatively common observation that while the rule of law is counter-posed to the 'rule of men', the rule of human individuals (of either gender) is reintroduced through the work of judges (and adjudication). On the one hand, the role of judges might be seen therefore to compromise the rule of law, making the norm partial or even nonsensical; on the other, the role of judges' practical reasoning is public, can be understood and is needed to apply general laws to specific situations. The latter position, made famous by Neil MacCormick (2005), posits that rather than counter-pose adjudication and judges' deliberations *to* the rule of law, judges (and judicial deliberation) must be seen as an important element by which the rule of law does what it is supposed to do: govern a society in a just and predictable manner. Judges are needed to resolve cases because it is unlikely that two opposed parties will agree completely either on the salient facts or the interpretation of the law; an independent, trusted and legitimate party is required to make these judgements and under all conceptions of the rule of law this is the role of the judge.

This then leads to two linked issues: the practice of judges themselves (which is the subject of MacCormick's work) and their position of independence from other branches of government. This independence is most clearly articulated in rule of law systems through the procedures of judicial review of governmental practices and decisions: reviews of the legality or otherwise of particular practices or decisions (are they in compliance with the wider system of laws of the state or system in question?); reviews of whether laws are fair, just and equitable (do the procedures of the state uphold the normative aspects of the rule of law?); and adjudication of appeals against irrationality or unreasonableness, again related to the normative elements established by an appeal to the rule of law (Jowell 2004, pp. 20–1). In the thinner conception of the rule of law the judge's role is to discover the facts of the case and to establish how they fit with the law as legislated; interpretation is only required inasmuch as general regulations need to be compared to specific (and complex) cases as presented to the court. However, in the thicker view, the judge is there to ensure that the rule of law is consistent with a wider range of considerations (encompassed by the thicker set of norms), thereby ensuring that the outcomes from a mechanical application of the law to the (found) facts still conforms to the rule of law's requirements for fairness, justice and other aspects of the thicker norm as understood by society in general and the judge in particular (Dyzenhaus 2010).

Unfortunately, as already noted, this can suggest that the rule of law may be to some extent indeterminate, although, as Robin West has pointed out, this is only surprising to those with no legal training; 'it is certainly one of the unsettling surprises of law school to realize how unclear, and indeterminate, and "open", is much of the law' (West 2003, p. 26). The discussion of the appropriate and legitimate role of judges therefore often revolves around the claimed indeterminacy of law, compromising accounts of the rule of law that do not accord a central and positive role to adjudication. If adjudication is rendered as a corruption of the rule of law, then given the practical requirement for the judgement of individuals in law courts, the rule of law can only be procedural and hence thin at best. If, on the other hand, the role of judges is accepted – that they by definition bring personal judgement to bear, albeit constrained by the requirements of their profession and through socialization into the rule of law – then the question becomes what values can judges legitimately use in their evaluations of cases before them?

In his criticism of much of the commentary on the rule of law, Jeremy Waldron argues that the rule of law requires a legal system that is centred on the court (and thus the role of judges). He sets out a list of five elements of such a system that were any one to be missing would fatally undermine any claim to be adjudged as acceding to the rule of law: the existence of courts (as open and accessible places in which the law is enacted); the norms by which the system functions are public and recognizable as society's own; our laws are made by us and are the result of a historical and social political process (they are not a foreign imposition); and are oriented towards the public good, or at least purport to be so; and all of this is articulated through a legal system in which it is possible to understand how the different elements relate to one another (Waldron 2008, pp. 20–36). This requires much greater attention to argumentation – how the courts deploy and engage with the systems' normative elements in any particular adjudication; judges are working to apply norms that are socially evident and accepted.

To ascertain what these public-regarding norms might be, a question posed by Jürgen Habermas is useful: 'What basic rights must free and equal citizens mutually accord one another if they want to regulate their common life legitimately by means of positive law?' (Habermas 2001, p. 116). This allows a start to be made to develop the sorts of normative or substantive content that might constitute a thicker reading of the rule of law. This question led Habermas himself to suggest that the

> internal relation between democracy and the rule of law consists in this: on the one hand, citizens can make appropriate use of their public autonomy only if, on the basis of their equally protected private autonomy, they are sufficiently independent; on the other hand, they can realize equality in their enjoyment of their private autonomy only if they make appropriate use of their political autonomy as citizens. Consequently, liberal and political basic rights are inseparable. (Habermas 2001, p. 118)

Here, the rule of law is linked with democracy, but perhaps as importantly with equality and citizenship. A society that excludes from citizenship groups of the population (within the area of jurisdiction), or mandates unequal treatment based not on behaviour but group membership, in Habermas's view fails to fulfil the standard for the appellation 'rule of law'. Indeed, in his defence of the thicker conception of the rule of law, the late Ronald Dworkin was moved to place the positive value of justice at its heart (Dworkin 1985). Whatever practical issues might lead us to defend the substantive content of the thicker norm, most importantly, the thicker reading of the norm must, in Dworkin's view, also encompass the commitment not merely to rule by law but also a commitment that justice be done through the law. Paul Craig (1997, p. 487) points out that Dworkin and Raz actually agree about the impact of including justice in the definition of the rule of law – it makes the two norms interdependent – but disagree as to whether this is advantageous (Dworkin) or a corruption of the norm (Raz).

Underlying any defensible and progressive claim for the legitimacy of the thicker rule of law is an appeal to a universal set of principles. This also indicates that any thicker depiction of the (global) rule of law must be established on grounds other than the mere invocation of supposedly self-evident liberal values, unless such values can be demonstrated to enjoy near universal applicability and support. If so, then a thicker view depends on the inculcation of the polity into a set of acceptable values; the rule of law must positively/actively be (re)produced if its thickness, its substantive content, is to become settled. For Nardin, this suggests that the values that the rule of law must be said to encompass are moral values directly related to the system of law itself: it should only refer to those systems that encompass 'an association of moral equals' and that protect the 'moral rights of all' (Nardin 2008, p. 397). This leads him to assert that: 'If law is not a relationship between independent agents, collective or individual, if its presumption is not the independence – the freedom from unwarranted coercive interference – of those agents, there is nothing to distinguish law from power' (Nardin 2008, p. 401). This is certainly the sort of (thicker) conception of the rule of law that often seems to lie behind the invocation of its developmental and progressive worth, as articulated across the global polity.

## LORD BINGHAM'S SYNTHESIS

With apologies for another list, I shall use the (late) Lord Bingham's exploration of the defining elements of the rule of law to summarize the analytical terrain traversed above. The reason I deploy Bingham's list is twofold: firstly, working in an extended tradition of the rule of law that can be traced back to Dicey's original formulation of the term, Bingham's work is anchored in the disciplinary discussion that has been subsequently globalized not least by his work as Lord Chief Justice in the UK; secondly, Bingham's final intervention in the debates about the rule of law was a book, from which I draw, that explicitly sought to set out his views on the content of the norm of the rule of law for a non-legal, or even popular audience. As such, his definition acts as a good bridge, it seems to me, between the legal and the common sense understandings of the rule of law that I seek to explore herein.

Tom Bingham did not seek to establish a simple definition of the rule of law but rather to introduce the non-legal reader to the range of issues that are encompassed by the term, and which it is vital for them to understand. To this end, he starts his account with a short and schematic history focusing on 12 moments he regards as vital to the development of the rule of law: starting with Magna Carta 1215, and ending with the Universal Declaration of Human Rights in 1948 (Bingham 2010, pp. 10–33). Unlike Harold Berman, who traced the origins of the norm to the Papal Revolution of the twelfth century (Berman 1983, pp. 94–9), Bingham prefers to keep his history firmly located in the British legal tradition, partly as a recognition of the central rhetorical role of A.V. Dicey (Bingham 2010, pp. 2–5). Bingham's is not so much the history of the norm itself but an account of its ascendance to a central ideal of (British) liberal politics. Unlike Raymond Plant's recent discussion of the *Neo-liberal State* (Plant 2010), Bingham does not seek to establish the veracity of the rule of law through an argument from jurisprudential or political theoretical principles; rather reflecting his understanding of common law, it is an account based on custom, precedent and the development of law in response to political pressure. Thus, while Plant tests neoliberalism against its internal logic, asking whether the rule of law can serve liberalism's moral ends without it becoming a threat to (a neoliberal idea of) freedom, Bingham sees the rule of law threatened and perhaps even undermined by the state itself.

The first of these threats is the (so-called) War on Terror. Bingham points out that unlike the US government, and drawing on the experience of Northern Ireland, the UK government has prosecuted terrorists as criminals not as combatants (Bingham 2010, p. 137). The UK government has also not sought the considerable extension of powers that has been accorded to the Executive in the USA, nor has it sought to use third countries (utilizing extraordinary rendition) as a site for extra-legal measures (Bingham 2010, pp. 138–42), although there are now some questions about how far the UK has actually distanced itself from these practices. Bingham then argues that unfortunately there are also issues where both countries have compromised the rule of law in their bid to confront terrorism: ranging from discrimination against non-nationals to detention without trial, and surveillance (Bingham 2010, pp. 143–58). Like others Bingham concludes that this merely lets the terrorist win; if we abrogate the rule of law, one of our key political values, then we compromise our own claims to be on the side of the good.

Bingham's second threat is perhaps a little more surprising than his critique of the government's actions in the War on Terror: he concludes that another major threat to the rule of law is the sovereignty of Parliament. While one can hope that Parliament will not legislate in a manner that conflicts with the rule of law, there is actually nothing to stop this happening (Bingham 2010, pp. 160–70). As someone who worked for Charter 88 in the early 1990s, such a conclusion has a familiar ring: one of Charter 88's key demands was a written constitution to ensure that our rights would not be dependent on the good will or good faith of Parliament. Thus, for Bingham, the rule of law seems under threat from two directions: from political actions and from a more general misapprehension of a term that however widely and frequently deployed remains insufficiently understood to act as a simple basis for political criticism; it is this second danger that his book is meant to address.

This short preamble returns us to Bingham's attempt to set out a range of issues that together can be said to constitute the rule of law. In a series of short chapters he sets out eight key components of the rule of law (many of which will be already familiar):

1. 'The law must be accessible and so far as possible intelligible, clear and predictable.' The key issue is that we can hardly expect law-abiding behaviour if it is impossible for those so governed to be unable to ascertain what the law actually is (Bingham 2010, pp. 37–47).
2. 'Questions of legal right and liability should ordinarily be resolved by application of the law and not the exercise of discretion.' This is not to argue that there can be no discretion, only that any discretion must be exercised within the bounds of the law; no decisions should be arbitrary and without recourse to some law or another (Bingham 2010, pp. 48–54).
3. 'The laws of the land should apply equally to all, save to the extent that objective differences justify differentiation.' All must be equal before the law, with no distinction between, for instance, the rich and the poor, the weak and the powerful. Where the law distinguishes responsibility by age, there may be some reason to treat people differently, but only when these differences are 'objective' and not social, political or economic (most importantly arguing against discrimination by race and gender) (Bingham 2010, pp. 55–9).
4. 'Ministers and public officers at all levels must exercise the powers conferred on them in good faith, fairly, for the purpose for which the powers were conferred, without exceeding the limits of such powers and not unreasonably.' This is intended to underpin judicial review, so that the state can be held accountable to the laws Parliament has enacted and does not go beyond that democratically grounded intent (Bingham 2010, pp. 60–5).

Up until this point Bingham's elements are essentially procedural, requiring little or no judgement about the content of the law they are compatible with a thin depiction of the norm as set out above. Even the invocation of objective differences under '3' can hardly be said to be normative towards a liberal sense of equality, as 'objective' differences are often in the eye of the (political) beholder; for instance, racists see differences between ethnicities as objective. These elements can often be differently ordered: to take one example, Gerald Postema puts Bingham's fourth element right at the centre of his depiction of the rule of law, making accountability (understood as a reciprocal recognition of the law by rulers and ruled) a vital and necessary element of the rule of law (Postema 2010). However, the next four elements of his depiction move Bingham firmly towards a thicker reading of the rule of law.

5. 'The law must afford adequate attention to fundamental human rights.' He explicitly rejects the thin reading of the rule of law, spending some time exploring various Articles of the European Convention on Human Rights. For Bingham, the rule of law cannot be said to obtain where the procedures of law explicitly are intended to underpin injustice (Bingham 2010, pp. 66–84).

6. 'Means must be provided for resolving, without prohibitive cost or inordinate delay, bona fide civil disputes which the parties themselves are unable to resolve.' This extends the point about accessibility; if effective representation is blocked by costs to all but wealthy defendants, then the law is not treating all equally. Here he offers a clear defence of legal aid and expeditious legal process as crucial to the maintenance of the rule of law. Given questions about the impact of economic inequality and the measures needed to ameliorate these difficulties, this element reflects a political position about the good society that evokes issues of extra-legal inequality (Bingham 2010, pp. 85–9).

7. 'Adjudicative procedures provided by the state should be fair.' The judiciary and legal profession must be independent of the state, allowing both sides (prosecution and defence) a fair trial. The defendant must know the charges against him or her and be able to properly interrogate the evidence. Given this requires a judgement about political organization rather than the procedures of the law itself, again this might be regarded as a thicker reading of the rule of law (Bingham 2010, pp. 90–109).

8. 'The rule of law requires compliance by the state with its obligations in international law as in national law.' Here, Bingham expands his purview from the previously rather domestic orientation of his discussion to argue that the state's obligations do not end with its own law, but rather extend to the realm of global politics. This includes his invocation of human rights, but also the rules of war and other international regulatory arrangements. Bingham does not recognize a moral difference between politics inside and outside the state (Bingham 2010, pp. 110–29).

His discussion of these elements of the rule of law is intended to demonstrate that the norm itself is multifaceted but also that merely recognizing procedural norms should not be sufficient for any state to be accorded the recognition of being governed by the rule of law. As this demonstrates, again using the metaphor of stuffing, moving towards the thick end of the continuum involves the addition of extra, often non-legal elements to the conception of the rule of law, but with the intent of ensuring the evaluation that the rule of law obtains also indicates something about the positive political values of the society examined.

## CONCLUSION(S) AND SOME RELATED ISSUES

All of this leads to the conclusion that the rule of law is hardly an uncontested norm, with various positions arrayed along the normative continuum between thin and thick depictions. This might collapse down into a distinction between approaches to law that see the rule of law as being focused on order, and those that include a set of substantive values of which justice is paramount, but this merely draws us back to the actual positions set out by specific commentators or analysts. Nevertheless, the crucial question remains: can the rule of law be regarded as universal in some manner, or can universality only be accomplished and defended if one is to regard the rule of law in thin, procedural, positive terms? If this question is a political issue of judgement, with the rule of law itself subject to argument and disagreement, then to make some sense of its role in the contemporary global political economy, we need to consider not only the manner in which it is deployed but also, as importantly, how its various meanings are (re)produced and maintained.

This means that firstly we need to recall that the 'rule of law' is a term of particularly Anglo-Saxon, British and American political discourse, although the European notion of the *Rechtstaat* is often linked to it (Fogelklou 1997; Praet 2010; Troper 2003). Certainly, like the rule of law the *Rechtstaat* has been relatively difficult to define and over the history of its deployment has oscillated in meaning (van Caenegem 1991, pp. 185–99), but we can see some intersections in conceptual grounds if we list some of its key elements:

1. The principle of legality and the subjugation of all three branches of government to a constitution.
2. The separation and differentiation of government power into a legislature, an executive and a judiciary.
3. The presence of a legal remedy and an independent judiciary.
4. Equality before the law.
5. A working system of fundamental rights (Praet 2010, p. 174).

Comparing these elements to aspects of the rule of law set out above suggests a significant realm of (at the very least) parallel politico-legal conception. Indeed the Council of Europe contends that notions of '*Rechtstaat, Etat de driot* and rule of law tend to amalgamate in the European legal order' (Council of Europe 2008, p. 7). Although there is some parallel with (and connection between) these ideas, as here I am concerned primarily with the rule of law as a political artefact and the (re)production of this (initially) Anglo-Saxon conception, I shall leave the political conceptual issue of the *Rechtstaat* to one side. However, while accepting there are some parallels I do not suggest that the two political concepts are necessarily interchangeable.

Returning to the issue of how we understand the normative impact of the rule of law that I raised earlier, it is worth (re-)emphasizing that if its normativity is to be regarded as an important element of the rule of law, then this means that the definitions we recognize need to go beyond the more generally accepted notion that law acts as social guidance, a leitmotif that can be found in most discussions of law from the Greek city states onwards (May 2012; Sampford 2006, pp. 56, 271). The rule of law cannot therefore just be a (social) mirror; rather it is a story about how the good life should be and why we ought to follow the law to that end. The obligations that are involved in the rule of law are not fixed; as we accede to the obligations of law so we reproduce its normativity, by our being guided by it. In this sense, the normativity of the law is underpinned by the rule of law itself as an 'internal' set of reasons for following the law. That said, at least in the thin view of the rule of law, for each locale, for each society seeking to expand (or support) the rule of law, there may be different 'ingredients' to how the law's normativity is articulated and internalized (Krygier 2004, p. 269), and we will return to this issue of pluralism near the end of the book.

A discussion of normativity suggests that there is a difference between compliance with the law and obedience to it. Compliance requires no real sense of obligation, but is rather an instrumental reading of the situation – following the law is less costly than breaking it, where costs may involve reputational issues, issues of (lost) incentives or other aspects of 'encouragement'. If we feel obligated to follow the law, we do so without necessary prior consideration of the costs of the required outcome, but, when we begin to doubt that our obligations are parallel to our social mores, the desire to follow the law may collapse back into compliance rather than obedience. It is likely mistaken to see these as opposed reasons; rather they overlap but are weighted differently in any specific instance; thus our acceptance of the rule of law underpins any obligation we may feel. Sylvie Delacroix suggests that our changing manner of acceding to the law may itself (re)shape the law and as such the changes in social mores that it 'promotes' (Delacroix 2011, p. 317). Thus, law's normativity is not necessarily fixed in its character, and it is apposite to ask how does it change? I look at this question when I discuss civil disobedience in Chapter 7. Crucially, any commitment to the rule of law implies an acceptance of its constraints on (political and social) actions. Only if we are willing to hold ourselves bound by the strictures of the rule of law can we legitimately require the fidelity by others.[8] That is to say, the rule of law is essentially a reciprocal norm; it requires a broadly symmetrical politics to be fully legitimate.

Finally, without a presupposition that there is a recognizable legal system in place, then it is unclear to what a discussion of the rule of law would refer or appeal to. The difficulty is that the rule of law itself may be (in developmental circumstances) the norm on which the legal system is to be built. This has led Martin Krygier to conclude:

> In societies where the rule of law has long been secure, the fact that it is mis-conceived might not matter too much, since to a considerable extent it runs on its own steam. However in conflictual, post-conflict and transitional societies, where efforts are made to catalyse the rule of law these problems can be catastrophic. (Krygier 2011, p. 32)

Krygier is dismayed at depictions of the rule of law as a form of technology (common among those who adopt a relatively thin definition) that can be applied with little account of the social milieu into which it is to be introduced. However, as Krygier also points out, given the clearly unsettled character of the rule of law norm,

> to point to an interpretation of the rule of law different from one's own, or to a tension between it (or an interpretation of it) and another value is not of itself to point to a misuse. On the other hand, failure to acknowledge that one's interpretation is an arguable choice, or that it is possible to deal or live with tensions between it and other values, might amount to misuse. (Krygier 2006, p. 157)

If, as I want to argue in this book, the rule of law has become the common sense of (global) politics, then the question is whether the lack of any emergent consensus undermines such a claim: can there be a common sense that lacks a commonly held understanding? Here, the suggestion that the rule of law is a social imaginary is an important route to an answer.

The rhetoric of the rule of law is widespread, treated as a positive norm and is widely appealed to in arguments about contemporary global politics. Certainly, one criticism of its wide currency has been that it is essentially vacuous, but I think it is worth retaining a wider perception of what the rule of law means; there may be much discussion and confusion,

---

[8] See Thakur (2012) for the international implications of such a normative invocation centred on the role of the UN and its legitimacy in humanitarian interventions.

but at bottom there is a clear understanding that the law can be counter-
posed to other political norms – monarchical or authoritarian power; the
rule of force – and as such there remains some *deminimus* reading of the
rule of law that underpins its function as a common sense; that may only
stretch some way along the continuum that I have defined above, but the
thin (procedural) elements of the rule of law seem to be relatively uncontentious, if their sufficiency as regards claims for the rule of law to obtain
is less settled. It is here that the flexibility of conceiving of the rule of law
as a social imaginary becomes so helpful in understanding what it might
represent in political-rhetorical terms. Thus, it may make more sense to
ask: what is the point of the rule of law? rather than ask what the rule
of law is (Krygier 2006). This is an excellent heuristic for considering the
legalization of (global) politics alongside the role of the rule of law norm
in these developments, to which I now turn.

# 3. The rule of law and the legalization of politics

> If the category of law itself is taken for granted, there is little reason for engagement with underlying questions of what law is and how it may be distinctive from other forms of social normativity. (Brunnée and Toope 2013, p. 136)

> It would be nice if one could take the rule of law without the rule of lawyers. But this is not possible. To have one, you get the other. (Weiler 2000, p. 7)

> Although savvy policy professionals rarely present themselves as naive voices of neutral science, they think of themselves as participants in something altogether less parochial or ideological than 'politics'. (Kennedy 2001, p. 471)

In this chapter I ask whether politics is becoming more patterned by legal considerations, in what is often termed the 'legalization' of (global) politics, before moving to develop an explicitly agent-centred account of this posited development. Having set out the rhetorical contours of the rule of law (both its incidence and its contested meaning), here I begin to look at the social processes and practices that are behind the increasingly common sense notion that the rule of law is the answer to most general political (and economic) issues.

To suggest that there has been a legalization of global politics implies that we can measure this development in some way.[1] Critical analyses of legalization (most obviously Mattei and Nader 2008) would suggest that what is evident is merely rule *by* law: the patina of law with none or little of its normative content. Conversely, most accounts of legalization implicitly or explicitly depict the process as introducing at the very least a thin form of the rule of law (as depicted in Chapter 2). This has established a minimal threshold against which any particular process of legalization can be compared, thereby reinforcing the links between legalization and the rule of law. At the margins there may be cases where legalization had produced legal-like regulation or governance that could be regarded as failing to fulfil even the minimal demands of the thinnest depiction of the rule of

---

[1] In addition to the sources cited in the text, see also the special issue of the *Hague Journal on the Rule of Law* dealing with measuring the rule of law (Botero et al. 2011).

law, but for my purposes here I regard these as a small subset that would require detailed and case-specific accounts; that is to say, I am going to assume that legalization involves the general expansion of the rule of law (even if there remain questions about any particular development's place on the continuum discussed in the previous chapter).

In his assessment of five different indexes that seek to measure the rule of law across the world, Wolfgang Merkel notes that none has a long time series (the oldest stretching only back to 1990) and as such there is little available evidence of longer-term trends that might (or might not) indicate legalization as a general political shift (Merkel 2012). Additionally, only one of the indexes (and unfortunately it is the most recent, from the World Justice Project) offers a complex (although lightly theorized) depiction of the rule of law as a basis for measurement, while the others are part of wider compendiums of development measures. A recent attempt to deal with this time series issue (by constructing data back to 1850) is unhelpfully dependent on the character of the constitution as an indicator of legal order alongside the existence of legal periodicals and the provision of legal education as a proxy for legal infrastructure (Nardulli et al. 2013). This certainly allows a much longer time frame for analysis but at the cost of no real consideration of the rule of law as practice rather than declaration.

Elsewhere, in an earlier survey of rule of law measures (focused on their link, or otherwise, with development), Kevin Davis suggests that the data used to capture the character and extent of the legal system is often far too dependent on proxies and subjectivity (opinion surveys) to allow any conclusions to be drawn about the real extent of a rule of law culture and its impact on development (Davis 2004). These surveys are in the main concerned with the rule of law as it impacts on the private sector and how it facilitates economic activity (with the World Bank's survey explicitly included under the rubric *Doing Business*), often with little guidance on meaning for those contributing their views. The difficulty is that where these measures become part of policy debates, the data produced can then shift the focus of rule of law development and support towards those aspects that offer the ability of demonstrating improvement in such data; thereby metrics can become standards (Krever 2013). However, the most recent attempt to measure the rule of law (and by extension trends in domestic legalization) tries to establish a richer and more complex data set.

The World Justice Project (WJP), funded by the Gates Foundation and Neukon Family Foundation (as well as a wide range of legally oriented organizations) produces an annual *Rule of Law Index* utilizing a range of 48 variables that attempts to look at the rule of law from the 'bottom up' (Agrast et al. 2012, p. 7). The WJP bases much of its assessment on survey evidence about perceptions of the character and practice(s) of the law in 97 countries surveyed (in 2012), but the research is not limited (as so often with other subjective measures) to practitioners or legal groups; using both expert questionnaires and public surveys the *Index* has the broadest evidence base of any current rule of law measurement project.[2] The *Index* looks at the rule of law in nine dimensions (or 'factors'): limited government powers (that is, how is the state held to the law); absence of corruption; order and security (related to personal perceptions of (in)security); (the recognition of) fundamental rights; open government; regulatory enforcement; civil justice; criminal justice; and informal justice (being often related to community dispute resolution) (Agrast et al. 2012, p. 11). This approach still suffers from the difficulty of coordinating respondents' differing interpretations of the same set of legal facts on the ground, but overall offers potentially dynamic assessments of individual countries through annual surveys and thus despite the short time series (2012–13 is only the third report to be published) offers considerable and useful data for assessing the rule of law's development in various countries. In the future, perhaps within a decade, the WJP *Index* will have some real purchase on trends in legalization. However, the *Index* only seeks to gather data on the domestic rule of law, and while this is an important aspect of legalization, for many commentators it is the international realm that is the subject of any major claim for a contemporary process of legalization.

A focus on the international realm suggests that a simpler way to measure the extent of legalization could be to count the number of international and regional courts across the global system. To give one example of this method, Karen Alter has argued in her extensive analysis of the European Union's legal system that a key shift has been the development and empowerment of an active European Court of Justice (ECJ). The expansion of the (European) rule of law can be measured by the rising incidence of cases referred to the ECJ, but also through the establishment of the court itself (Alter 2001). Likewise, it is often observed that there has been an expansion of the activities of international courts, and the international reach of national courts (Archibugi et al. 2012, pp. 12–13) with the role of emulation (especially of the ECJ in the case of human rights courts) being crucial (Alter 2012). The rule of law is appealed to as a reason for the recourse to courts but also reflects the establishment of special purpose tribunals as part of post-conflict arrangements sponsored by the UN after the end of the Cold War. These UN-sponsored courts are

[2] The most recent *Rule of Law Index* can be downloaded from http://worldjusticeproject. org/rule-of-law-index where the data sets are also available alongside online tools for exploring the data in detail.

explicitly seen to be extending the reach or scope of the rule of law where it has been deficient, utilizing tried and tested models of institutional establishment.

Reflecting this approach to measurement, Kal Raustiala has surveyed the extent of legalization under the rubric of the 'density' of law, including the number of international courts cited by Alter, the often noted rapid expansion of international organizations in the second half of the twentieth century and the doubling of the rate of treaty registrations at the UN, from 4318 between 1950–59, to 9809 between 2000–09, with a cumulative total of over 48,000 international treaties registered (Raustiala 2013, p. 306; see also Brütsch and Lehmkhul 2007). Thus, we might crudely measure the rate of legalization by the number of law-like social facts found in the global political economy. The difficulty with such an approach is that this does not account for their character. For instance, criticisms of the international investment treaty arbitration system, directly focused on its lack of rule of law principles (van Harten 2007), suggest that merely assembling law-like mechanisms may not be enough. The lack of tenure in arbitration courts, alongside the one-sided initiation system (where only investors can seek recourse against states, and not the other way around), have undermined the key principle of judicial independence, as arbitrators unwilling to find for the plaintiff are unlikely to work again (see also CEO 2012). Counting courts and legal-like procedures therefore does not necessarily measure the extent or growth of support for the rule of law.

Alternatively, we might posit the expansion of the international criminal law as indicative of legalization. In Kathryn Sikkink's account of the 'justice cascade' (the move to prosecute officials and political leaders responsible for human rights violations), she argues that the expansion of such prosecutions while to some extent depending on the rule of law also helped build and develop the rule of law in the countries concerned (Sikkink 2011, pp. 155–6, *passim*; see also Sikkink 2002). These developments are not self-propelling and she notes that there were specific groups (human rights non-governmental organizations (NGOs) primarily) that strove to develop individual criminal accountability and by achieving this acted as a spur and influence on the 'justice cascade' that has seen the human rights norms around accountability becoming increasingly globalized. If human rights are by no means the totality of the rule of law, there remains a clear link (as noted in the previous chapter) between these norms, with the rule of law including the rights so identified, but also being a mechanism by which such rights can be protected and instituted (Guilhot 2005; Keck and Sikkink 1998; Risse and Sikkink 1999; Sikkink 2011). Frequently, the discourse of the rule of law is preferred to that of human rights because it can be presented as non-political (or depoliticized). Thus, the rise of the global rule of law norm (legalization) while not coterminous with the politics of human rights is nevertheless likely closely linked with these developments.

The expansion of international courts and the rise of human rights alongside the expansion in numbers of treaties all go some way to supporting the observation that the process of (global) legalization is not misidentified; there seems to be some move towards an increased utilization of legal instruments (and an appeal to the rule of law), and these developments may well be linked. However, it may be the case that legalization and the establishment of the rule of law as the common sense of global politics is actually over-determined (Comaroff and Comaroff 2009, p. 38), with the complex of causes and stimuli behind this development difficult if not impossible to untangle. In the second half of this chapter I do not try to replace previous accounts of legalization but rather seek to complement them with an important element of agency that has hitherto been severely underplayed, making a clear and parsimonious cause of legalization even more elusive than might be hoped; but first I explore the character of analyses of legalization in a little more detail.

## THE LEGALIZATION OF GLOBAL POLITICS

The legalization of (global) politics is often presented as a development without agents or even cause(s), with much work focusing only on the consequences and effects of legalization. The contemporary analytical claim in International Relations (IR) and IPE is most easily traced back to a special issue of *International Organisation* (reprinted as Goldstein et al. 2001), which discussed legalization in terms of three dimensions: obligation or legally binding rules; precision in that ambiguities are removed from regulatory relations; and delegation by which third parties have the authority to implement, interpret and apply rules as well as offering effective dispute resolution between states. Taking a self-denying ordinance on the dynamic of legalization, the authors presented in the special issue explicitly only seek to compare different issue areas to assess whether one or other is more (or less) legalized, and by doing so explain the extent of legalization through the characteristics of the issue area. While there is much of value in this approach, the dependence by the contributors on a collective definition of legalization as a political situation involving a set of characteristic legal processes driven by the functional advantages law brings, itself narrows the view of what is happening (and perhaps more importantly, why). This comparative approach reveals much about the contemporary system but offers little other than a sometimes implicit, sometimes explicit functionalism. This collective analysis broadly takes the process of legalization (and the rule of law) for granted and is concerned almost exclusively with its impact.

However, in the closing essay of the special issue Miles Kahler offers a partial corrective; while recognizing the strong functional character of much of the volume, he teases out some further aspects of the process, including a brief recognition of the role of lawyers and other groups in pursuing an agenda of legalization. Unfortunately, this expansion is seldom taken up in subsequent work. Anne-Marie Slaughter in her own later work (she contributed to the legalization volume) is concerned with the manner in which international, intergovernmental networks work together to produce the forms of regulation that currently pattern the international system (Slaughter 2004), not the underlying (and necessary) appeal of the rule of law itself. Certainly, this offers an appealing heuristic with clear potential for measurement, but does little to explain causes of the shift (other than an implied rational choice among contracting partners).

More recently, Nicole Deitelhoff, deploying legalization as the under-lying analysis, looked at the development of the International Criminal Court using a constructivist framework. She argues that her 'public interest frame' includes an allusion to the rule of law, but again the more overarching normative framing of the rule of law is either ignored, or perhaps taken for granted, with her analysis only looking in detail on the development of a political justification for the Court itself (Deitelhoff 2009). This is not to suggest Deitelhoff's work is at fault, more that the notion of legalization seems to normalize the rule of law so comprehen-sively that the norm of the rule of law itself is removed from the range of developments that need to be explained. Interestingly, some five years before the legalization special issue appeared, Abram and Antonia Handler Chayes, in their influential discussion of compliance with treaties and other legal instruments in international relations, were clear that it is 'almost always an adequate explanation for an action, at least prima facie, that it follows a legal rule' (Chayes and Chayes 1995, p. 119), but spent little time exploring the underlying norm that makes this statement coher-ent, other than identifying the legitimacy of (legal) norms (Chayes and Chayes 1995, pp. 127–34). Their discussion of legitimacy certainly touches on elements of the rule of law but not under this rubric. This indicates (perhaps) an acceptance of the founding character of these norms, which are distinguished by the Chayeses from 'parochial' norms. However, they offer no explanation of how these norms arose to become legitimate (how they were made less parochial).

More usefully, work on finance and private law has sometimes explicitly linked the move to standards and regulatory rules to the role of specific groups of agents (lawyers, accountants) and as such here legalization *is* linked to a causal mechanism (Arts and Kerwer 2007; Cohen 2007; Wüstermann and Kierzek 2007). Likewise, Adler and Bernstein suggest that the impetus to legalization comes from 'corporations and investors who want a stable, transparent, and rule-governed policy environment that they expect to protect them from what they might perceive as arbitrary political or regulatory interference' (Adler and Bernstein 2005, p. 310), and drawing on earlier work on epistemic communities to which I return below they are clear (if brief) about the role of agents in (re)producing the legal mindset that underpins legalization.

These seem to be the exceptions; in the main, analysts who allude to legalization in their work remain focused on its political impact rather than the practices that have prompted this dynamic, other than broad structural issues such as globalization or the influence of market regulation in the USA (influential by virtue of the size of the national market for imports). The limits of the identification of legalization become clear in Benjamin Cohen's summary of the approach in his 'intellectual history' of the (sub)discipline of IPE; he merely notes there that (international) legalization has the three dimensions noted above: obligation; precision; and delegation (Cohen 2008, p. 112). These are presented as issues of 'raising costs' of non-compliance, rather than having any relation to the propensity or otherwise to accept the notion of legal rules in the first place.[3] This leads Martti Koskenniemi to criticize the notion of legalization, as deployed in IR and IPE, as merely presenting the use of law as one policy choice among others (Koskenniemi 2007a, p. 21) and thereby not according its more generalized normative importance sufficient weight.

Moreover, as Yves Dezalay and Bryant Garth have stressed (and as I will develop further below), the legalization approach misses the

> role of lawyers as activists and moral entrepreneurs, combining access to media resources and the law as part of a political strategy, or the role of international corporate lawyers serving as brokers between multinational corporations and domestic states or private companies. (Dezalay and Garth 2011a, p. 3)[4]

Lawyers in their role as 'brokers' help define the problems that the law is then brought into solve. For instance, as Dezalay and Garth have explored at length, the appeal to internationalized commercial arbitration has the

---

[3] Indeed, even in this survey of the field, apart from this brief treatment of the legalization approach, any consideration of the rule of law as being an issue for discussion is completely absent.

[4] This might be regarded as a specific case of the wider lack of recognition in IR of the role and impact of transnational advocacy networks (Keck and Sikkink 1998).

effect of normalizing specific forms of legal problem solving for externally focused companies in states where the rule of law is as yet not Westernized (Dezalay and Garth 1996). Thus, the analysis of legalization may be subject to methodological critique for mostly concentrating on benefits to states (Brütsch and Lehmkhul 2007) as it fails to fully encompass the larger political-normative issue that underpins the recourse to the law. As an analytical approach legalization seems to offer little analysis of the characteristics of the rule of law (other than to suggest it is centred on a relatively narrow but important conception of obligation) and misses its role as a globalized political process underpinning the legitimacy of regulation (Finnemore and Toope 2001). Indeed, despite its identification of a process (legalization), analyses adopting this focus seem to miss the dynamic character of the rule of law itself and are uninterested in the actual mechanisms or practices of normative (re)production behind the effects with which they *are* concerned.

One response to these problems has been to stress constitutionalism as the process of change, rather than legalization (Dunoff and Trachtman 2009). Here, the rise of the increasingly globalized rule of law reflects a functional need among states in an increasingly interconnected international system. For instance, in one statement of this position, Sabino Cassese argues that:

> [L]egal globalization is a consequence of problems emerging that no domestic legal order can solve on its own . . . There exists a circle: the more communication, the more we apprehend the world, the more differences are manifest, the more global instruments are applied to resolve these differences, the more we care about the democracy and accountability of these instruments, the more we seek to strengthen the ties between global institutions and civil society, and the greater the frustration with a world that has 'governance' without having a government.
>
> This is ultimately a cumulative process, marked by both the ongoing development of a global legal order and the growing dissatisfaction with it; this dissatisfaction in turn drives further developments. (Cassese 2005, p. 989)

This suggests that the utilization of the rule of law as a political tool for reform is a response to global institutions that have been developed to engage emerging international problems in an interdependent system, and that operate on the basis of a set of legal procedures and practices for which legitimacy can be claimed (through an appeal to the rule of law norm). In turn, pressures for reform of the system further embed its key processes in the international political economy and prompt recourse to constitutionalism, which seeks to both establish the rule of law as part of an overarching logic while setting the limitations on legal obligations and requirements.[5] This is an important theme in the treatment of the rule of law and hence I devote an entire later chapter to discussing the idea of constitutionalism in global politics and its relation to (or in my view dependence on) the rule of law.

An additional and relatively easy explanation of legalization is to note that, as Paul Kahn contends, in general terms American political identity is 'peculiarly dependent on the idea of law' (Kahn 1999, p. 9; see also van Waarden 2009). Indeed Curtis Milhaupt and Katharina Pistor have suggested that 'legal governance is probably more crucial to the US economic system than to that of any other country in the world' (Milhaupt and Pistor 2008, p. 186). Thus, the rise of American global power would also be expected to impact on the manner in which (global) politics was perceived and characterized.[6] Certainly, Pierre Bourdieu agrees that the social and political role of law (and in his terms, therefore, the relative strength of the juridical field) is notably stronger in the USA than elsewhere and hence the weight accorded the rule of law is that much greater (Bourdieu 1987, p. 823). This allows the rise of the rule of law as norm and rhetoric to be directly (and simply) linked to the post-1989 (political) establishment of a single general (US-inspired) development trajectory focused on democratization and liberal market economy (Carothers 2006, pp. 6–7). The defeat of communism and the triumph of neoliberalism (or more accurately the ongoing process of neoliberalization) shifted the focus of developmental political economy, bringing with it a clear and established role for the rule of law, based on an American set of preferences (variously articulated) often gathered together under the term the Washington Consensus.

This has a certain simple appeal but again leaves the rule of law norm as merely a functional reflection of larger structural developments, for instance: the expansion of an hegemonic American political identity, an argument that has been extensively developed in IPE (see, for instance, Gill 2003); or the shift in US foreign policy to the promotion of a specific form of democracy ('polyarchy') that seeks to institute, among other things, the social support for legal forms and practices that support the expansion of capitalist markets, and inoculates such developments from popular political criticism (Robinson 1996). It is also possible to gloss such moves as a responsible hegemonic power seeking to apply models developed by the

---

[5] See also Zangel (2005), and as regards the need for law where international interactions are expanding see North (1990) for a classic treatment based on transaction cost analysis suggesting that in trade relations laws around property and contract become internationalized alongside the relations they seek to govern in a self-reinforcing dynamic.

[6] See Sklar (1988) for an account of the development of American corporate capitalism before the First World War that focuses on the adaption of the legal order to the specific needs of US-based corporations.

New Deal state during the 1930s to a damaged international system after the Second World War (Burley 1993). To be clear, I am not suggesting that such arguments have no merit, merely that this can hardly be the whole story. The constitutionalism account largely lacks a process by which such a shift was prosecuted, while the polyarchy account is light on discussion of the legal systems in such sites of aid and development, and its more positive version is merely concerned with the mechanisms and institutions of multilateral institutionalism rather than the processes of international-ized normative reconfiguration required to peacefully bring about such changes in perspective.

Finally, we might also observe that law abhors a vacuum and as such is likely to be expansionary. Peter Schuck summarizes this position in a rather colourful and evocative manner: Law 'does not simply share social space with other forms [of regulation]; it proliferates like weeds in a garden, occupying more and more of the remaining space and crowding out the others' (Schuck 2000, p. 433). Once regulation is enacted there are always marginal issues, practices or actions that the regulators believe should be brought within the purview of the regulatory system, and thus the system expands through political action, often justified by extreme cases and talk of risk. In the analysis of the political history of the European Union this is discussed under the term 'spill-over'. Indeed, Sigrid Quack suggests this is a strategy adopted by international legal professionals: the move to establish a shift from 'soft' norms to rules and laws that will then enable them to exercise their legal expertise (Quack 2007, p. 655). Of course, the interconnectivity of the international system needs to have developed enough to make this an (at least apparently) sensible approach to regulat-ing international political and/or economic relations and as such it is no surprise that globalization is itself often cited as a contributory factor in legalization (for instance, see Flood 2007; Reich 1997; van Waarden 2009; Zangel 2005). The increasing interdependence of societies and thus our increasing dependence of (distant) strangers for all sorts of socially valu-able services and goods means in times of difficulty, rather than social, family or clan mechanisms of resolution that depended on knowledge and trust of the other party, the rule of law is invoked as a way of resolving problems (Friedman 1994, p. 123; North 1990). However, the combina-tion of an increasingly interdependent global political economy, and an increasingly complex legal/regulatory environment may actually reduce the very certainly that the rule of law is claimed to promote (Raustiala 2013, p. 314). Forum shopping between courts and organizations, diverse interpretations of the 'rules' and the multiplication of judicial opinions can all lead to less certainty, not more. However, this is not how the rise of the rule of law is presented by the key agents of its normative (re)production, and it is to the under-recognized political role of the (professional) community of the rule of law that I now turn.

## THE EPISTEMIC COMMUNITY OF LAW(YERS)

James Gardner once suggested that one of the key outcomes of the law and development movement in Latin America and elsewhere (when US lawyers offered assistance to develop developing countries' legal systems) was to prompt a lawyerly elite to become much more interested in and active in national politics (Gardner 1980, p. 286). This may have also built on foundations laid by the ICJ, which, especially during the 1950s and early 1960s, worked to expand the adherence to and valuing of the rule of law (Tolley 1994, pp. 68–78; Weeramantry 2000, *passim*; also see ICJ 1959, 1966).[7] Bryant Garth further emphasizes the normative pull of US approaches to law especially through US law schools; when non-US students returned home 'fortified with US degrees and the credibility they brought, they invested their imported ideas and technologies in their own legal professions and countries, multiplying the influence of US law' (Garth 2008, p. 261). Major (and smaller) advocacy-focused NGOs, such as Amnesty International, also have supported the development of cause lawyering networks in many developing countries to expand the utilization of the legal system for legal-political campaigns around human rights and other causes such as gender rights or ethnically based discrimination (Ellmann 1998), again enhancing the value of the rule of law in (and to) those societies. However, as Stuart Scheingold has concluded, 'cause lawyers wishing to call upon external resources from transnational networks are likely to find that this funding is only available for an agenda compatible with neoliberal values' (Scheingold 2001, p. 397). In different ways, these examples suggest that the (re)production of some characterizations of the rule of law might be better supported than others.

Jennifer Beard argues that the rule of law is a belief that must be internalized, and that the inculcation of the subject (and society) is required for the rule of law to be achieved.

> Just as the early Christian was trained to confess his sins to the clergy, contemporary underdeveloped peoples are trained within development practices to speak of the economic and cultural practices in terms of their 'willingness to reform' to the rule of law instituted and structured by various development agencies. These agencies, in turn, claim to be able to mediate and transform

---

[7] The ICJ remains active and still works to promote the rule of law. See http://www.icj.org/.

these peoples into a truer, more developed form of subject. Arguably, the result being sought by rule of law development is for underdeveloped peoples to look to Western nations for salvation from themselves. (Beard 2006, p. 412)

Complementing Beard's argument here, John Flood compares international law firms (collectively) to the Jesuits (Flood 2007, p. 39), on the basis of the centrality to the culture of such firms of processes of inculcation into well-tested norms and rules. This sort of perspective suggests (again) that the process by which the rule of law has risen up the normative agenda is both more complex and more political than is often acknowledged; it is more than merely a process of legalization caused by historical shifts.

Before continuing, it is worth setting out how we might understand the (global) legal community collectively.[8] As I discussed when introducing Margaret Archer's approach to how ideational shifts take place, individuals as both actors *and* collectivities (or 'corporate actors' in Archer's terminology) are important. I am going to use the idea of an epistemic community to capture some key aspects of the legal profession(s') collectivity, as very helpfully Mai'a Davis Cross has recently reviewed and rethought the concept. Therefore, rather than going back to the original work from the late 1980s and early 1990s, here I will draw on this more recent reformulation. She suggests that the original conception of the epistemic community as a network of experts 'who persuade others of their shared causal beliefs and policy goals by virtue of their professional knowledge' (Davis Cross 2013, p. 142), even if originally quite permissive has been subsequently too often narrowly interpreted (presuming that the only sort of expertise that qualifies as epistemic is scientific). This leads her to set out some key aspects to a (reformulated) analysis of epistemic communities.

Firstly, Davis Cross suggests that the concept should be permissive and widely interpreted when identifying such possible communities; what is important is not the issue area so much as the internal coherence of the group (Davis Cross 2013, p. 148). This leads her to identify a central role for professionalism as a key mode of establishing and enhancing intra-group coherence. This does not mean that an epistemic community is necessarily coterminous with a profession indeed there may be

---

[8] A key reason that I do not rely in this analysis on the analytical approach developed by Kathryn Sikkink and others is that rather than norm entrepreneurs driving the emergence/ development of the norm(s) of the rule of law, it seems to me this is much more of a process of collective inculcation. It may be that an adaptation of Sikkink's approach would serve my purposes (based, for instance, on Finnemore and Sikkink 1998), but here a (reworked) epistemic community analysis seems to dovetail better with my perspective (drawing as it does on Margaret Archer's work – see the earlier methodological interlude).

competing communities within a single profession. These communities build coherence through networking, education and socialization into the communities' norms, developing a common culture. The more coherent the epistemic community, the more likely it is to have an impact on global politics. Secondly, epistemic communities are able to establish influence when policy makers and other actors are uncertain or lack specialized knowledge about aspects of the issue area in which the epistemic community has demonstrated expertise. Thirdly, while an epistemic community will have a range of formal networks into states and major organizations, they will also have numerous casual and mediated channels for expressing and communicating their expertise (Davis Cross 2013, pp. 147–54). Thus, to recognize and start to explore the role of a putative epistemic community, we would expect to find a relatively high level of coherence and professionalism among the group, a focus on an area where in-depth knowledge and expertise is at a premium, leading to considerable uncertainty by non-adepts about how to proceed, and the group would have a highly developed set of formal and informal networks through which their influence flows.

Lawyers are pretty clearly such a group. They certainly see themselves as a guild of accredited individuals sharing common beliefs, of which the importance and value of the rule of law is central (Olson 2000, pp. 23–4). They also (almost self-evidently) regard themselves as enjoying significant expertise in an area that others find mysterious (a perception lawyers often perpetuate). Thus, drawing a parallel with epistemic communities, Ian Johnstone has suggested that (international) lawyers are an interpretive community, not least of all as legal norms are not necessarily fixed (as noted earlier) but rather are shaped and reshaped through inter-subjective practices of interpretation (Johnstone 2005, p. 192). Patterned by authority in interpretative opinion, this community can be seen as a series of concentric circles with varying levels of ability to interpret the rule of law episteme's elements, most obviously as regards issues of acceptable practices and at its most extreme the distinction between the civilized and the barbaric (Adler and Bernstein 2005, pp. 309–11).[9] The epistemic community is perhaps most coherent in the centre of Johnstone's circles, where interpretive authority is greatest and consolidated through shared socialization, while further out putative members of the community must serve their dues (as it were) before becoming fully adept at the range of interpretations allowed by the central epistemic authority. This authority

---

[9] This is a softer presentation of the interpretive community than is usually drawn from the work of Stanley Fish. For a review and critique of Fish's 'hard' position on interpretive communities as related to lawyers and judges see Patterson (1996, pp. 99–127).

is dynamic with the potential for new legal interpretations to be developed through processes of complementarity and contradiction that I drew from Archer's work in the methodological interlude.

This epistemic community of law(yers) is patterned by inter-firm/ practice networks, what might be called 'practice communities' (Bessy 2012, p. 23; Davis Cross 2013), which intermingle at training seminars and professional conferences, and extend networks initially established through legal education and law school alumni networks, including internationally focused efforts such as the International Development Law Organization (IDLO).[10] Likewise, the International Bar Association (IBA), the ICJ, international practitioner organizations (such as the European Federation of Insolvency Practitioners), alongside internationally facing national bar associations (such as the American Bar Association or City of London Law Society) all foster and support these networks. They convene conferences where opinions are exchanged and establish standing committees to work on developing authoritative readings of the law and its (international) practice. They offer guidance on standard and accepted practices to lawyers, but also importantly to international organizations and other actors in the global political economy (not least as they seldom limit their membership strictly to legal professionals) (Quack 2007, p. 651). These (collective) actors help maintain and develop a 'community of practice' that works with the norms of the rule of law across the global system to produce a practice 'capable of generating fidelity or an internalized obligation' to the idea of the rule of law (Brunnée and Toope 2011, p. 117). Thus, for instance, the IBA's *The Rule of Law: Perspectives from Around the Globe* collects together a range of papers on the rule of law from events in Chicago, Moscow, Russia, Brisbane, Singapore, Buenos Aires, Nairobi and Cambridge, all of which respond to the IBA's self-proclaimed project to stimulate more attention to the rule of law, following the IBA Council Resolution of 2005, which sought to underpin worldwide adherence to its principles (Neate 2009, pp. vii, 8). The events represented therein were explicitly intended to help encourage a wider adherence to the rule of law.

International law firms are also involved in processes of socialization that build on these networks and activities, but as John Flood points out, in the international realm of contending legal systems,

---

[10] See http://www.idlo.int/HomeIDLO/index.html. Interestingly the IDLO's origins include assistance from Ibrahim Shihata, then at Organization of the Petroleum Exporting Countries (OPEC) (Hager 1986), who would later work to transform the World Bank's position on the rule of law (see the earlier discussion).

[f]inding ways of dovetailing sometimes incommensurable systems has led to the globalisation of legal education and training. Young lawyers from jurisdictions outside the Anglo-American nexus now find it essential to obtain an LL.M degree at a major U.S. or U.K. law school otherwise they will not be conversant with global legal techniques. (Flood 2007, p. 54)

These graduates then often go on to judge any system to which they return against an internalized benchmark of US or UK common law and as such act in ways that start to move legal systems towards the normal characteristics with which they have become familiar at law school (Milhaupt and Pistor 2008, pp. 214–15). The community has clearly evident routes into its more central and influential areas with education and socialization encouraging the uptake of specific forms of understandings of the rule of law, its techniques, practices and procedures.

Within this community much is shared and shifts in its culture are always (relatively) collective. Innovative reading(s) of any particular aspect of the law only really gain traction as they are adopted across a widening range of legally focused groups (Watson 1983, p. 1153). One of the chief reasons that it makes sense to talk of an epistemic community of lawyers is that their work has been partly to normalize the law and inculcate a consciousness of the law both within the group itself (as regards micro-techniques/ readings) and outside in (global) political 'communities'. However, it would be a mistake to assume, therefore, that the epistemic community of law(yers) is fully globalized: by far the majority of those working in law are likely to be working in national jurisdictions, mobilizing local community mores and working within historically and socially transmitted understandings of the rule of law. These may well coincide to a significant degree across borders, but equally national variances and even significant differences cannot be just wished away.[11]

This epistemic community of law(yers) is not limited to practising lawyers of course; national and international judges are part of a lively and well-developed network (Berman 2005, pp. 503–4), as are other related professions (Kennedy 2001). For judges, this may lead not so much to the adoption of precedents across national borders but to a convergence of rhetoric in legal opinions expressed in courts (Berman 2005, p. 537). Those within the epistemic community of law(yers) are often the clearest about the limits of law and the role of discretion and exceptions in the manner in which law actually works (Kennedy 2001, p. 480). This tendency is not

---

[11] See van Waarden and Hildebrand (2009) for a discussion of the impact of American notions of legalism on Dutch legal practice, resulting in changes to the legal system's practices but which retained nonetheless significant, crucial and continuing national (Dutch) characteristics.

limited to common law systems where precedent and judicial interpretation are often regarded as underpinning significant flexibility, but also in civil law systems where, despite formal fixity, there remains significant scope for 'inventiveness' in legal practice (Bessy 2012). Rather, it is those who may have adopted the legal mindset but have less actual experience with law who may have less notion of what the rule of law entails.

This epistemic community of law has 'promoted' a legal mode of thought. Like other transnational networks identified by Margaret Keck and Kathryn Sikkink, lawyers 'try to frame issues in ways that make them fit into particular institutional venues' (Keck and Sikkink 1998, p. 201), and their preferred venue, unsurprisingly, is the legal system. Paul Berman observes that this 'legal consciousness may be so much part of an individual's world view that it is present even when law is seemingly absent from an understanding or construction of life events' (Berman 2005, p. 495). Law is waiting in the wings ready to be deployed on demand. This is what legalization has wrought: the recourse to law as a tool for resolution of a wide range of social tensions, conflicts and decisions is always available and legitimate. The 'legal episteme' is spread by the actions and practices of lawyers and their sympathetic political interlocutors.

This community is growing, as indicated, for instance, by the fivefold increase in the number of lawyers in China between 1986 and 2005, a period in which economic development was also accelerating and lawyers were seen as 'economic police requiring no government outlay' (Weidong 2008, p. 59); or the 'dramatic' increase in in-house lawyers in major global corporations (Shaffer 2009, pp. 167–8). Moreover, as a profession, in developed countries at least, lawyers seem to dominate politics, even if they are not so well represented in the governments of developing states (where engineers and the military are more pronounced),[12] while lawyers have also played a key role in the development of governance in the European Union (Vauchez 2012). The epistemic community of law(yers) is not merely reproducing itself but rather expanding its reach by force of numbers and the range of its (political) activity.

Perhaps one of the major effects of the mainstream legal epsteme is the acceptance of the rule of law as a technology, where law can be treated, in Martin Krygier's words, as 'technical equipment, social machinery, which can be transported and plugged in wherever the need for them arises' (Krygier 1999, p. 82). This is not necessarily a recent development (see Friedman 1969, pp. 29–30), with the ICJ already indentifying the lawyer

---

[12] 'There was a lawyer, an engineer and a politician', *The Economist*, 18 April 2009, pp. 65–6 – reporting on a survey carried out by the magazine's researchers on the almost 5000 politicians listed in that year's *International Who's Who*.

as a social engineer in 1965 (ICJ 1965, p. 72), and was an important contributory factor in the World Bank's expansion of its legal technical assistance. Nevertheless, the epistemic (sub)community of international public
lawyers has taken command of the 'technology' to promote the expansion
of international customary law with less regard to particular state interests
than might be found in international treaty law. Andy Olson observes that
this community has forcefully argued that 'customary international law is
*created* through the convergence of the opinions of members of that community' (Olson 2000, p. 24, emphasis in original), dividing law off from its
subjects. Here, the professional project (discussed below) is surely pushed
to its extreme limits. More generally, as Shirley Scott has argued:

> If the system of international law were not perceived to have a considerable
> degree of autonomy, then legal argument would be no more useful than a policy
> rationale. International lawyers serve as guardians of the relative autonomy,
> cohesion and consistency of international law. (Scott 2007, p. 420)

As with legal argument more generally, this is not to say that such opinions are wholly indeterminate, but it *is* the epistemic community itself
that informs and shapes the boundaries of the acceptable and unacceptable reach of legal opinion (even if these boundaries may move through
dynamic processes within this community) (Scott 2007, p. 417). This helps
explain why while particular laws may be subject to change and shifting
political pressures, the underlying logic of the rule of law remains remarkably constant as a political foundation.

Because lawyers know how the law works (and how to make it work for
their clients), pressure for change in law frequently comes from outside the
epistemic community rather than from within (although for some 'cause
lawyers' linked to campaigns of civil disobedience this is less the case)
(Watson 1983, pp. 1156–7). Thus, for instance, in his revisionist account
of the rise of human rights as a global norm, Samuel Moyn (2010) has
suggested that international lawyers were behind the curve, with the drive
for this innovation in recent international law driven more by social movements and other political actors, with the legal community being initially
concerned about the enforceability of such rights before swinging behind
human rights as a persuasive international norm. It is likely that the initial
reticence about human rights by international lawyers (as identified by
Moyn) was actually a reflection of their own concern for the rule of law,
and it is only the careful dovetailing of human rights and the rule of law in
thicker accounts of the norm that have then made these two norms compatible (in the minds of international lawyers at least). More generally, the
consolidation of the epistemic community of law(yers) and the expansion

of their role in global politics represents in one sense a successful project of professionalization. That is to say, across (global) politics professionals have usurped the non-specialist or self-empowered activist. This process remains partial and incomplete, but nevertheless far from negligible.

## THE PROFESSIONALIZATION OF GLOBAL POLITICS

The professionalization of global politics has prompted an increasingly important role for lawyers and legally trained or legally adept individuals, while the professionalization of law itself has also had some impact on how the rule of law has developed.[13] Examining the English legal profession, Richard Abel has observed that as professionalization advanced, so law firms ceased to be satisfied with a passive (waiting) role; rather they sought to manage their relations with clients better and develop ways of creating demand for their services (Abel 2003, pp. 484–8). Historically, in the UK at least, this involved the support for third-party payment (through legal aid and other mechanisms), but more generally, the move from passive/ reactive forms of practice to proactive lawyering also involves the argument that issues previously regarded otherwise are actually matters of law and thus require the work (and retention) of lawyers for their resolution. This aspect of professionalization is particularly relevant as it implies that lawyers, by reinterpreting issues as legal issues, also (re)produce the normative value of the rule of law for the non-law adept.

By the professionalization of global politics I also mean to identify the move of individuals who have had specific training in recognized professions into the institutions and organizations involved with politics beyond the state. This trend is of course much wider than the professions(s) of law, and is not only (or even primarily) an international phenomenon. For instance, Christopher McKenna has linked the development of new forms of (national) regulation with the rise of management consultants, who through 'economies of knowledge' professionalize processes of change navigated by both commercial and non-profit organizations dealing with new laws that impact on their operations (McKenna 2006). Thus, the trends I seek to identify and relate to the discussion of legalization are, firstly, the move to reinterpret political issues as legal issues and, secondly,

---

[13] Space precludes a detailed discussion of the shift of law from a trade to a profession; although Perkin (1990) is concerned with the development of the professions generally, more focused treatments can be found in Ariens (1992) examining the USA and Sugarman (1993) concerned with the UK.

the increasing deployment (and employment) of lawyers in international organizations and in the civil society organizations with which they interact.

This professionalization of global society (not least among civil society groups or organizations) has led to a move to regard the terrain of the professional as an increasingly important element of understanding the polity (Guilhot 2005). As Harold Perkin also notes, ideas of social justice and fairness are embedded within the internal value system of the professions (Perkin 1990, p. 402) and contribute to (although do not determine) the move to put these values at the heart of the new millennium's global politics. Thus, one simple way to explain the rise of the rule of law in global politics is to stress the number of lawyers entering politics alongside a more general professionalization of the global polity that has moved legal forms of organization to the forefront. The political self-maintenance of the legal profession alongside trends towards professionalization in modern society have reinforced each of these, prompting the increasing deployment of the rule of law.

This has led to transnational advocacy networks expending significant energy on helping to draft new legal rules, before then (empowered by these very same rules) seeking to publicize where national and international practices fall short (Sikkink 2002). By expanding the utilization of legal mechanisms to address political issues, these networks have prompted a further normalization of the rule of law (Tamanaha 2011, p. 236). To some extent this represents the recognition by these networks of new opportunities that have been established through new elements of international law (such as new treaties or international organizations' review processes) (Graubart 2004), but equally by turning to these mechanisms (international) advocacy groups have expanded the political role of the legalized debates that take place in such fora. However, as Boaventura de Sousa Santos and César Rodríguez-Garavito (2005, p. 11) have cautioned, we must avoid conflating the influence of radical lawyers working for civil society groups and corporate lawyers who work for multinational corporations or for international organizations as part of various global governance networks; these groups see the rule of law very differently and, thus, while likely agreeing on its importance will differ on what it actually means. Even within NGOs it is not necessarily the case that lawyers can shape collective views. Based on a review of US civil society organizations' experience, Michael McCann (1998) rejects the crude argument that lawyers co-opt (otherwise) radical campaigns into legally circumscribed activity/foci because it fails to recognize that most campaigns are pluralist organizations/groups well able to resist lawyerly cries for 'moderation' if necessary.

Whatever this normative role among such organizations, the move to the rule of law as a set of assumptions (a common sense) is often missed while organizations' normative entrepreneurship on (perhaps) narrower issues is more easily identified and analysed.[14] This may be because the impact of the preference for the rule of law most often takes place in meeting after (dull) meeting, a slow incremental accretion of normative weight over successive iterations of discussions (Braithwaite and Drahos 2000, pp. 502–4). Allied to a historic preference for individualism among professional development practitioners (drawn initially from former colonial officers, military personal and other international organizations) (Chabbott 1999, p. 243), this has likely led to a preference for rights talk and its attendant legal discourse.

Examining the professionalization of French NGOs, Gordon Cumming (2008) argues that this move is leading to a development 'mono-culture' that has been supported (or even promoted) by states' governments (in this case France) seeking to distinguish those groups worthy of funds from those not. Here, professionalization is driven by the fragmentation or diversification of advocacy and civil society groups alongside increasingly scarce resources to support this segment of the international policy community. This has increased the use of contracts to frame and manage the delivery of a wide range of assistance projects, moving from relations of trust and informal delegation to relations relying on executable (legally constituted) contracts for the 'delivery' of aid and assistance measured through performance indicators (Cooley 2010), where professional accreditation is a useful risk management indicator for funders. Here, the political, economic and social constitutive roles of the law have a considerable impact, reforming relations between parties along the formal lines familiar and common to neoliberal capitalist practice: buyer of service and provider/contractor.

For Perkin, the professionalization of society also includes a move from a focus on capital either as investment or activity-based to a focus on property (that is, scarcity) in the delivery of services (Perkin 1990, pp. 377–80, *passim*). This shift is a move from the discussion of power based on territory and/or resources to the notion of power based on knowledge and expertise, the very attributes claimed by professionals. The 'professional project' undertaken by many professions includes the development and promotion of a higher status for themselves in the social (and political) order (Macdonald 1995, pp. 187–207). This status is established by the control exercised over the discourse and definition of the field in which the

---

[14] See, for instance, the contributions to Khagram et al. (2002) that cover a good range of norms but are silent on the question of the normalization of the rule of law.

(nascent) profession seeks to operate, which is then extended through the process of abstraction and reduction: particular problems are reconceived in abstract terms and then reduced to problems that fall within the jurisdiction of the profession (Abbott 1988, p. 98). Professionalization is therefore the result of professions seeking to capture political terrain on which to operate, as much as it is about shifts and changes in that terrain caused by material factors. The legal profession's ability to establish and maintain the scarcity (and thus value) of its expertise is exemplary of this development (Bourdieu 1987). Social problems are increasingly reconceptualized as issues of regulation, and then reduced to issues of the development, application and interpretation of law, where lawyers can claim expertise.

This can easily be detected in the contemporary international realm, where political questions are becoming more frequently rendered as questions about the choice of jurisdiction (the choice of which set of rules, and/or organization) where adjudication should be sought (Koskenniemi 2007a). This leads to (international) lawyers being asked to pronounce on political issues, deploying a perspective that appeals to (nascent) cosmopolitan values and norms, 'rescuing' issues from politics. As noted above, this has led to an interest in constitutionalism, seen either, critically, as a move to establish the rule of capitalism across the global system (Gill 2003) or more positively as a response to the increasing fragmentation of governance, a shift away from states' sovereignty towards a range of issue-based international organizations. Jan Klabbers has concluded that: 'constitutionalism carries the promise that there is some system in all the madness, some way in which the whole system hangs together and is not merely the aggregate of isolated and often contradictory movements' (Klabbers 2004, p. 49). As I will discuss in Chapter 7, the rule of law is the foundation on which the notion of an emergent global constitution must sit, allowing the continual competition for authority over contentious issues, to be presented not as political contest, but rather as technical choice, overseen by lawyers and technologists, not politicians with sectional interests. The rule of law appeals to two powerful elements of contemporary (global) political thought: the desire for universal truths and a mistrust of politics (Upham 2004). Legal techniques seem to simplify and dissolve social difference, while removing politics from difficult social choices and placing professionals at the centre of decision making.

Historically, David Sugarman points out, lawyers' political role has been partly facilitated by the written form of the Western legal tradition.

> Writing enabled lawyers to claim to be, and sometimes to appear to be, above and beyond the individual acts of power involved in legal practices and the application of the law. In manifold ways, the written form of law abrogated

power to those lawyers claiming specialist expertise in the 'interpretation' of the
law. (Sugarman 1993, pp. 292–3)

This has not been a passive nor reactive development but rather is linked
to the professional project of lawyers to promote their expertise and skills
(and to reify the law, thereby ensuring it needs interpretation). As Ugo
Mattei and Laura Nader put it:

> the rule of law, an early tool used by lawyers to claim a special professional
> status as guardians of a government of laws, was in fact born out of their role as
> guardians of a given, highly unequal, and certainly non-democratic distribution
> of property in society. (Mattei and Nader 2008, p. 12)

Working in the Western political tradition that Sugarman identifies,
lawyers continue to promote law as a technical ordering device that supports the development of the good (political) life; they emphasize the
specialist and technical character of their undertaking, while seeking to
maintain and increase their social status by closely guarding entry to the
profession and underemphasizing the origin of law in legislatures. The
professional project of lawyering involves both the careful fostering of a
closed group, the epistemic community of law(yers) alongside the promotion of their tool (law) as a solution to problems of order.

However, the value of professions to politics is by no means uncontested; Perkin notes that the idea of a scarcity in expertise and professional
service (driving the increase of value of the profession's work) was firmly
rejected by the new right in the UK and elsewhere in the 1980s (Perkin
1990, pp. 472–519). Alan Paterson has recently argued that in response,
professionalism in the legal system of the UK has undergone a period of
renegotiation, seeing a rebalancing from a system that prioritized benefits
– status, reasonable rewards, restricted competition and autonomy – to
one that has emphasized instead the profession's obligations – reliable
expertise, access to the law, public service and public protection (Paterson
2012, pp. 16–17). However, while this has moved the profession of lawyers
into a more commercial service-focused logic (which he compares to
plumbers, not altogether jokingly), Paterson suggests the profession
retains the expectation of adherence to professional values, such as independence, loyalty and confidentiality, alongside a commitment to uphold
the rule of law (Paterson 2012, p. 13). Thus, while the ethos of the lawyer
may be shifting, the rule of law remains a constant refrain.

In many developing countries professional inculcation into the rule of
law is not always as successful due to its incompatibility with (local) politics 'on the ground'. This leads Dezalay and Garth, who have developed a
substantial body of work on the role of lawyers in global politics, to argue

that the wide variance in the successes of US-led legal exports in Latin America is largely the result of the character of the legal culture (and legal politics) of the recipient countries (Dezalay and Garth 2002).[15] Indeed, Gardner points out that earlier during the 'law and development decades' developing country lawyers

> generally turned American legal assistance to their own ends, and in this they were reasonably consistent: they wanted resources, better training for entry into the public sector, and an implicit legitimation of their move away from what they, too, perceived to be 'antiquated' legal doctrines, toward the problem-solving, technocratic public sector role they were adopting and advancing. (Gardner 1980, p. 287)

This may give one indication of why at the global level much of the work on rule of law has been driven by critical and oppositional groups of one sort or another. Some groups of lawyers have adopted the neoliberal/new right agenda that proposes law (to simplify a little) as merely a procedural mechanism to deliver the order required for capitalist expansion (focused primarily on property rights and the sanctity of contracts, with some interest in corruption). Conversely, other (mainstream as well as oppositional) lawyers have developed a much more substantive (expanded) conception of the rule of law that supports the values of social justice and fairness, and lies at the heart of their professional project. Both these self-conceptions can be maintained by the professionals' representative bodies acting in a guild-like manner as the guardians of debates about their (local and wider) community's character and practices. Indeed, over 40 years ago Lawrence Friedman suggested that law reform was one of the key components of the project of professionalization for lawyers, allowing them to present themselves as progressive and responsible (Friedman 1969, p. 42). He went on to draw a parallel between law reforms and the then emerging law and development (modernization of law) movement (Friedman 1969, p. 45). Here, debates about the character of law reform as a professional concern are not limited to national jurisdictions but are a key issue for the (globalized) epistemic community itself.

Finally, in terms of developmental support, professionalization may also have been driven by a reaction against perceived imperial/colonial forms of knowledge in the post-colonial period; formalized technical legal expertise can be presented as non-political by both its suppliers and its recipients. Less formalized modes of developmental support were to a large extent compromised by the imperial relation in which they were

---

[15] They have also undertaken an extensive analysis of the history of legal transplants in Asia to reach a similar conclusion (Dezalay and Garth 2010).

articulated, but even so the move to a (claimed) universal technical knowledge often merely reflects another set of political economic assumptions and power relations (Kothari 2005, pp. 36–38; Mattei and Nader 2008, pp. 28–34). Nevertheless, Gardner suggests that the model of the professional lawyer was perhaps the most influential export of the law and development movement of the 1960s and 1970s, offering some support to 'problem-solving' lawyers for their work with the public sector and legal system (Gardner 1980, p. 257). This move to what has sometimes been called 'managerialism' can be presented as depoliticizing the process of post-imperial developmental aid, offering a set of technical solutions ('delivered' by professionals), but such a claim for technical expertise ignores the wider issue of the political economic role and social constitutive role of the law, and its links with values such as human rights or justice.

To summarize: there are clearly identifiable agents whose interests (political and professional) are served by the move to normalize the rule of law, and whose modes of practice drive and reinforce the normalization of the rule of law. I should caution that this is not to suggest that such developments are merely undertaken cynically,[16] but are more likely to reflect a particular understanding of the way societies develop and the role of law in that development – the legal episteme. This perspective remains ideological and not merely technical and needs to be understood as such, but also reflects a good faith belief in the value of the rule of law by most lawyers.

## CONCLUSION: THE RULE OF LAW AS PARADIGM MAINTENANCE?

The rule of law mindset, or the legal episteme (Adler and Bernstein 2005), is being spread both by the professionalization of global politics and through the widespread activities associated with programmes of technical assistance and capacity building, promoting the rule of law undertaken by lawyers, to which I turn in the next two chapters. Perhaps the most important aspect of these developments is the attraction that non-lawyers often now feel towards the rule of law. The rule of law provides, especially in its thicker depictions, a series of political values (including the constraint of executive power) that appeal much more widely than the legal profession.

---

[16] Although for some commentators this is less obvious; for instance, in 1969 commenting on the early years of the law and development movement, Lawrence Friedman suggested that the 'major interest that [the law] serves is that of the legal profession itself' not least of all because 'lawyers develop the inner rationality of the legal system to suit their own purposes and pretensions' (Friedman 1969, pp. 49, 51).

The political appeal to the law may in any specific instance be motivated by tactical considerations but more generally the (global) legal profession has been pretty successful in its promotion and maintenance of the rule of law as a reliable and legitimate solution to myriad problems of order and governance in both domestic and international politics.

So far in the foregoing chapters I have, in one sense, been following Kennedy, who suggests that these 'professional vocabularies give us a window into [the] more general establishment consciousness, both because they are influential, and because they articulate what is common sense in the broader society of cosmopolitan people who influence international policy making' (Kennedy 2001, p. 471). However, while the normative (re)production of the rule of law seems to be proceeding across the global polity, any convergence on a single form of legal practice that might be recognized as characterizing the rule of law is absent in both analytical and practical terms. This leads to a paradox: the rule of law is increasingly appealed to while its empirical existence seems to lag well behind such political proclamations. Adopting a phrase used by Robert Wade, one way of understanding the normative activity around the rule of law is to see it as a form of 'paradigm maintenance' rather than any substantive reflection of political reality; a social imaginary with a purpose.

When Wade deployed the term 'paradigm maintenance' to discuss the process of writing the World Bank's 1993 WDR, *The East Asian Miracle*, he identified relatively formal processes including the choice of staff (employed by the Bank), alongside an implicit promotions system that influenced the entire internal review and editing process of WDRs (Wade 1996, pp. 30–3). While the rule of law field does not approach the organizational cohesion of the Bank, we can see in the professionaliza-tion of global politics a parallel process of choice of individuals who are able to pronounce on the value of the rule of law, albeit a process that is always incomplete in its attempted limitation on commentary on the rule of law. Again, unlike the Bank there is no single review and editorial locus for discussion of the rule of law, but rather a continuing and seemingly irresolvable discussion about the norm's actual meaning. However, this indeterminacy has pushed the rhetoric to a level of generality that enables it to work as a political touchstone. Thus, in a mirror of the processes at the Bank, the lack of consensus in the process of deliberation of analysis/ meaning allows claims to remain defensible in the face of difficulties on the ground as there remains no consensual criteria against which we might 'measure' the rule of law (Merkel 2012; Samuels 2006; Tamanaha 2011, p. 228). Thus, paradigm maintenance in the rule of law may be concerned with holding experience and norm at some distance from each other, while at the very same time the imaginary is deployed for political ends.

This may be because, as Tamanaha has concluded:

> Rule of law initiatives are dominated by the agendas and ideological views (including modernization assumptions) of the promoters on the delivery side – whether transnational corporations or investors seeking legal protections, or selfless advocates of human rights – more than they are about finding concrete ways to serve the pressing needs of the receiving populace. (Tamanaha 2011, pp. 244)

The rule of law is therefore often a solution seeking a problem. This should not be such a surprise as most lawyers involved in development programmes, unlike other groups of development practitioners, have little if any prior experience of the countries they are working in, and therefore only see how these systems lack the forms and practices they are used to (and which they regard as normal) (Golub 2006, p. 127). They are working within the paradigm of a specific rule of law because it is what they know and expect, but this can then involve extensive interventions to attempt to build 'normal' legal institutions where there is little that looks like a liberal legal realm or system. The difficulty is that in this (re)building of the legal realm local and customary law systems are dismantled or sidelined even when they might be easily modified to fulfil rule of law strictures, and elites are able to capture (for their ends) the new structures, where and when they are successfully established. Rule of law programmes therefore may fall considerably short of their liberal emancipatory intent (Richmond 2011; see also Krygier 1999). In searching for a solution to the problems in developing countries, lawyers reach for the law, and as global politics has become increasingly professionalized with more lawyers (and the legally trained) working in these policy areas, so more reach for the rule of law as a solution because it seems to be absent from the societies with which they are concerned. In the next two chapters I explore these programmes and ask how they relate to ideas about the rule of law and what they suggest about the legalization of global politics.

# 4.  Building the rule of law with a political focus

The rule of law has become a new rallying cry for global missionaries. (Garth and Dezalay 2002, p. 1)

Today's export of democracy occurs in a context of much diminished expectations for non-Western states in the wake of the perceived failure (for the most part) in the experiment in post-colonial independence. (Chandler 2006, pp. 490–1)

The rule of law that peace-building missions are mandated to inculcate cannot exist where either rulers or ruled (or both) feel free to ignore them. (McAuliffe 2011, p. 135)

In this chapter I explore the way the rule of law is linked to political development most often with the intent of restoring order in post-conflict states. In the following chapter, I'll look at how economic arguments are then used to buttress the political development of specific forms of the rule of law. In the most general terms, the purpose of much of the activity discussed in this and the next chapter is to make the law count in ways that previously it has not. Moreover, the rule of law is tied up with the articulation and mobilization of political power; any radical change or reform of the rule of law in a country at the very least will change the way the country's rulers govern, but may also (and not infrequently) shift the locus of power in ways that previous rulers find uncomfortable or (indeed) unacceptable (Friedman 1969, p. 47). To supporters the crucial difference a rule of law programme can make is the transfer of power from arbitrary and violent sources to a stable structure of legality. Unsurprisingly, when programmes have failed it is often (as in Afghanistan) the difficulty, or failure, to affect this shift of power that is indentified as the problem: the rule of men, and/or violence, is not supplanted effectively by the rule of law in the eyes of the recipients.

How the law is perceived as ruling in transitional states is crucial; as Martin Krygier puts it, a general social recognition of the ascendance of the rule of law is evident when:

- 'citizens generally obey the law and expect their fellows to do so too';
- obedience to the law is voluntary (not based on fear);
- the law counts for the people who count (the ruling elite);
- and the 'law should not merely serve the purposes of the rulers but also those of citizens, as a protective and facilitative device available to them in their relations both with the state and with each other' (Krygier 2001, pp. 14–15).

Only when these four conditions are largely fulfilled might the introduction of the rule of law be regarded as a success by the general population. As rule *by* law does not necessarily equate to the rule *of* law, rule of law programmes often are not addressing the complete absence of a legal system, but rather are focused on the distinction between the extant systems and processes of law as understood as legitimate in the countries (and societies) from which aid and support is delivered, and the forms of legality that exist in the host/target countries. However, the rhetoric (and celebration) of the rule of law is a lot easier in policy debates than when attempting to fill the (politically) identified 'lack' to which rule of law programmes are responding.

In RAND Corporation's useful survey of nation building, the key challenges confronted, and thus actions required, by rule of law programmes are identified as follows:

- *Pre-conflict legal planning*: in the pre-intervention stage a 'quick-start' package of laws and immediate legal requirements is helpful and should be based on a needs assessment. To some extent this represents recognition (as noted below) that programmes have often been ill-prepared and have lacked knowledge of the previous (and possibly existing) local legal system (Dobbins et al. 2007, pp. 77–8). Here, the treatment or perception of the rule of law as a generally applicable legal technology may undermine such preparation or render it as an un-needed diversion.
- *Establishing applicable law*: it may not be feasible to merely reinstall a previous legal system and indeed choosing among past systems itself may be a political problem of some magnitude (as in the case of Kosovo, discussed below). However, to begin to get a system of law to actually work, programmes need to either establish which previous legal code will now be applicable or provide a comprehensive new legal code (from public administration to vehicle codes/laws; from commercial laws to criminal statures) (Dobbins et al. 2007, pp. 78–81). The former, often after (civil) wars, requires one or other sides' legal preferences to be recognized, however, and one

(or others) to be dismissed, unless a new constitutional process is begun to find a consensual system of laws (in itself by no means an easy task); the latter requires not merely extensive preparation (legal systems are complex) but also a programme to quickly establish the new laws' legitimacy.

- *Recruiting, vetting and training judges and lawyers*: legal systems are dependent on courts and thus lawyers and judges. This involves not merely the (re)training of existing and past post-holders and advocates but also the recruitment and selection of viable new candidates. Moreover, rule of law programmes need to work through this process more than once; they need to set up legal education systems that support a sustainable system to prepare expert court personnel committed to the rule of law (Dobbins et al. 2007, pp. 83–5). Part of the problem here is that many in-post and/or lapsed judges and legal personnel may have been compromised by the previous regime, or conversely by their resistance to it, making it difficult for a case to be made that the (new) courts are neutral and fair in the early period of transition while new trainees are still undergoing whatever educational programmes are being delivered.
- *Building infrastructure and providing equipment*: leading on from the above item, there are plenty of legal facilities that may require attention, from court buildings to law schools (Dobbins et al. 2007, p. 86). Legal infrastructure is both physical and social, but funding these programmes requires a staged approach to rebuilding, suggesting that the Supreme Court and Ministry of Justice might be prioritized for their potential demonstration effect, to emphasize the rejection of 'lawlessness'.
- *Improving the corrections system*: if the population is to feel secure in the new environment, then RAND suggests the (re)building of the correctional system must be a priority (Dobbins et al. 2007, p. 87). Although this may reflect the American culture of incarceration to some extent, nevertheless, if order is to be maintained (and providing the court system is seen as largely fair), it is important to ensure that law breakers are sanctioned effectively. A failure to sanction offenders can quickly bleed away any emerging legitimacy the (new) legal system may have gained.
- *Establishing a rule of law culture*: all of the above feed into the key requirement that if the rule of law is to be sustained in the long run a supportive (legal) culture must exist. Indeed, without such a culture there is little chance that the (new) legal system will be seen as legitimate. This involves both the support of citizens and civil society in the working of the legal system, and the requirement that the

system is seen as fair, equitable and generally accessible. This may involve outreach programmes, training assistance to local NGOs and work to legally empower groups whom the previous system was prejudiced against (Dobbins et al. 2007, pp. 88–91). This is easy to say, but may well confront the persistence of legitimate and locally respected legal cultures that do not reflect the (new) rule of law in some or all of its various elements. Building a rule of law culture may confront differing views of how the law might work for the population (a theme we return to later).

- *Supporting transitional justice*: the RAND report also suggests that Truth Commissions and war crimes trials should be included in the process of establishing the rule of law (Dobbins et al. 2007, pp. 91–100), and certainly the establishment of the International Criminal Court and the expanding experience of Truth Commissions suggest that they can serve a useful cathartic role in post-conflict societies, although there may be issues around the problem of retrospective application of more recent laws, or political problems related to the need to engage previous enemies in joint processes of political development. As there is a considerable literature discussing transitional justice,[1] for my purposes I shall merely note that such processes require and are built on the development of the rule of law and while they may enhance such a culture, if politicized they can also become part of the critical debate about the meaning of the rule of law more generally in a given society.

As these elements indicate, programmes to build the rule of law are wide-ranging and potentially complex with many inter-related developments and so failure (or difficulty) in any particular dimension may (but may not) compromise the overall project of establishing the rule of law.

Support for the enhancement or fuller implementation of the rule of law may come from external pressure based on conditionality linked to some clear political outcome, of which the European Union's link between standards of governance and membership is the most explicit. It may also come from external 'change-agents' who are working on the basis of foreign aid priorities focused on internal/domestic benefits for the recipient community. In both cases it is presumed that the domestic political system will not be able to proceed towards the establishment of the rule of law spontaneously and without external help through either

---

[1] See, for instance, Almqvist and Esposito (2012), Elster (2004), McAdams (1997), McAuliffe (2010), Nalepa (2010), Sikkink (2011), Stromseth et al. (2006, pp. 249–309) and Teitel (2000).

incentives or direct involvement in the legal sector; this might be called the 'implied causal story of the rule of law'.[2] This causal story is related to progress, development and the achievement of the good life (as perceived by the supporters of law reform at least). It also involves a debate about the sequencing of reforms, and the context (or circumstances) in which the rule of law is being promoted (Prado 2010), whether each programme of reform(s) is dependent on the society and polity into which it is being introduced or not.

Reflecting this question of a pre-existing political context, sequencing is often alighted on when analysts are looking for simple explanations for the (relative) failure of rule of law programmes. Francis Fukuyama argues that a thin (proceduralist) rule of law may be possible to establish without many of the (liberal) norms of the thicker perception being in place when societies are not yet ready for the full 'liberal' rule of law. Moreover, in his view even a spatially limited development of the rule of law (limited to urban areas, for instance) may be a good start (Fukuyama 2010). Here, the promotion of a universalized liberal rule of law is not merely too difficult and expensive to achieve quickly but is likely to fail as it can never fulfil (or even approach) such ambition by trying to do everything at once. Conversely, as his critics maintain, autocracy is inherently in tension with the rule of law and those gradualists who claim to be partially reforming the law may not be on the road to democratization at all, but merely seeking to consolidate their own positions and repel further external political intervention.[3] Debates about sequencing are a useful corrective to the idea that rule of law reform can be achieved quickly, and thus introduce a (perhaps more sensible) appreciation of gradualism, even if they raise (again) questions of threshold conditions.

Thus, while the rule of law is often treated as a key element in the process of democratization it does not follow that this relationship works the other way: it may be entirely possible (in thin views of the rule of law at least) to establish the rule of law without the full panoply of liberal democracy and indeed without the expectation that in the near future such a democratic structure might be reached. Here, as Paddy Ashdown argued (drawing lessons for Iraq from his experience in Bosnia), the sequence of reforms places the rule of law well before political liberalization and democratic process (cited in Chandler 2006, p. 483). Indeed, it is not only

---

[2] Although I do not develop this point here particularly, Deborah Stone (1989) offers a useful analysis of causal stories and their importance in the formation of policy agendas, not least as they often involve the identification of crucial actors, either as agents of, or impediments to, political change; this is picked up in the section on culture below.

[3] For more on sequencing see Fukuyama et al. (2007) where Carothers (2007) is the subject of a series of exchanges.

authoritarian regimes that seek to introduce a thin rule of law for their own ends. The manner in which post-conflict states come to be managed by the 'international community' with internationally appointed administrators (such as Carlos Westendorp and then later Paddy Ashdown in Bosnia) who seek to present their work as technical authority above popular accountability, appealing to their own knowledge of the common good (Chandler 2006, pp. 479–80), depends on a largely procedural (thin) rule of law.

On the other hand, it does not always play out like this, as the case of the European Union's work in accession states demonstrates; here the rule of law and democracy are entwined much more clearly and therefore it is here that I will start to explore how rule of law programmes can work when the focus is primarily political, before moving to the case of rule of law programmes in post-conflict states.

## THE EUROPEAN UNION, ACCESSION STATES AND THE RULE OF LAW

The European Union (EU) has been extensively involved in the (regional) promotion of the rule of law, often using the promise of association or even membership to drive adoption of its various elements. The EU's accession-linked programmes only developed a significant dynamic after the end of the Cold War and the dissolution of the Soviet bloc, but subsequently these programmes, which are linked to clear entry criteria to the Union, have contributed to considerable socio-legal change in the recipient countries. This work stems from the Programme of Community aid to the countries of Central and Eastern Europe (PHARE) that while initially focused on economic and market issues, was quickly reoriented towards a concern with a range of social and political issues once neighbouring states in Central and Eastern Europe expressed interest in joining the EU (Berling 2006, p. 81; Kleinfeld and Nicolaïdis 2009, p. 154). This also reflected the Council of Europe's central concern with the promotion of the rule of law across a widely conceived Europe. The PHARE programme developed a series of activities intended to support potential accession and given the centrality of the rule of law to Europe's self-image (Walker 2009), this was included as a central element of these activities. The use of the Copenhagen criteria[4] to assess the candidate countries'

---

[4] To join the EU, a new Member State must meet three criteria:

- political: stability of institutions guaranteeing democracy, the rule of law, human rights and respect for and protection of minorities;

readiness to be admitted to the Union meant that states were adjudged on a wide range of legal issues as a requirement to adopt European rule of law practices (Kleinfeld and Nicolaïdis 2009, p. 154). Interestingly, this extensive accession programme also equipped a growing band of EU staff with clear appreciation and understanding of the rule of law and therefore underpinned the expansion of the EU's wider legal reform work in the Palestinian Occupied Territories and elsewhere.

These rule of law programmes also shifted from what has sometimes been referred to as 'market and demand driven', focused on the forms of legal reform required by countries to receive grants and aid they wished to access, to accession-driven reforms, related to the Council of Europe and EU criteria statements (Hammerslev 2011, p. 145). As accession loomed large in particular states' policy making so the balance between rule of law development assistance provided by US-based contractors and that which was being supplied and funded by the EU shifted towards the latter. This also involved a further move from programmes formalized and conducted by economists (often British) to ones run by bureaucratic/administrative law specialists (often from France) (Hammerslev 2011, p. 148). However, while EU programmes focused on state capacity and the development of state institutions, US-funded programmes were still continuing to focus on the private sector. Although these activities could be complementary, equally different segments of a country's elites often were being inculcated into the rule of law differently, understanding its central normative value in differing ways and potentially using reforms for differing (preferred) ends.

In their consideration of the EU's rule of law activities, Amichai Magen and Leonardo Morlino (2009) disaggregate adoption into three elements: rule adoption; rule implementation; and rule internalization. There may be widespread adoption of various laws but they may not be so well implemented, and perhaps most obviously, as demonstrated in many of their project's studies, there can be a lack of normative commitment by elites to the rule of law itself. This involvement and commitment of political elites is often regarded as crucial to the success of programmes; for instance, in the cases of the United Nations Transitional Authority in Cambodia (UNTAC) and the United Nations Interim Administration in Kosovo

- economic: existence of a functioning market economy and the capacity to cope with competitive pressure and market forces within the Union;
- acceptance of the Community acquis: ability to take on the obligations of member ship, including adherence to the aims of political, economic and monetary union.

Available at http://europa.eu/legislation_summaries/glossary/accession_criteria_copenha gue_en.htm (accessed 10 October 2013).

(UNMIK), Carolyn Bull (2008, pp. 93–6, 148–52) argues that the lack of any substantial elite support, alongside the inability of the mission to build popular support, was one of the major factors for the lack of progress in establishing even some elements of a recognizable rule of law. Likewise, in a study of criminal law reform in Russia, Matthew Spence identifies the impact of elite attitudes complementing an inferred US influence as producing positive, if small-scale, improvements in the rule of law (Spence 2006). The socialization of elites into a rule of law mindset cannot be taken for granted nor left for later.

That the EU accession programmes have been successful seems uncontroversial; in the last decade over ten countries have reached the democratic standards required for accession to the EU, which included significant achievements in the realm of the rule of law across all the elements listed above by RAND. These states now confront the problems of collective governance and the relation of their split sovereignty to domestic democracy, rather than the chaos of arbitrary rule and totalitarianism (Ganev 2009), although some governments and electorates may hanker after the previous certainties. Additionally, the EU's rule of law standards are relatively robust as demonstrated by the continuing difficulties for Turkey's candidacy for membership (although there are other contributing political factors at play in this specific case). Indeed, the EU membership programme includes what Rachel Kleinfeld calls 'strong enmeshment'; candidate states have been offered the benefits of membership but on the very clear condition that they reform and (among other things) adopt a legal system that conforms to the EU's own membership standards (Kleinfeld 2012, pp. 135, 141). Whether such incentives can be developed outside the special case of EU accession is another matter, with no easy answer to hand, although Kleinfeld suggests (focused) international organizations such as the World Trade Organization and/or the North Atlantic Treaty Organization have the best opportunity to help incentivize reform as part of their accession/membership processes.

Conversely, and returning to the role of local populations, reflecting on the EU experience, Esa Paasivirta has suggested that these programmes (and their success) have demonstrated that reforming the rule of law (towards the standards envisaged by liberal states) can only be achieved with extensive local/domestic ownership of the programmes themselves. This requires extensive engagement and dialogue between various stakeholder groups and/or communities and the careful management of expectations for the process of reform. Perhaps most strikingly, Paasivirta suggests that the EU experience demonstrates that sector-wide, wide-spectrum approaches work better than focused attention on one or other aspect of the legal system (Paasivirta 2010). However, Morlino and

Magen's analysis of the EU's programmes concludes that the development of the rule of law is much stronger where there have been clear and specific regulations or laws to be adopted rather than where the change required has been more normative (Morlino and Magen 2009, p. 238). These conclusions may not be necessarily contradictory; dialogue and discussion may better support developmental outcomes where the subject of discussion is relatively formal rather than attitudinal, but framed by the imaginary of the rule of law. Even then these conclusions may reflect the particular circumstances of the EU accession case(s); in post-conflict situations, it is unlikely that there will be an opportunity for such wide-ranging reform programmes or detailed negotiations between widely legitimated partners.

## POST-CONFLICT PROGRAMMES TO (RE)INTRODUCE THE RULE OF LAW

While the EU's rule of law programmes have been primarily about persuading strong states to relinquish power, to work within the rule of law (and to be constrained by it), post-conflict rule of law programmes often have a more basic intent: the replacement of chaos by some form of (hopefully acceptable) order (Magen 2009, p. 73). In the new millennium the rule of law has become an almost universal prescription for the management of post-conflict societies and their progression towards peace and order (Charlesworth 2010, p. 47). This has led to a common focus on law and order, including the reform and 'cleaning up' of police forces to underpin changes wrought in the name of the rule of law. Thus, all UN peace operations that explicitly had a rule of law component between 1999 and 2006 included a specific reference to reforming the police, while all but two also included specific references to judicial reform and the majority included reform of the prison system (Smith et al. 2007. p. 35). In Africa between 1989 and 2010 the number of UN peace operations that included rule of law assistance went from around half to all, at the same time that the overall number of missions expanded from two to twelve (in any particular year), although again the focus has been on law and order issues (Sannerholm 2012a, p. 364). Of course, this is not to claim that such deployments succeeded but merely to indentify the centrality of order to rule of law programme conception and planning, with only one mission explicitly focusing on constitutional or public administration issues (Sannerholm 2012a, p. 367). As noted above, populations who see criminals acting with impunity will not see the worth of any laws.

In an evaluation report for the World Bank, Kirsti Samuels suggests that rule of law projects in post-conflict societies have five clear priorities: the restoration of human security and basic law and order; the development of a system to resolve property-related and commercial disputes; the introduction of basic economic regulation; the support for human rights and transitional justice; and the provision of access to justice and maintenance of equality before the law (Samuels 2006, p. 7). This requires a programme of social change, not merely the introduction of formal legal structures. Because people will have likely found their own methods to resolve local conflicts where the state has failed, or will distrust formal law due to the manner in which it may have been mobilized prior to external intervention, rule of law programmes can confront a difficult task in developing trust and legitimacy in the institutions and practices they introduce (Stromseth et al. 2006, p. 311). Establishing the rule of law in post-conflict states is always going to be more than the importation or revival of formal legal mechanisms, institutions and practices.

Afghanistan has become a well-documented case of post-conflict rule of law programmes, although of course there are many others from which evidence could be drawn. The mosaic of donors and providers of technical assistance led to problems of implementation; for instance, reform of the Afghanistan judiciary was led by an Italian team whose efforts were not particularly successful, but given this programme's 'ownership', other aid teams were reluctant to intervene or contribute to the effort (Lister 2007, p. 14). Different external agencies may not agree about particular issues; in the case of international Romanian adoptions, for example, the EU position demanding a ban, linked to its work on the domestic rule of law, directly conflicted with pressure brought to bear by other governments to help the orphans (Demsorean et al. 2009, p. 94). Coordination between agencies and state programmes is also often lacking, leading Sebastian Astrada in a study of Mongolian reforms to suggest that one of the key elements for its (relative) success in the promotion of the rule of law was the World Bank's Legal Needs Assessment (Astrada 2009, pp. 58–61), which prompted wider coordination and cooperation between the various donors and agencies involved.

Unfortunately, as the Afghan mission has been conducted by a coalition, not only are there a range of stakeholders in the Afghan communities, they are being engaged by a range of (not particularly well-coordinated) national teams (Tondini 2007). Alongside a lack of funds and the absence of a clear set of strategic priorities, the establishment of the rule of law in Afghanistan is at best partial and certainly not entirely evident beyond urban enclaves, although the country has always had a fragmented governance system (Lister 2007). Reflecting on a decade's worth of attempts to reform the rule of law, Whit Mason suggested that the real difficulty in Afghanistan was that the rule of law was a late addition to the programmes considered by the occupying powers. By the time it was recognized as a major factor in helping to restore order and security too many Faustian bargains had been made with powerful local political players resulting in impunity and lawlessness among the elite (Mason 2011, pp. 322–3). Rather caustically, he concludes that the administration in occupied Afghanistan while it might be interested in security as regards external actors has little interest in the rule of law for the Afghan people (Mason 2011, pp. 327–8). It may be that trying to establish the rule of law in a country that continues to be on the edge of a civil war is impossible.

Additionally, and due to the security environment, in Afghanistan much of the rule of law work was conducted by US Army Judge Advocate General (JAG) units that, as Vasilios Tasikas reports, often had difficulty applying what was perceived as a relatively abstract concept – the rule of law – to the activities and practices on the ground (Tasikas 2007, p. 57). Nevertheless, even within the JAG units there was a recognition that it was unsatisfactory to deal with the rule of law as a technology with little reference to the local circumstances. As elsewhere, there was a lack of understanding or any early appreciation of the forms and practices of existing local justice and (legal-like) community dispute settlement mechanisms (Pimentel 2010; Rőder 2012, p. 226), which led to difficulties for the JAGs in implementing or supporting developments towards the establishment of the rule of law as envisaged by the overall US Afghan mission. Tilmann Rőder observes that the main instruments to build the rule of law in Afghanistan have been 'positive incentives, conditionality, persuasion and capacity building' with many 'incentives' to adopt particular programmes shading into outright corruption (Rőder 2012, p. 225). Nevertheless, the use of 'persuasion' and capacity building are/were regarded as legitimate in Afghani society, although the programmes often were focused on the development of rule of law 'technologies' unrelated to the prior legal culture of the country.

While there remain a number of education institutions (such as Kabul University) that have a long record of legal training, they remain beset by the (relatively) common academic difficulties of infighting and struggles over curriculum development between academics and government; this is in addition to the particular problems of Afghanistan, not least of all the reformation of education by the Taliban. In 2004 the lack of reliable and well-developed legal (re)training for judges prompted the Italian-led scheme mentioned above to establish the Independent National Legal Training Centre (Swenson and Sugerman 2011, pp. 141–2). While this has not been overly successful at raising the legal knowledge of the fragmented and diverse Afghan judiciary (who have been appointed under varying regimes and legal arrangements), it has emphasized the need for the rule of law to include not just physical and institutional capacity building but also the need to build human (judicial and legal) capacities.

Additionally, and albeit working differently from peace-keeping forces of various sorts, the International Monetary Fund (IMF) and the World Bank as well as operating with established states also offer rule of law assistance in post-conflict states. Interestingly, due to their established modes of activity, both usually work with transitional authorities as if they were 'normal' sovereign states, and often end up fulfilling the legislative function of these states themselves (Boon 2007, p. 531). In Iraq, for instance, the IMF and the World Bank had considerable advantages over the occupying forces when it came to work on the rule of law. While the occupying forces (due to the character of their presence) were constrained from wholesale legal change by the international laws on occupation that constrain legal transformation and require occupying forces, in most circumstances, to uphold the existing civil law, and were largely focused on the criminal law (and supporting institutions) (Rőder 2012, p. 219), such constraints or tight focus did not apply to the international financial institutions (Boon 2007, pp. 538–42). Thus, for the period the Coalition Provisional Authority was in power, the IMF and Bank were able to conduct a major programme of legislative reform, including the moves to instigate laws to support international trade as well as new laws on foreign investment. As I will discuss in the next chapter, these types of reform are seen as central to economic development, but in the Iraqi case, as in other post-conflict situations, there were also more basic requirements to (re)build the rule of law in more general terms including access to justice and the reformation of the Iraqi police force.

Often internationally constituted institutions enjoy support that the national legal system does not (especially after the end of a conflict) and as such enhancing the rule of law via criminal law needs to include capacity building in the local societies to help embed rule of law values into local legal systems (Stromseth 2011, pp. 182–3). The development of the rule of law in post-conflict states therefore starts from a different (perhaps more basic) set of needs than EU programmes, but remains recognizably part of the same spectrum of elements that make up the rule of law as a common sense (even if there are debates about which elements should be prioritized practically).

## COMMON PROBLEMS IN RULE OF LAW PROGRAMMES

There is no shortage of overviews of rule of law programmes seeking to draw the lessons from a least a decade's experience. One of the best of these is the report assembled by Kirsti Samuels (2006) for the World Bank. Here she raises 11 problems.

1. Lack of coherent strategy and expertise: rule of law programmes often have little strategic vision of how one might change the local system, and may indeed know little if anything about this system.
2. Insufficient knowledge of how to bring about change: not only do programmes' staff know little about the local (legal) circumstances, often they also have little knowledge of how to successfully transform (legal) institutions.
3. The priority of form over function: by focusing on the institutions and forms of law, the importance of legal practice is missed, leading to a disconnect between formal changes and continuing (local) practices.
4. The preference for formal over informal and traditional mechanisms: rule of law programmes frequently miss, downplay or misunderstand the role of the local legal culture.
5. The focus on tangible short-term reforms over long-term strategies: programmes are much too focused on short-term 'wins' rather than longer-term and sustainable systemic changes.
6. Wholesale over incremental and contextual-determined change: programmes sometimes assume that comprehensive change is needed now rather than seeing the rule of law as a goal towards which a society may move in stages and steps.
7. The need for local 'agents of change': the imposition of the rule of law by external actors (or the supply mode) misses the vital requirement that there must be a demand for change (for the rule of law) if it is to become embedded in custom and practice as well as formal (legal) mechanisms.
8. The paradox of local ownership: while local involvement is important, the 'right' local owners can make or break a rule of law intervention. Finding the right stakeholder groups is therefore vital to success, yet often not achieved.
9. Rushed and compromised constitution-making: constitution writing is a fraught process and needs to carefully balance the interests of diverse groups and/or communities, which too often is compromised by the perceived need to have a document promptly finalized and in place.
10. Poorly designed training and legal education programmes: few programmes seem to foster sustained change, and are often pitched at too high a level, supposing a level of knowledge of and familiarity with the rule of law that may not be evident.

11. The problem of sequencing and prioritizing: as indicated above, there is no real clear idea about what (if any) sequence of reforms might be preferred, leading all too often to an advance on all fronts (universalism), which is prone to compromise and failure, impacting on the reception of the rule of law itself (Samuels 2006, pp. 16–23).[5]

Difficulties in one or two of these areas does not necessarily undermine a rule of law programme, but the list is a reasonable account of the range of issues the promotion of the rule of law may confront in post-conflict situations (and elsewhere), and which may frustrate attempts to quickly produce the rule of law where it has hitherto been lacking.

Due to resource constraints, even willing countries' governments keen to progress such programmes are often dependent on external funders for support, and the resulting short-term funding cycles promote the erection of buildings and the training of elites – which produce outcome data for funders – rather than more long-term social capacity activities (Berling 2006, p. 203; Charlesworth 2010, p. 53). Moreover, and unsurprisingly, these external funders bring their particular view of the rule of law, preferred areas of work and sequence of changes, and by doing so downplay the local needs and priorities of the recipients of aid or support (Carfield 2011, p. 785). The donors have defined the 'problem' and the solution, and often seem to have little interest in the individual circumstances of recipient countries.

As Thomas Carothers observed (reflecting on his experiences in the 1990s in Guatemala, Romania and Nepal):

> Merely sponsoring the writing of new laws, especially by copying models from the United States and other donor countries, barely scratches the surface. The shiny new drafts are often not enacted into law, or if they are, the relevant state institutions usually lack the capacity to implement or enforce them and no budgetary provisions have been made to pay the costs of implementation. (Carothers 1999, p. 173)[6]

Once the new laws/constitutions have been delivered, for some programmes this is sufficient to claim that change has been achieved, even if on the ground such change has little impact. This re-emphasizes the pervasiveness of the view of the rule of law as a (social) technology that can be applied to a legal system without any real concern for the existing circumstances (Krygier 2011, p. 21). Such rule of law programmes

---

[5] For a broadly similar list but drawn from an analysis of African case studies see Sriram et al. (2011).

[6] Although for a defence of the use of 'model' legal codes see Rausch and O'Connor (2008).

are supply driven and not demand led; targets set for programmes may not only be ambitious but also (due to the contractual relationships that pattern much aid work that is linked to the process of professionalization noted earlier) be set with short time horizons for success, and programme evaluations only concerned with narrowly defined activities and outcomes (Jenkins and Plowden 2006, pp. 156–7). Rule of law programmes frequently appear to have been pulled off the shelf with little regard to the local conditions and context of the recipient societies, and as such it may be no surprise that the rule of law is subsequently treated as the imposition of foreign norms and mores rather than the delivery of an empowering social technology.

Additionally, the use of personnel, from judges to police officers from previous regimes, while pragmatically necessary can also often undermine rule of law objectives as they retain a cultural and personal commitment to previous practices. Judicial reform can be a long(ish) process requiring both political will and the ability to reform powerful, well-entrenched institutions and political communities. As Carothers points out, for 'many judges who have spent the career in dysfunctional systems, the vision of a reformed judiciary may well be unappealing' not least as it may constrain their previous personal power or reduce their 'income' from side payments or bribes (Carothers 1999, p. 175). Thus, part of many rule of law programmes is the move to enhance both the pay and professional prestige of judges to try to nullify or side-step these inherited attitudes (Humphreys 2010, pp. 199–201). Indeed, rule of law programmes in Europe, Latin America and elsewhere have needed to confront some common difficulties regarding governments and elites. Firstly, prior actions by the state may have undermined confidence in the rule of law, as authoritarian regimes may have ruled *by* law, where supposed constitutional safeguards have meant little. (When I worked for Charter 88 a popular way to criticize our campaign was to describe a wonderful constitution to an audience, and then reveal it to be that of the Soviet Union!) Secondly, elites and rulers have often escaped the reach of the law, with elites and their network often enjoying impunity from prosecution whatever their actions. Lastly, the mere fact there is a legal system often has done little to stem violence and insecurity for the mass of the population prior to any period to transition and thus they may remain sceptical of the potential of rule of law programmes to deliver real social improvement.[7]

Programmes in the early post-Cold War period, such as the UN programme in Cambodia (Bull 2008, pp. 72–119), were conceptualized as

---

[7] This list follows in its general contours the account of programmes in Latin America in Domingo and Sieder (2001).

reinvigorating already existing legal institutions rather than establishing a new rule of law. Thus, to some extent, the 'rule of law revival' (to use Carothers's phrase) was a period of (re)learning how the rule of law might be supported through political intervention. In contrast, the UN transitional mission to East Timor was explicitly mandated to reform the rule of law in the territory (Bull 2008, pp. 191–2). However, when the UN team went to work on building the rule of law in East Timor, there was little knowledge of or interest in the previous legal system nor in building on its foundations a sustainable set of institutions that would outlast the intervention itself (Samuels 2006, p. 16). This was perhaps understandable as the UN confronted a situation where most Indonesian and pro-autonomy legal personnel (judges, prosecutors and others) had left the country, and there were few if any remaining people with knowledge of the prior system who were untainted by the conflict (McAuliffe 2011, p. 115). Like the situation in Kosovo (discussed below) the UN Transitional Administration in East Timor found itself having to define the applicable law as well as building a (new) legal system.

Using a system of Special Panels (each with one Timorese and two international judges) was intended to move beyond prior experiences of political interference (both in practice and, as importantly, in the perception of the local population) and to engage in a programme of transitional justice (McAuliffe 2011, pp. 117–19). The difficulty has subsequently been that successive political leaders in East Timor have clashed with the UN about the impunity extended to cover political crimes of the crisis. This has led to a weakening of the perception that the rule of law might obtain, not least of all as the UN teams have in the end opted out of these disputes, leaving the institutions they initiated to be shaped (or undermined) by East Timorese political developments (McAuliffe 2011, p. 134). Moreover, once the UN decided to wind up the panels when the mission ended, leaving many suspects and crimes still to be investigated or tried in the courts, the rule of law values that were being built through the panel's activities were immediately undermined (Stromseth 2011, pp. 190–3). This is not the place to reflect on the rights and wrongs at stake in East Timorese politics, but it does demonstrate that merely building institutions is hardly sufficient to foster a sustainable rule of law.

Although to some extent anomalous, the difficulties encountered by UNMIK around applicable law are illustrative of another difficulty that can be encountered even if the courts are to some extent functional. Generally, the rule of law norm includes a supposition that there is a single legal system, with no competing formal legal system in place. Indeed, it is a common aspect of histories of the modern state (and law) that the rule of law requires the domination over, and then dismissal of, parallel formal systems (such as British church courts) (Spruyt 1994). In Kosovo in the 1990s the post-conflict mission initially declared that the laws of the Federal Republic of Yugoslavia would be the applicable law. However, Kosovar-Albanian judges objected to applying this set of laws as the laws were identified with the Serbian system through which the Kosovans had been marginalized (Bassu 2008, p. 26). After some months with different sets of judges applying different laws, UNMIK reversed its decision, although this was more to do with gaining compliance from an important set of actors than any necessary consideration about the advantages of the laws themselves; it was the implementation of the Serbian laws that was more of a problem than their substance (Peterson 2010, p. S24; Stromseth et al. 2006, p. 317). This did little to deal with the problem of local judges being put under pressure as regards their judgments in locally fraught trials in the post-conflict upheaval in the region, and also merely reversed the direction of disquiet with the courts. However, it was not clear whether UNMIK really had the authority to reform the legal system (although it had done so) (Bassu 2008, p. 27), leaving the idea of the rule of law somewhat compromised by its partial and formal (re)introduction, not least of all as it was only four years into the intervention that UNMIK finally formulated a clear rule of law position and programme (Bull 2008, p. 181). Indeed, the idea of rule of law was not only technically compromised; the actions of UNMIK suggested to the population that the law was merely a political tool of the external (foreign) administrators.[8] This reiterates the importance of the underlying assumptions of rule of law programmes; in this case, that there was one legal system to which reforms could be applied, and to which the population might owe fealty.

Reviewing the failure of three UN Transitional Administrations to fully establish elements of the rule of law in the countries they were working in (Cambodia, East Timor and Kosovo), Bull concludes that there are three 'deal breakers' in such deployments: the failure to establish effective state justice systems; the inability to build domestic commitment to the rule of law; and the failure to address informal justice mechanisms. Many other factors contributed to potential successes, but these three undermined any move towards the expansion of the rule of law in all three cases (Bull 2008, pp. 254–5). I have explored the first of these deal breakers above, and now turn to the second and third in the guise of the question of the persistence of local cultural commitments.

---

[8] The rule of law programme(s) in Kosovo are covered in considerable detail in Sannerholm (2012b) and he notes that, like other post-conflict programmes, the bulk of effort has been relatively narrowly focused on the criminal law and justice sector rather than on a wider understanding of the character of the rule of law.

# THE PERSISTENCE OF LOCAL (LEGAL) CULTURE

While many of the problems noted above might be regarded as practical or even technical it is also clear that they are often symptoms of a bigger and more general problem: the tension between the norms that rule of law programmes are attempting to transplant, and the local cultures of justice and legality that are regarded as lacking or not fulfilling rule of law criteria by the programme personnel (and their employing agencies). Indeed, for John Reitz:

> The most important way for a legal exporter to avoid wasting time and money in the export of the rule of law is to concentrate on exporting, not statutory language, but the *values underlying the rule of law*. Thus the most important long-term goal of activities to export the rule of law has to be to try and change the legal culture. (Reitz 2003, p. 484, emphasis added)

As might be expected, however, often rule of law programme operatives, in Deborah Stone's words, 'attempt to push the interpretation of a bad condition out of a realm of accident and into the realm of human control' (Stone 1989, p. 299). Thus, reformers try to identify a group who are impeding the conditions for introducing (or expanding) the rule of law, and as such must bear the burden of reform.

The focus of this attention is the persistence of 'unhelpful' local norms, and therefore one approach to this issue is to attempt to bring the rule of law (as understood by the technical support teams) and the local norms together so that the tension is resolved through reformulation (mainly and usually of the local norms). As part of the co-option of the ruling elites into a discourse of the rule of law, programmes of legal reform often therefore have the effect of promoting state-based/centralized law over the competing (and localized) non-state (customary) law of a society (Rajagopal 2008, p. 1369). Because rule of law programmes (especially those built on a thin conception of the rule of law) usually do not regard local norms as particularly important this is supported by centralized ruling elites with little recognition of the risks of failure in implementation that may result from programmes' confrontation with incompatible norms of (local) legality.

This situation is compounded by rule of law reform teams being made up mostly, if not exclusively, of lawyers, who are more at home and easy with codes and rules that in thinking about normative and/or cultural change as a requirement of their work (Stromseth et al. 2006, p. 314), and whose relationship to the legal epistemic community is much more meaningful than any perception of the local legal environment. This leaves the manner in which existing informal and traditional justice processes

and cultures of dispute settlement are integrated into the rule of law programmes' objectives and aims underdeveloped, with many programmes
having no procedures in place to deal with this issue when they start. One
option can be to integrate local resolution systems as the lower (initial)
justice structure for local communities recognizing the established local
legitimacy of such processes that may have survived both colonialism and
decolonialization (Obarrio 2011). However, this can cause tensions where
the underlying norms are divergent; local practices related to religious and
traditional norms may be regarded as part of the problem that the rule of
law is intended to resolve when the rule of law is understood as a thick
norm freighted with Western values (around gender, for instance). This
can also be a problem of the level of government that is being targeted by
assistance efforts.

As Sarah Lister (2007) argues in her account of the ongoing Afghanistan
programmes, for the first four years, the focus of activity was on national-
level administrations and practices, leaving local government time to
adjust its traditional practices to the new post-Taliban realities with which
they were confronted. By the time this was seen as a problem, the window
of opportunity for consensual reform seemed to have passed. Indeed,
many Islamic legal norms that still shape adjudication in Afghan courts
can, as Matteo Tondini concludes, 'be easily considered to contradict the
international human rights treaties signed by Afghanistan and the 2004
Constitution' (Tondini 2007). On the other hand, Jennifer Lee suggests
that in Afghanistan, Sharia law could be interpreted as being consistent
with (Western) appeals for the rights of women. She argues that already
this has been achieved in Egypt and Iran with courts accepting that the
women's rights normally regarded as human rights can be upheld through
Sharia (Lee 2009, pp. 553–60). However, this may be dependent on
'progressive' courts and this can hardly be counted on in Afghanistan or
elsewhere (the criticism that supporters of the thin view of the rule of law
make of expansive or substantive descriptions of the norm). Such an invocation merely shifts the 'problem' from socialization of the population to
socialization of an elite, which leaves (again) a potentially difficult tension
between the rule of law and the society (overall) with which it would be
concerned.

This leads David Ellerman to argue that 'Much "bad development assistance" consists in getting countries to "pass good laws" and then expecting
everyone to wake up the next morning and start acting like the people in
the donor's or helper's own developed country' (Ellerman 2008, p. 175).
Unfortunately elites and policy makers often want the 'best laws' and as
such favour laws that are current in the funding country (or in the states
that have provided the lawyers) but which may well have been developed

over years with that country's own cultural mores embedded within them (Ellerman 2008, p. 177). The difficulty is this process of social embedding is often under-recognized by the experts in the field and thus not factored into the choice of legal development pathway. Local partners themselves may be impatient and seeking prompt resolutions to perceived (legal) problems. In this, although the issue of local culture is likely to be more visible to them than to incoming experts, there is still a temptation not to 'reinvent the wheel' and to look to the programmes to deliver ready-made (rule of) law systems (Reitz 2003, p. 449). This approach also dovetails well with notions related to a thin reading of the rule of law norm that sees it as a generalizable technology.

More problematically, local 'partners' may not be able to tell the rule of law programme staff exactly what the local and prevailing norms around the law are. For instance, in the early 1990s, despite being initiated by the Vietnamese government (via an invitation to help), the Swedish International Development Authority (SIDA) was unable to quickly develop an understanding of the domestic legal culture; the government staff involved were reluctant to discuss the underlying norms of the legal system and in the end the project workers had to expend considerable time developing *An Introduction to the Vietnamese Legal System* describing the system that was to be reformed (Berling 2006, pp. 53–4). However, as Stephen Toope (who had been a consultant for the Canadian International Development Agency – CIDA) points out, the Vietnamese government at this time was committed by its 1992 constitution to instigate a 'state ruled by law', and, given the role of the state in Vietnam, this therefore was likely to be some distance from anything that the SIDA, CIDA or others would regard as the rule of law (Toope 2003, pp. 412–13). Here, the state wished to import or adapt non-domestic laws and practices, but did so with a formal view of the law; that is to say, they were uninterested in the political and social (normative) context in which such laws operated (Toope 2003, p. 406). In the end, as neither CIDA nor SIDA (nor other actors in the developmental field) had the appetite to try to establish the independence of the judiciary, courts relied on the 'guidance' of the party in their judgments (Toope 2003, p. 407) – and as such any move towards the rule of law was likely to be partial. However, this is not to say the approach was uncontentious: local lawyers supportive of a court system able to hold the government to account (drawing on thick depictions of the rule of law norm) have been vocal and active in this regard, although this has led to imprisonments and harassment by the state (Nicholson and Low 2013, p. 24). Conversely, other locals have worked within these constraints to achieve partial reform, further confirming that there are varying positions here (as in other countries) about how best to develop the rule of law, and the relationship between its local/political and the general/normative aspects.

Many accounts of the difficulty of instigating the rule of law end up asserting that if (local) culture is the problem, then local culture needs to be changed. In this view the 'people' lack the appropriate and fully formed legal consciousness, and it is therefore a question of education to produce a change in behaviour. This is intended to produce self-regulating individuals who, recognizing the rule of law can help, work to expand the rule of law as a (newly domesticated) cultural value (Cohen 2009). As Maggi Carfield summarizes this approach: 'The changing culture approach seeks to assess what is best for a community, to identify norms that stand in the way, and then to develop strategies aimed at shifting the errant norm *regardless of how the norm is perceived in the community*' (Carfield 2011, p. 782, emphasis in original). One's attitude to this issue depends on how the rule of law is conceived, with this position reflecting an understanding of the rule of law as a universal norm, as opposed to a more pluralist notion of how the rule of law might relate to local circumstance (which I will explore in Chapter 7).

If the rule of law is understood as the manner in which societies govern themselves, and keep authority within bounds, then some aspects of self-determination are likely to be highlighted (and here Amartya Sen's work, specifically *Development as Freedom* (Sen 2001) has been influential). Sen's focus on human capabilities and the ability to make informed choices chimes well with the rule of law's values of certainty and predictability in law alongside (as the next chapter will suggest) the role that law can play in establishing and maintaining open and well-operating markets (which again Sen sees as largely beneficial) (Ringer 2007). However, the shape of these developments can only be driven by an assessment of local needs, not the imposition of a one-size-fits-all (legal) solution. To put this slightly differently, as Brian Tamanaha has pointed out: 'to operate effectively, legal systems require respect and support from the populace, but to secure this respect and support, the legal system must serve the needs of the populace' (Tamanaha 2011, p. 214; see also Bassu 2008, pp. 33–4). These 'needs' are constructed and reproduced in the culture of the society in question, and any externally driven change of accepted norms, while frequently justified by an appeal to human rights, will present difficulties if it confronts strongly held local values and traditions. 'Education' may be able to resolve this tension, but does such normative change fit with the rule of law? For thin readings of the rule of law many such local norms may not be an issue provided the 'correct' mechanisms and procedures are in place, while for thicker readings they present some difficulties as regards the sort of political values that Sen identifies.

The importance of local norms can be missed because in the developed countries from where the rule of law programmes (and their staff) mostly originate the rule of law has become so normalized (as common sense) that the idea that there might be different ways of proceeding towards order have been submerged. This has led to what Rosa Brooks (2003) has termed a new imperialism of the rule of law. Interestingly, while sceptical of the ability of promoters to import Westernized notions of the rule of law into societies without them developing some knowledge and sensitivity to local norms, she does not suggest that therefore local norms should be accorded any predetermined weight; rather hers is an approach that while recognizing the worth and value of Western notions of the rule of law accepts that socialization into these (new) norms may take time and requires considerable self-knowledge and reflexivity among promoters, which she believes is often absent. Likewise, Stromseth and her co-authors recommend that rule of law programmes' practitioners need to start from the position that like doctors they will seek to do no harm (Stromseth et al. 2006, p. 314) before planning to make a long-term commitment to community engagement about the local ends of the rule of law. This will likely require adding a series of cultural elements to programmes, from investing in civil society organizations to a commitment to localized legal education and recognition of the legitimacy (and utility) of local/traditional conflict resolutions practices (Stromseth et al. 2006, pp. 326–39). However, cultural programmes of this sort are not only slowly moving; they also involve the hybridization of customs, practices and understandings.

The rule of law so implemented is unlikely to be the (fully liberal) rule of law that thick proponents of the norm expect and desire. Only when the rule of law is being discussed in similar terms to its appearance in Westernized political discussions (as a common sense) can the norm really be said to start having some local salience (Cortell and Davis 2000, pp. 71, 74). And indeed only when the local political cultural landscape includes some notion of the rule of law can the more detailed work of making it real really get under way. It therefore seems that Lawrence Friedman's observation from 1994 remains true today:

> Law reformers, traditionally, do not bother to understand *why* something has gone wrong; they act as if errors and inconsistencies and gaps in the legal system are some sort of technical error or failure, that the system, like some sort of computer, is simply 'down' and the repairmen (jurists, technicians of law, drafters of documents) must simply come to the house, bring their tools and fix the system. But legal systems are products of society – more specifically of legal culture; hence reform is a subtle and complex task. One has to take into account the *limits* imposed by culture; one has to re-examine whether the 'failures' of law are real failures, or whether we are neglecting to cut with instead of against the grain. (Friedman 1994, p. 130)

Sadly, this indictment remains apposite 20 years after it was written. That said, as Martin Krygier warns, we should not reify 'culture' into a catch-all residual category where the impediments to introducing the rule of law can be located and blame shifted to the recipients of technical assistance (Krygier 2011, p. 31). Some commentators do perceive a shift in processes prompted by the recognition of the 'problem' of culture. Kleinfeld argues in her analysis of American rule of law programmes that a new (or second) generation of reform is gaining credence; here, the local and particular are recognized and rather than the rule of law being seen as a universal technology, a prior engagement with the local specifics alongside a clear understanding of the goal (or ends) of reform is changing the manner in which programmes are being conducted (Kleinfeld 2012). It is too early to say whether this will be a successful innovation, but even if it is on one level it merely reiterates the common sense notion of the rule of law as the way of the world, albeit now with local characteristics.

## CONCLUSION

Some critics have identified an almost complete disconnect between commentary and evaluation of rule of law programmes (often undertaken at distance and through data sets) and the practitioners who undertake them (Jenkins and Plowden 2006, p. 159; Staton 2010, p. 1512). The practitioners, driven by their understanding of the common sense of the rule of law, focus on the 'big picture', while evaluations often focus on the ends achieved (or not achieved) by the legal reforms undertaken as depicted in (sometimes synthetic) indicators. Additionally, the expectations of rule of law programme practitioners and of recipients are often over-ambitious and optimistic; this may be because there is a frequent over-estimation of the likely impact of formal changes, and an underestimation (as discussed above) of the need for social changes to support any institutional reform. Judicial training, law reform and other forms of technical assistance on their own will not produce the rule of law (Stromseth et al. 2006, p. 389). There is often little appreciation of the risk of failure involved in programmes (partly due to this disconnect between evaluation and practice), leaving the question of what are the reasonable expectations and timescales for a rule of law programme often unanswered (Jenkins and Plowden 2006, p. 161). This leads Jane Stromseth and her co-authors to conclude that

> [p]rogress towards the rule of law is rarely linear but instead involves fre-
> quent movement back and forth: a success in reforming legislation may be

counterbalanced by a walkout from the political processes by a disgruntled group of stakeholders; a programme to train women in effective legal advocacy and community organising may be counterbalanced by restrictions on women's movements resulting from a surge in insecurity. (Stromseth et al. 2006, p. 391)

The rule of law is both complex and multidimensional and the attempt to move forward on all fronts (especially in post-conflict countries) is frequently the triumph of hope over experience. Thus, the management of expectations is often a problem, as it proved in Kosovo (Bull 2008, pp. 150–2; Stromseth et al. 2006, p. 320) where even the mission itself was unable to meet its own legal standards, or even the slacker/weaker standards that had been followed prior to the conflict. This did little for the expectation that UNMIK would really introduce the rule of law, given that its own attempt to follow human rights standards that it had instigated itself was seemingly impossible. Likewise, American practices at Abu Ghraib once they became public did little to support claims that the occupation forces where seeking to expand and consolidate the rule of law in Iraq.

In post-conflict societies rule of law programmes have also been required to deal with issues of reconciliation, war crimes adjudication and other issues pre-dating the programme intervention (Bull 2008). This is of course to be expected as without such problems there would be less need for intervention, but as most programmes have been forward-looking development programmes, this has not necessarily been fully appreciated prior to deployment (although for the transitional work by the UN in East Timor, this was part of the remit of the mission from the start). To be fair to practitioners, lack of preparation can be an aspect of the speed of post-conflict deployment where the time to develop clear strategic plans to deal with both the past and current societal needs in anything other than general terms is absent.

In post-conflict societies this can be compounded by the military playing a major role in rule of law programmes, as the conception of the rule of law they work with can be narrowly focused on criminal justice (reform) (Röder 2012, p. 230) and does not include many of the other issues that might even be included in a thin view of the norm. This is not to say the criminal law is marginal to the rule of law, but it is by no means coterminous with it. However, even the focus on the criminal law can be partial, with much more attention paid to issues around punishment, enforcement and policing than to other (just as important) aspects of the rule of law as usually understood, such as rights of the accused and even well-developed due process for suspects (Humphreys 2010, p. 163). This is especially the case where the rule of law is being 'introduced' into societies (still) wracked by terrorism, leading to a major tension between perceived effective action against terrorists and the protection or expansion of civil liberties and personal rights (Huang 2008).[9] Here, the normative character of the rule of law is not so much thinner as tightly focused on specific social order issues, leaving wider considerations of what the norm might entail to one side.

The difficulty with importing the rule of law from outside then is that it is not tied to the political history of the society in which it is being transplanted. Whatever the merits of the rule of law, without a clear link to the society that it is intended to govern the political history may prove too strong to overcome, and this is especially the case in post-conflict states where the social divisions are often merely reproduced through the rule of law. Indeed, the frequent depoliticization of the rule of law has often served to mask the political motives of programmes' initiators (such as support for a 'liberal' democratic peace) when they work in post-conflict societies (Peterson 2010, p. S31; Sriram et al. 2011). The development of the rule of law on the ground, as much of the above indicates, is a long process, and much of the difficulty encountered by rule of law programmes stems from (at least initial) failure to recognize this, driven at least partly by the depoliticized and technical understanding of the rule of law that underpins many assistance and aid programmes.

Comprehensive programmes of rule of law reform may be compromised or undermined by failure in one or more parts of the package of reforms (Prado 2010; see also Samuels 2006, p. 19). Avoiding sequencing difficulties is not easy, but often the local circumstances and history may suggest certain areas where a lack of early remedial action will ensure that subsequent incremental rule of law reforms will be compromised, although only a detailed knowledge of the local legal realm will allow such judgements to be made. Finally, the problems identified above also reflect one further critique of the earlier phase of law and development programmes; law cannot be introduced in this manner, whatever its value, but must rather be the result of a *political* struggle to establish a just rule of law (Dhavan 1994; see also Ellerman 2008). In this sense, the Western or European rule of law that has become the touchstone of development work was itself the product of a long political history and there may in the end be no way to bypass such social processes, and hence law and development work is doomed to failure in the short term as it can only (metaphorically) plant seeds for long-term growth not transplant fully grown plants. This, of course, is obscured by the universalism of the rule of law in its role as the common sense of global politics.

---

[9] This is not a problem limited to post-conflict states of course – see Dyzenhaus (2006).

# 5. Building the rule of law with an economic focus

> There is no way a market system can work efficiently in the absence of clear, enforceable laws regarding property and contractual rights and obligations. (Shihata 1991b, p. 228)

> [E]stablishing the rule of law is a long-term project which no-one knows how to accomplish. Meanwhile, recent experience confirms that explosive economic progress can occur in the absence of the rule of law. (Tamanaha 2011, p. 245)

> [P]roof that economic growth and stronger law can go hand in hand does not prove that law reform can actually cause economic growth in the first place. (Dam 2006, p. 231)

Having examined the rhetoric and practice of the rule of law from the perspective of law and order, I now move to look at it from the perspective of economic development, not least as the latter is an often-posited reason for focusing on the rule of law as a developmental priority. While I sometimes draw on material that would be broadly included under the rubric of the new institutional economics (Nye 2008) in this chapter, I do not present the relationship between law and economics in the same manner. Rather than focusing on transaction costs, or considering primarily property rights, I am more concerned to understand both the rhetorical link made between law and development (widely promulgated by the World Bank),[1] and a wider range of intersections between economic behaviour(s) and legal aspects of development. In this chapter, I look at the manner in which individuals' social actions are patterned by their beliefs about the surrounding structures, and how these beliefs and actions then work on such structures; this makes explicit the link between the rule of law and political economy that underlies the whole book.

The relatively new field of behavioural economics offers an interesting way of thinking about the rule of law and economics, and by drawing on George Akerlof and Robert Shiller's recent summary and synthesis of

---

[1] In addition to the discussion of the World Bank's position on the rule of law in the Introduction (and the sources cited there), see also Decker (2010) and Krever (2011) for an indication of the range of Bank activities and programmes in this area.

this perspective, in the second half of this chapter I review five aspects of human psychology and then relate these to the discussion of the rule of law as a political economic imperative. This suggests that the reason capitalism needs the rule of law is directly related to the shape and thrust of human economic behaviour, just as much as it is based on the functional provision of the structures that underpin its economic relations. However, before moving to this aspect of the discussion I briefly map out two other well-known approaches that account for the link between economic development and the rule of law. As many of the legal developments suggested by a focus on economics are broadly the same as those discussed in the previous chapter, what I am more interested in here is the manner in which economic arguments are used to justify legal change rather than a further analysis of the conduct of rule of law programmes themselves, although where appropriate I will again cite specific instances of law-related technical assistance, capacity building and developmental aid.

## ECONOMICS AND THE RULE OF LAW

There is a general acceptance by policy makers and in the wider academic community that the rule of law is central to the successful establishment of market societies (Haggard and Tiede 2011; Haggard et al. 2008).[2] To take one (further) example: Svetozar Pejovich argues that the rule of law is made up four institutional elements – private property rights; law of contract; independent judiciary; and a formal constitution – which exist in all countries in the West. He argues that the relative strengths and levels of development of each of these institutions goes a long way to explaining divergence in economic performance, with the clear conclusion being that an improvement overall in the rule of law pays economic dividends (Pejovich 2008, pp. 41–3). As he summarizes this position: 'Private property rights and the law of contract generate efficiency-friendly incentives that move resources to their highest-values uses. An independent judiciary and a constitution protect those incentives from decision makers in government, rent-seeking coalitions, and majority rule' (Pejovich 2008, p. 165).[3] This focus on property and contract has also been stressed by

---

[2] See the survey of literature in Trebilcock and Prado (2011, pp. 41–79) and much of the rhetoric discussed in my introduction to this book.

[3] This is also similar to the position that was set out by Ibrahim Shihata in the 1990s when at the World Bank he was instrumental in moving the Bank towards an engagement with law and governance (as development technologies) – see Shihata (1991a) and the earlier discussion of the development of the World Bank's position on the rule of law.

Judge Richard Posner (an influential proponent of the law and economics perspective):

> Legal reform is an important part of the modernisation process of poor countries, but the focus of such reform should be on creating substantive and procedurally efficient rules of contract and property *rather than on creating a first-class judiciary or an extensive system of civil liberties.* (Posner 1998, p. 9, emphasis added)

Here, law is instrumental in promoting economic growth but only if relatively unencumbered by demands emanating from non-economic interests. Other authors certainly agree that the property rights/contract rights development nexus is important, but there may also be a wider set of laws that need to be considered as part of the underpinnings of successful development (Trebilcock and Prado 2011). One of the aspects of the rule of law that distinguishes the approaches discussed here and those explored in the previous chapter is that while in this approach contract law issues are often emphasized, in accounts focused on post-conflict societies or failed states, the question of private law issues (like contract) are largely absent.

In general terms, the economic development approach might be summarized as good law + good enforcement = improved economic outcomes (Milhaupt and Pistor 2008, p. 5). However, overzealous enforcement of laws can in itself present a difficulty with strict (and formalistic) adherence to laws potentially impeding economic development (Cross 2002, p. 1772). Thus, a number of the measurements deployed by the World Bank Doing Business Group are concerned with the regulations and laws that may slow down (or stifle) the development of new businesses, and by doing so slow down (or even halt) economic growth.[4] This is not to say that regulation in this perspective is seen as the enemy of competition; rather, as Ibrahim Shihata suggested, what is needed are 'regulations which aim at clearly agreed economic and social objectives, continuously serve these objectives, avoid excesses and arbitrariness, and prevent the concentration of the market in a few hands' (Shihata 1997, p. 1585). Even so, for Shihata, regulation should be largely permissive; that is to say, like the common law it should focus on explicit prohibitions rather than setting out to shape activity through proactive (legal) characterization. Shihata refers to this as creating a legal environment that is 'enabling' for business (Shihata 1991b, p. 212). Whatever other benefits it may bring to society, in this argument

---

[4] Up to date data (and guidance to the figures) is available at http://www.doingbusiness.org/rankings (accessed 24 January 2014).

the rule of law is essential if a country is to successfully develop a market-based (capitalist) economy.

This view of the importance of the rule of law for capitalism is hardly new and demonstrates (again) the continuing influence of Max Weber. The rule of law contributes to the rationalization of contemporary capitalist society, and reflects this rationalization, although for Weber it is the law that is the more important element in the relationship between law and society. The rise of legalism in Europe, the development of a law that was largely autonomous and that was (relatively) unchallenged as a social authority, lay behind the successful expansion of European capitalism. The reduction (or obstructing) of other normative schemes in society allowed rationalization (parallel to the professionalization of the law) to underpin the development of capitalist society (Trubek 1972), and as such only as legalism became widespread did capitalism prosper in Weber's view. Thus, the move to reduce the role of local practices and customs (which encompass competing norms) draws at least some sustenance as an analytical position from Weber's work.

Likewise, some decades later, Franz Neumann, in developing a critique of capitalism in the run-up to the Second World War, also emphasized the law's rationality. The rule of law is

> necessary as a precondition of capitalist competition. The need for calculability and dependability in the legal system and administration was one of the motives for restricting the power of the patrimonial princes and of feudalism . . . Free competition requires the generality of law because it is the highest form of formal rationality. (Neumann 1937 [1957], p. 40)

Equality in law reinforces the approach to the (posited) equality between market actors, allowing freedom of contract to be transformed from a social concept 'implying the exchange of equal values among equally strong competitors' to a legal mechanism equalizing the ability to contract but not requiring equality in the pre-contractual starting conditions (Neumann 1937 [1957], pp. 41–2). The rule of law facilitates economic development by diluting social barriers to the deployment of resources, and through formalization reduces the impact of prior social constraints (Neumann 1937 [1957], p. 59). The rule of law removes socially obstructive local customs and practices, replacing them with a universal economic rationalism.

Likewise, Ugo Mattei and Laura Nader have argued (while criticizing this view) that in the 'contemporary neo-liberal view of the law, less developed economies are seen as lacking something very simple and universal . . . [a] valid *minimal institutional* system necessary for the unfolding of an efficient market' (Mattei and Nader 2008, p. 74, emphasis added). Much of the mainstream development commentary takes for granted that for a country to develop a capitalist economy it needs to establish a broadly 'liberal' rule of law. This also leads to the position that local laws (and forms of legality) can then become the scapegoat for a lack of economic development (von Benda-Beckmann 1989). For instance, Timur Kuran has recently argued that a different and specific form of legality (Islamic Law) has held back the development of modern capitalism across the Middle East (Kuran 2011). The lack is not of procedures of legality as such (rule *by* law) but the particular 'Western' ideal/norm of the rule of law that has underpinned the history of capitalist development. This position begins to suggest that the rule of law that underpins capitalism is not merely the existence of law-like regulation (the thinnest rule of law) but rather the more substantive form of the norm.

Although the rule of law may be necessary for (capitalist) economic development, it is unlikely to be sufficient, with law interacting with other aspects of society to either promote (or hinder) development (Dam 2006). Parallel to the discussion about law, order and local conflict resolution (in the previous chapter), local culture(s) also may in various ways counteract or come into tension with the rule of law as it relates to market relations (Cross 2002, pp. 1753–64). There may be considerable interaction (and thus hybridization) between a rule of law culture and other socially evident culture(s) that inform social practices and norms, especially in the economic realm. However, analyses that link law and development often seem to start from the proposition that if it doesn't look like the liberal and Western rule of law then it cannot support economic development 'properly'. Conversely, if legal systems are the result of legislative history and an accumulation of politico-legal decisions, it may make more sense to ask initially what purposes and interests the prevailing legal system serves before setting out to transform it into a system that more closely approximates to the rule of law as perceived by the external reformers (Goodpaster 2003, p. 691). The focus of reform needs to be on political interests and the social context more than the rule of law; it needs to ask why the rule of law is not formulated to serve the economic interests that developmental programmes might regard as indispensable.

## THE RULE OF LAW AND THE HISTORY OF PROPERTY

From the perspective of economics, one of the key benefits of the rule of law is that it facilitates activities by reducing levels of uncertainty, producing predictable patterned behaviour that can be easily understood and followed. This is often expressed as law's support for efficiency: shared rules governing markets dispense with the duplication of effort that would be required constantly to renegotiate bilateral coordination between social actors, and this is especially valuable for the expansion of markets beyond a local community. The rule of law makes the risk of breakdown of economic exchanges lower, freeing extensive reserves (of food and fuel, for instance), which it might be prudent to hoard when the risks of 'dishonest dealing' are higher. The social institutions of law serve a particular function: efficient coordination of social, political and economic activities.[5]

Although the rule of law generally may be important for social stability, the law of property is often emphasized by economists as being crucial for the establishment of working markets. In a stylized history, pre-property ideas of legitimate ownership emerged between individuals whose activities required some form of coordination due to their competition over scarce resources. Institutions (property rights) were then developed by rulers to structure the expectations that individuals have regarding the behaviour of others towards them. Here, an important advantage of property rights is the internalization of external costs and benefits; all activities have costs and benefits to those who indulge in them. Property is an institution that aims to attach costs and benefits to the 'owner' of the property which produces them (Demsetz 1967, pp. 348–50). However, part of the continuing fluidity in the legal constitution of property rights has been prompted by the frequent attempt by 'owners' to secure benefits while keeping costs externalized. Social efficiency might be best served by costs accruing to the property that delivers the benefit; however, for individual owners it is more 'efficient' to have the costs met by others.

Gains from cooperation and coordination can be explained and located as part of social development in an abstract sense, but property rights do not just emerge; they are constructed to serve particular interests, not only efficiency. It may be that economic efficiency is a crucial element of (capitalist) development but this is only one and not necessarily the most important aspect to the history of property as a social institution. As Douglass North points out: 'institutions are not necessarily or even usually created to be socially efficient; rather they, or at least the formal rules, are created to serve the interests of those with the bargaining power to devise new rules' (North 1990, p. 16). The assumption that the social location of

---

[5] I have discussed the history of property laws (and related it to the issue of intellectual property) elsewhere – see May (2010, pp. 16–48), where I discuss John Locke's particular views on the justification of property and its relation to law more generally – and therefore do not seek to offer an extended treatment here.

an activity is neutral, as it costs nothing to transfer the product from one 'owner' to another, produces a different result from that which is found in the real political economy. Although in abstract terms the location of activities might be decided by the efficient use of resources, the ability of some actors to extract a transaction cost for transfer (either monetary or social) may shift the location on grounds other than efficiency. The same is the case for the development of the rule of law: while in the abstract world of zero transaction costs, such institutions can be developed that produce an economically efficient coordination of social activities, when power differentials are taken into account, the forms of law (and legality) that actually occur may well serve very different purposes (Williamson 1985, p. 26ff). The establishment of particular institutions (such as the rule of law) is therefore tied up with the need to reduce costs of certain behaviour and to maximize the benefits obtained by specific (that is to say, powerful) social actors.[6]

In his treatment of the interaction between legality and exchange, North suggests three overlapping historical types of exchange. Each has different levels of transaction costs and thus different needs relative to the emergence of particular institutions (North 1990, pp. 34–5). The first is small-scale interpersonal exchange, which is characterized by repeat-dealing, a substantial amount of cultural homogeneity and the lack of third-party enforcement. Here, few if any laws are required, but while transaction costs are low, the development of the division of labour and specialization is also rudimentary, and therefore the costs of transforming inputs into goods are relatively high. The next type of exchange develops as the scope and extent of exchange expands. Now exchange becomes impersonal by virtue of the increasing quantity of individual exchanges, but behaviour remains regulated through kinship ties, bonding, merchant codes of conduct or in extreme cases hostages, and as such a formalized rule of law is still not vital. This sort of development underpinned a geographic expansion of trade along international trade routes and at the fairs of Medieval Europe. It led to an increased role for the proto-state in protecting merchants' interests and to the use of such merchants as a revenue source through taxation and the sale of monopolies (Spruyt 1994, pp. 61–76; Tigar 2000, pp. 61–168). In this second stage, in certain respects pre-state rulers increased rather than decreased transaction costs. As protectors and enforcers of property rights they intervened in transactions that were being concluded through informal links and ties.

In North's third type of exchange (the modern), enforcement hardly relies on informal links between contracting parties (Guilds or families) at

---

[6] Rodrik et al. (2002) is one well-cited attempt to test these ideas empirically.

all, but is enforced by a third party through formalized legal instruments. Even greater proliferation of exchanges is supported as there is now no need for any sort of personal link between parties. As third-party involvement, by virtue of its imprecise and generalized nature, is more costly in any particular circumstance relative to first and second stage exchanges, returns for cheating and opportunism expand through the anonymity of the market. If enforcement was entirely dependent on active policing and force, the advantages of complex economic exchange would be unlikely to be extensive due to the increased costs of direct enforcement. Thus, as North suggests, 'effective third-party enforcement is best realised by creating a set of rules that then make a variety of informal constraints effective' (North 1990, p. 35). This leads to efforts to produce a legitimized and socially embedded set of norms and principles (the rule of law) that will in most cases ensure behaviour accords with the formal rules without being policed: legislators build on rather than contradict broad patterns of traditional practice and embed them within a generalized and legitimated rule of law.

Generally, if property is to be something more than possession, then the rights accorded to possession (or under property law 'ownership') need to be embedded within a legal framework that can be enforced by the state. Moreover, the rights to specific properties need to be enjoyed by either individuals or clearly legally defined (and constituted) bodies, otherwise the voluntary exchange of property (on which markets are built) becomes difficult if not infeasible because initial ownership is difficult to establish and any subsequent transfer (sale) may confront difficulties of demonstrating the right of disposal by the posited 'owner' (Holderness 1985). Thus, the rule of law (when closely related to property rights) seems likely to prompt more individualized notions of 'ownership'. Property, while being related to pre-legal practices, can only be recognized *qua* property to which rights are accorded by the intervention and sanction of the state to emphasize the rights of individuals. Legitimate disputes are no longer concerned with the actual institution itself but rather with boundary issues (what is and is not property) and ownership issues (the control and legitimization of sales and rents, alongside the punishment of theft and other infringements of the rights of owners, such as damage by third parties).

This (idealized) history of property carries with it the implicit notion that it fulfils a certain function, and therefore justifications founded on the emergence of property as a support for the operation of markets relate the function of property as the efficient allocation of scarce economic resources. This allocation may not be 'optimal' but property markets are still presented as the most efficient method of allocation available, even if they can be less than 'perfect'.[7] There is a complementary function that may equally well be seen as the root of certain developments. The emergence of property furthers the interests of specific groups in society: those in possession of such resources that can be utilized to accumulate more resources, the nascent capitalists. While the institution of property may support efficiency of allocation there is a need to remember exactly what such efficiency means and whose benefit it serves.

Much of the commentary on the rule of law and economic development parallels this (brief) discussion of the development of property rights; the rule of law is presented as a functional response to the needs of economic exchange, and indeed the law and economics approach is focused on understanding the law's economic benefits (and of criticizing those laws that seem to be either suboptimal or even obstructive to the efficient management of economic relations). The rule of law and the market economy evolve together, with markets requiring regulations to enhance the opportunities for 'free' exchange, while the problems that may arise from the exercise of this freedom then prompt further refinements to individual laws and the legal system more generally.[8] This approach is relatively ambivalent as regards the content of the rule of law (Goodpaster 2003, pp. 679–80, 687), allowing for similar effects to be achieved by rule *by* law or a thin rule of law. Nevertheless, the rule of law remains widely promoted as the most efficient (and perhaps elegant?) solution to the issue of facilitative regulation of markets.

## THE RULE OF LAW AND THE MYSTERY OF CAPITAL

If individuals appear only quite schematically in the institutional (property rights) approach, in Hendando de Soto's work they are more central; legal empowerment of the economically excluded fosters their integration into the economy and is vital for growth and development. His work has been well received in the international aid community and multilateral development institutions, including the World Bank (Gilbert 2012; *World Policy Journal* 2011), but for those already active in the field of legal empowerment, the rule of law and legal reform, it is sometimes difficult to understand why this analysis has become so influential in certain quarters, not least of all as there are severe doubts about its empirical basis.

[7] Haggard and Tiede (2011) include a summary of the empirical studies supporting this link.
[8] This perspective on legal change can also be found in the work of Friedrich Hayek (1988, p. 36).

However, as Jan Michiel Otto points out, de Soto is a great story-teller, sets out a position that policy makers are very willing to hear (there is a relatively easy solution to development) and it is a story that fits well with dominant economic analyses; even his critics accept that de Soto has at least brought widespread attention to their field (Otto 2009, p. 180). For the purposes of my argument here, it is his contribution to continuing normalization of the rule of law that is most significant. Although sometimes legal empowerment approaches are presented as an alternative to rule of law programmes (van Rooij 2012, p. 313), I want to emphasize the link between legal empowerment of the poor and an overarching normative commitment to the rule of law.

Initially, de Soto's position was focused rather tightly on the issue of developing titling systems for customary holdings (drawing on his analysis of land 'ownership' in Peru). More recently, and perhaps responding to a criticism that one cannot understand people's willingness to utilize property law separately from the legitimacy (or otherwise) of the legal system itself (Davidson 2010), de Soto's interest has widened to the legal empowerment of the poor more generally. His starting point is that capitalism needs capital to develop and accelerate. This much is uncontroversial, but he also argues that far from being excluded from capitalist endeavour by their poverty, 'most of the poor already possess the assets they need to make a success of capitalism' (de Soto 2000, p. 5). The problem is that these 'assets' are held in forms that are unrecognized by the states in which they live, and as such the 'poor' are unable to capitalize on them; they are unable to lever their assets into financial instruments (loans primarily) to develop their enterprise(s) into nascent capitalist businesses. This is often unrecognized, he contends, because economists often seem to believe that if the property of elites (or the urban population more generally) is secure, then everyone else's property is also.[9] The *Mystery of Capital* (the title of his most famous book) is the manner in which the Western developed states have engineered a legal system where titles to property (or more widely possessions) are widely generated and secured, allowing them to act as security for the provision of 'financial' capital, which can then be deployed in myriad ways impossible for the initial forms on which the financial capital is secured.

This leads de Soto to focus on how societies might recognize this 'missing' capital, including some startling large estimates of how much these assets might be worth if capitalized by the developing countries that are as yet to be fully exploited (in this manner, at least). Recognizing

---

[9] See the study by Terry Lawson-Remmer cited in *The Economist*, 'Free exchange: property and the lady', 30 March 2013, p. 80.

these assets, he argues, allows an assessment of their economic potential, so that future market utility can be assessed, and thereby a value assessed (de Soto 2000, pp. 42–4). This valuing is made easy by the information that is built up as titles are awarded and assets evaluated; as the system expands so more and more information is available through a formalized property system and thus judgements are improved (de Soto 2000, p. 46). This allows owners to be made (economically) responsible for their asset(s), and begins to make these assets fungible; by allowing assets to be capitalized (used as collateral) the money so generated can be deployed for other investments and/or activities (de Soto 2000, p. 49). Once this system is developing, de Soto argues, a network of economic actors can be established and formalized (stable) contractual relations between them become possible (de Soto 2000, pp. 50–4). It is because development economists from Western states have forgotten this aspect of their own countries' development that their efforts have often been frustrated (de Soto 2000, pp. 60–136). Failure to establish property titling constrains the ability of the poor to take advantage of their own energy and creativity to become more self-sufficient and economically independent.

This means the development of the rule of law is central to the success of empowering the poor to make the most of their abilities and assets, with a long chapter in de Soto's *The Mystery of Capital* devoted to legal failure. Here, he recognizes that there may be formal property systems in place but the poor may seek recourse to extra-legal systems of regulation for all sorts of reasons, thereby maintaining their exclusion from the potential developments that he identifies (de Soto 2000, pp. 137–88). Using a metaphor of the bell jar (drawn from Fernand Braudel) he suggests that inside the elites utilize a (reasonably) modern form of law to further their interests, but the poor are kept outside by a combination of administration costs and complexity (de Soto 2000, p. 140). This exclusion is detrimental to enterprise as many of the protections and advantages of property are not accessible and thus a wide range of costs are imposed on the poor (from lack of insurance for loss, to lack of security of tenure) reducing any surplus for development. Interestingly, de Soto sees this problem in political terms and as such locates ameliorative action in the political sphere not the legal (de Soto 2000, pp. 171–88), to some extent differentiating his approach from the World Bank's.

In contrast to some of the developmental practices discussed in the previous chapter, de Soto advocates the building of the rule of law on the foundations of local arrangements (the localized social contract) rather than merely imposing a top-down (technical/legal) 'solution' (de Soto 2000, pp. 158–61). Notably, he identifies lawyers both as potential agents of change and as potential conservative barriers to expanding the rule of law (de Soto 2000, pp. 180–3). However, as the problem is a 'political' issue in his view, in the end only political leadership can bring the rule of law to a wider range of people in developing and transitional economies and by doing so can enable them to capitalize on their own potential to prosper. As Sundhya Pahija has pointed out, this is a powerful and influential argument for development-focused actors from the West as it renders the capitalist economy 'both universal and axiomatically good through its connection to the rule of law' (Pahija 2011, p. 218); the (technical) rule of law provides support for the (political) development towards capitalism.

To take one example of how this might play out; some accounts of the experience of legal empowerment in Tanzania suggest that de Soto's approach has merely ushered in a neoliberalism that has had an (ironically) devastating effect on the very local businesses he sought to help (Shivji 2006). De Soto's own view of Tanzania is rather different, seeing a positive move towards formalization of economic relations and the 'spontaneous' adoption by the poor of legal practices of documentation and regulation that help them expand their economic activities (de Soto 2008). However, Michal Lyons (2013) examined the case of changes in the law around Tanzanian street traders and concluded that while potentially useful, the reforms were undermined by a lack of commitment by government to shift bureaucratic practices, a lack of prior consultation with stakeholders and a lack of consideration of the local social circumstances of the street traders that might compromise their ability to utilize legal forms. In the case of local water provision in Tanzania, Ellen Hillbom found that for the poor legal empowerment was actually about the protection of, and indeed expansion of, traditional law-based solutions to resource allocation in the face of encouragement towards privatization, suggesting that even if legal forms are preferred they may not be in line with mainstream notions of the rule of law (Hillbom 2011). It is often difficult to ascertain whether the impact(s) of a closely focused legal empowerment intervention (that is, with paralegal support and tailored advice to local situations) has then spilled over into more general changes (van Rooij 2012, p. 309). Here, perhaps the difference is based on whether one is concerned with the legal changes at a general level (de Soto) or with actual changes on the ground (his critics). To some extent this may also be indicative of the difficulty of compiling clear and compelling evidence of the impact of such interventions.[10]

---

[10] Stephen Golub (2010) has edited a report with a range of practitioners' perspectives to examine the issue of impact, but (again) one of the clear conclusions is that evidence (one way or the other) is actually difficult to formulate and/or obtain due to the manner in which empowerment develops within a complex situation-dependent political economy.

As the case of Tanzania indicates, de Soto's position is hardly uncontroversial, with criticisms made in a number of areas,[11] although this seems to have little impact on the influence of his work in the major development agencies (Gilbert 2012). One of the most salient critiques is that property rights themselves are an imperfect communication medium; de Soto's position is at least partly built on the value that titling brings to those wishing to communicate to holders of credit that they have assets ready to act as security for loan capital. Property records are hardly neutral however; they may distort and (re)shape the position on the ground and by doing so continue to exclude or disadvantage the groups de Soto seeks to empower (Davidson 2010). Likewise, in his early work (though less so with his more recent approach to legal empowerment), one might regard de Soto as taking for granted the acceptance of the rule of law in an abstract sense by the aspirant property 'owner' (seeking title) even if their particular experiences of the legal system were far from satisfactory. The argument in *The Mystery of Capital* does recognize the need for normative shifts to encourage a move from the extra-legal into the rule of law realm but it is not always clear once legality has been rejected, how a move in the opposite direction might be encouraged in light of prior experience. Here, presumably the states' government and civil service need to make a wider credible commitment to the rule of law, taking the political issue into a much wider realm and as such this might suggest that these developments may be more difficult than de Soto hopes. Here the difficulties in establishing a commitment to the rule of law in post-conflict societies (discussed in the previous chapter) may well be instructive.

Certainly, the more recent Commission on Legal Empowerment of the Poor (CLEP) report regards the (partial or complete) absence of the rule of law as a primary cause of the continued incidence of poverty of around four billion people.[12] Drawing inspiration from de Soto (one of the Commission's chairs), their report identifies four pillars that form the basis for empowerment of the poor: access to justice and the rule of law (generally); property rights; labour rights; and 'business rights' (specifically) (CLEP 2008, pp. 5–9, *passim*). The Commission argues that these rights are in fact human rights, and as such should be regarded as uncontroversial. While there may be some discussion about property and labour rights as human rights, even the Commission recognizes that it may be a stretch to seek the imprimatur of human rights (and thereby

---

[11] Barros (2010), for instance, contains a range of engagements with and criticisms of de Soto's position from property law scholars and a further overview of criticisms based on the implementation of de Soto's suggested policies can be found in Gilbert (2012).

[12] For the background to the formation of the Commission see Brøther (2008).

some easy legitimation) for 'business rights'. The report argues that 'business activities are an expression of an entire class of liberties, namely freedom of association, freedom of movement, freedom to develop one's own talents, and freedom to exchange legitimately acquired goods and services' (CLEP 2008, p. 31). One can see the advantage of claiming that the freedom to run your own business is a human right, but this seems an optimistic reinterpretation of internationally recognized norms. While this is certainly an area for discussion, it does allow the Commission to make a further link to the jurisprudence around the rule of law.

Most importantly, and more generally, the Commission report asserts that strengthening and expanding the rule of law is the key element that would transform local and national political economies into successful and prosperous capitalist societies. Offering a (slightly veiled) criticism of other attempts to build the rule of law, the Commission notes that its

> recommended approach to legal empowerment is different from traditional approaches to legal and institutional reform and does not involve off-the-shelf blueprints for implementation. National and local contexts differ ... Knowledge of, and being attuned to, the political context and reforms based on a deep and shared understanding of the local conditions in both the formal and informal economy is essential. (CLEP 2008, p. 9)

Ironically, of course, for a report making this potentially bottom-up call for change, it remains targeted at policy makers and governments rather than the poor themselves (Golub 2009, p. 111). Although there is a wider understanding of legal empowerment in *Making the Law Work for Everyone* (CLEP 2008), repeatedly as the report moves into detail, the economic aspects of the rule of law are highlighted.[13]

In one sense, this is hardly surprising as the report is ostensibly about poverty and economic exclusion, but, equally the view of the rule of law that is encompassed in the report is one that sees legal reform as primarily a way of freeing the poor from the (political and social) constraints that hold them back from all prospering as entrepreneurs rather than any of its wider social benefits. The project focuses on four types of access: to justice; to assets; to decent work; and to markets (CLEP 2008, p. 27, *passim*), which are seen as offering both 'protection' and 'opportunity'. However, while access to justice might relate to a wider understanding of the benefits of the rule of law (CLEP 2008, p. 49), the other three are clearly economic issues. Indeed, the explicit focus on access to assets and markets makes clear that much of the interest of legal empowerment (in the report) is in

---

[13] For examples of this tendency see, for instance, CLEP (2008, pp. 20, 25–6).

the facilitation of business. This is not to argue that this might be unwelcome, only that it is a relatively tightly focused appreciation of why the rule of law is beneficial.

However, Franklin Obeng-Odoom (2013) suggests that even then de Soto's and the Commission's view of the entrepreneurial potential of the poor is much too simplified and fails to account for the political economic context in which they are embedded. He argues that de Soto's solution could worsen inequality and poverty in the medium term as 'owners' are (legally) divested of their (now) transferable property. Likewise, the discussion of the informal economy in the report envisages the extension of various protections to informal workers without any consideration of the political economy of their situation and non-legal constraints on enjoying their legal rights (Faundez 2009). Finally, doubts have been raised about the (self-presented) novelty of the approach; Stephen Golub (2009) suggests that similar approaches to legal empowerment have been used for some decades, and the Commission's presentation of their perspective as relatively novel leads them to ignore the lessons that might be learned from this prior experience, most notably about the ability of powerful elites to undermine the social changes expected, if not the legal developments envisaged. In the end, whatever the accuracy of de Soto's analysis and the success (or otherwise) of his and the Commission's prescriptions, the rhetoric of the link between the rule of law and the unleashing of entrepreneurial spirits has been widely reproduced.

## ANIMAL SPIRITS AND THE HUMAN PSYCHOLOGY OF ECONOMICS

Although quite widely supported by academics and organizations involved in economic development projects of one sort or another, the above account of humans as economic agents is relatively one-dimensional. However, there is another way of thinking about the relations between law and economics that better suggests why economic actors might be disposed to, and benefit from, adopting the norms of the rule of law. In *Animal Spirits* George Akerlof and Robert Shiller set out an account of contemporary economics that seeks to re-establish a central place for human psychology, drawing their inspiration from the work of John Maynard Keynes, from whom they take the phrase 'animal spirits' (Akerlof and Shiller 2010). Broadly working within an approach now often referred to as 'behavioural economics', they set out five aspects of these 'animal spirits', four of which I will lay out below before amending and (slightly) refocusing their fifth element for the purposes of my argument. Firstly, I will briefly summarize this overall perspective before moving on to establish the analytical link that I make between the 'animal spirits' and the rule of law.

## Confidence

Recognizing that economists have been focusing on the central role of confidence, trust and belief in capitalist markets for some time, Akerlof and Shiller suggest that nevertheless such analysis has still accorded too much weight to rationality. The idea that market confidence, trust in economic progress and belief in the future spring from a rational appreciation of available information about the economy is mistaken. Despite some recent interest in the role of trust, they point out that actually, the

> very meaning of trust is that we go beyond the rational. Indeed, the truly trusting person often discards or discounts certain information. She may not even process the information that is available to her rationally; even if she has *processed* it rationally, she may not *act* on it rationally. She acts according to what she *trusts* to be true. (Akerlof and Shiller 2010, p. 12, emphasis in original)

Linking confidence, trust and belief to a positive (or negative) attitude to economic activity but removing any dependence on rationality allows Akerlof and Shiller to argue that while confidence may have a major impact on levels of economic activity, it has no necessary link with anyone's view of 'economic fundamentals'. Our knowledge of the future is only ever conjectural, but drives a wide range of economic decision making, from consumption decisions to questions of saving and investment. Swings in activity in a market economy cannot be predicted from a 'rational' account of economic information or data but rather are linked to individuals' sentiment and belief, often based on non-economic factors, linked to other aspects of their 'animal spirits'.

Drawing on Keynes's notion of the (economic) multiplier, where economic activity prompts further economic activity as money flows to market participants and is (re)spent, Akerlof and Shiller point out that multiplier effects are not only related to exchange itself. A 'confidence multiplier' impacts on the direction of markets: both surfeits and absences of confidence feed on each other (as they are socialized among market actors) to produce accelerated positive and negative movements (Akerlof and Shiller 2010, pp. 14–17). Articulations of confidence prompt wider confidence in the future and a propensity to act on such beliefs, but equally (and more seriously) an adverse shift in sentiment can very swiftly become market rout prompting a self-fulfilling downwards spiral of economic activity, without any necessary initial material change of similar magnitude in the underlying economy. Economies can 'talk themselves into a recession'. Thus, while it is a contemporary commonplace that restoring confidence in financial markets is required for any recovery from recession, for Akerlof and Shiller it is a much wider issue: the general economically active population needs to have their confidence in their own futures restored after a recession before the next period of positive economic development can get underway.

The key point that Akerlof and Shiller make is that although confidence is all about trust and belief in the future, it cannot be based only on 'rational' expectations: belief cannot itself be rational as then it would not be belief as properly understood. However, because capitalism is a system focused on future rewards (profit, capital accumulation) and individuals are likely to focus on survival within a system that requires them to be dependent for their personal wellbeing on their own economic situation, judgements based on beliefs about the future play a major role in influencing a wide range of economic activity. Mechanisms that build and restore confidence of private/individual economic actors in their future help support relatively stable economic activity, although over-confidence can also (quite easily) set in and prompt booms (which eventually run sufficiently far ahead of real potential to turn to bust). For Akerlof and Shiller, the role of confidence and changes in such confidence vary in importance across time, becoming crucial at potential turning points for an economy. However, trust and belief in the future shape of economic activity (what we might call predictability) are never absent from economic considerations, and such consideration must not presume that confidence will be built on rational calculations or even be mostly responsive to rational considerations.

**Fairness**

Having argued that confidence in the future is a key driver of economic activity, Akerlof and Shiller then turn to how perceptions of fairness may impact on the maintenance of confidence. This is not to say that economists have ignored the role of fairness; rather, although coverage of fairness has increased, it has not been accorded as important a role in analysis as behavioural economics would suggest it should (Akerlof and Shiller 2010, pp. 20–1). Detailing a number of empirical studies on the role of fairness in individuals' economic behaviour, they move beyond seeing fairness merely as reciprocity and argue that there are clear norms of fairness that play a significant role in how economically active individuals understand and then adjust their own behaviour especially as it relates to others. They suggest that a great deal of what makes people happy is living up to what they think they should be doing. In this sense most of the time people want to be fair. They consider it an insult if others do not think they are fair. At the same time, people also want others to live up to what they think those others should be doing. People get upset . . . when they think others are not being fair. (Akerlof and Shiller 2010, p. 25)

There are important economic effects flowing from how people expect themselves and others to behave fairly.

Scholars and commentators have examined specific aspects of political economy to ascertain whether these might be regarded as fair or not, but Akerlof and Shiller see the notion of evaluation based on the analysts' view of fairness as a secondary (albeit significant) concern: it has not led to much understanding of how individuals act on the perceptions of fairness in their own market interactions. For instance, one way of understanding how wages are set is not merely to focus on supply and demand but also to look at how the role of wage levels within organizations is perceived by those who receive them (Akerlof and Shiller 2010, pp. 97–106). Here, wage levels do not merely respond mechanically to supply and demand factors but are also determined in part by questions of workforce morale and perceptions of fairness (longevity of service and seniority may play a bigger role than would be expected on the basis of exclusively economic/ performance or 'rational' grounds).

It is likely that perceptions of fairness have prompted contemporary interest in fair trade, forms of ethical consumerism and approaches to corporate social responsibility, as well as a general dismay at the increasing inequalities of pay in the UK economy (see Hutton 2010). Thus, Akerlof and Shiller conclude that we can only understand actual behaviour in markets by according more weight to a general understanding of fairness. The acceptance of all sorts of price differentials reflect an acceptance of differing levels of service, reliability, convenience and other factors, which consumers are willing to reward accordingly (Akerlof and Shiller 2010, p. 22). To understand how markets actually work, we have to understand that fairness is valued and is often 'priced in' by consumers not based on some rational notion of accounting but on the basis of a perception of a fair reward for an aspect of provision. The wider issue here, beyond the question of pricing, is that economic activity responds to perceptions of fairness, and equally can be expected to also respond when fairness is violated in one way or another. Thus, confidence in the workings of the economy is tied up with perceptions of fairness, but it is not only questions of unfairness that lead to adverse judgements about prospects for future prosperity; the desire to avoid corruption and misdirection in market relations is also a key element of economic behaviour.

## Corruption and Bad Faith

Noting the importance of corrupt and fraudulent activities in the financial markets, Akerlof and Shiller make the wider point that although much bad and sharp practice is constrained by the knowledge built up by consumers undertaking recurring business, it is not always easy to spot sharp practice immediately (Akerlof and Shiller 2010, p. 27). The vendor who regularly misleads will not survive long where they are dependent on repeat purchases, whether they are the purveyor of rotten fruit or provide products that fail to do what they say they will, but in complex societies it is not always the case that social relations are close enough to ensure such knowledge is promptly and effectively socialized. Thus, in modern market societies, political pressures and scandals have prompted the development of extensive product regulations intended to ensure that consumers are not unfairly misled by unscrupulous merchants and producers.

Furthermore, where specific purchases or commitments are infrequent (investments, buying a house) it is much more likely that consumers will lack the social knowledge to help them make an appropriate market choice. Akerlof and Shiller argue that this is especially the case in the financial sector, given the increasing complexity of financial instruments and consumers' lack of experience (Akerlof and Shiller 2010, p. 39). Like the confidence multiplier, as bad practice and corrupt behaviour become more widespread, and are perceived as being unpunished (or even celebrated in popular culture), this feeds back and reinforces the tendency for economic actors to act without the constraints of morality, fairness or honesty. To some extent, regulation always follows misbehaviour but corruption and bad faith also respond to new unregulated economic opportunities (prompted by social and/or technological changes), and as such are often linked to booms prompted by new technologies.

Cultural changes, in response to new social and technological developments, often free the unscrupulous from the fear of punishment or retribution, as their 'crimes' may not be fully understood (Akerlof and Shiller 2010, p. 39). The widening incidence of corruption may undermine confidence and indeed will likely have a profound impact on the general perception of fairness in any market society where corruption is rife; here, the post-1989 example of Russia's (so-called) klepto capitalism is a recent example of the corrosive economic effect of widespread corruption and bad faith in economic relations. Only as society catches up with these developments, developing regulatory structures that constrain behaviour or mandate full disclosure of salient facts (ingredients, expectations or dangers), can confidence be rebuilt either in that sector or more generally.

## Stories

Akerlof and Shiller also argue that the stories societies tell themselves (or are told by influential leaders, commentators and others) have a major role in determining levels of confidence, and thereby the direction of economic activity. For instance, the story about the information society has been a major factor in the successive investment booms around internet-related technologies (Akerlof and Shiller 2010, p. 55), even if the story itself was not always particularly coherent (see May 2002). This leads them to argue that confidence is always a

> view of other people's confidence, and of other people's perceptions of other people's confidence. It is also a view of the world – a popular model of current events, a public understanding of the mechanism of economic change as informed by the news media and by popular discussions. High confidence tends to be associated with inspirational stories about new business initiatives, tales of how others are getting rich . . . [and therefore] the economic confidence of times past cannot be understood without reference to the details of these stories. (Akerlof and Shiller 2010, p. 55)

Equally, if we forget or ignore the stories of the past we are condemned to repeat the crises they had recounted. The slow forgetting of the story of the New Deal and specifically the need to separate investment and retail banking influenced the period of deregulation that many would regard as directly responsible for the economic crisis of 2008 (Akerlof and Shiller 2010, pp. 59–73). The act of wilfully forgetting and indeed the move to discredit specific stories can be just as important for the political economy as those that are current and celebrated. This, of course, also directly relates to the process of social change that my reading of Margaret Archer's work puts at the centre of *my* approach to political economy.

Akerlof and Shiller see stories spreading like viruses (Akerlof and Shiller 2010, p. 56) infecting those that they come into contact with, and thereby changing economic behaviour and actions. We make sense of the world by telling ourselves stories about our lives, our societies, and as such we try to impose narratives even when we have imperfect knowledge or information. Even when confronted with random episodes, in life or in markets, we try to concoct stories that make sense of what we see before us (Akerlof and Shiller 2010, pp. 51–2; see also Mlodinow 2008; Taleb 2007). One of the most powerful stories we are told is about economic man, although in contrast to its presentation as being about human nature, its genealogy reveals it to be historically contingent with different times having different economic men (Morgan 2006). And although we are often told that 'men' equals human, Nancy Folbre has (re)told that story as one of 'greed, lust and gender' where gender differences are not insignificant but constitutive of the story of economic man (Folbre 2009). Stories may compete and be in tension with one another, but nevertheless those we choose (or are convinced by) help us shape our economic actions and interactions. Our animal spirits require us to seek patterns from which we form explanatory narratives. This suggests to Akerlof and Shiller that changes in levels of confidence are often caused by a shift in the form and content of stories about the economy that are current and plausible to important groups of economically active individuals. As noted in their discussion of confidence, there is no necessary link between these stories and 'economic fundamentals', but the stories themselves may have significant and widespread economic consequences.

**Legal Illusion as an Analogue to Money Illusion**

The last element of Akerlof and Shiller's account concerns money illusion, which for the purposes of my account of the rule of law, I will (re)focus on the psychology concerned rather than the specific question of its relation to money. Money illusion – the focus on the nominal price of things including labour rather than their 'real' inflation-adjusted price – is a key element in Akerlof and Shiller's discussion of inflation and wage levels (Akerlof and Shiller 2010, pp. 41–50, 107–15). A key aspect of money illusion is that focusing on nominal prices, especially by wage earners, leads to misrecognition of the levels of real purchasing power and a general resistance to wage reductions even when general prices are subject to deflation. However, here I want to draw out of this an assumption about fixity; that is to say, their analysis of money illusion suggests that our animal spirits encourage us to have a relatively static view, especially in the short to medium term, disregarding the real value of money (expressed in actual purchasing power over available products and/or services) and focusing on its nominal value (expressed in prices).

This can be seen as analogous to the view that the legal system is a fixed system of laws. Certainly, most people in any jurisdiction will understand that new laws are passed, and sometimes old laws are removed from the legal system (although less often). However, mostly people encounter the legal system as a static set of laws that are known and shape or regulate social relations; law is seen as fixed not dynamic. Thus, although it is clear that a legal system is changing and (mostly) growing as regards the number of laws that have been adopted by the governing institutions of society, this movement and development is largely ignored in everyday life; we all work with an illusion of legal fixity. This, in parallel to Akerlof and Shiller's account, I will term 'legal illusion' for convenience.

# RULING MARKETS: ANIMAL SPIRITS AND THE RULE OF LAW

These five elements of our animal spirits shape economic relations according to Akerlof and Shiller, and if this is so, it makes it easier to see how the rule of law may allow these 'spirits' to support the development of capitalist market societies. Because I have been concerned with what we might term the narratives (or rhetoric) of the rule of law, here I will start with the issue of story-telling that Akerlof and Shiller finish with, which in many ways is an analogue to Taylor's idea of the social imaginary. The use of the rule of law as an evaluative term, where states and societies are gauged by perceptions of their accordance with the rule of law, might imply that there is some clear way of measuring the extent of any society's achievement of political standards that the rule of law obtains. However, as I have already noted, this is far from true (see also Rodriguez et al. 2010); rather, what we encounter is widespread agreement that the rule of law is a 'good thing' but almost no agreement about which aspects take priority. There is also no clear agreement even regarding the absence of which elements of the rule of law is fatal to an evaluation of its existence, and thus no clear agreement on the measurement of magnitudes or movement towards some defined threshold of attainment. Even a relatively simple account of the rule of law encompasses a range of discrete elements, but it does not seem plausible that the inability of a society to effectively deliver on one or two of these aspects would then suggest there was a total lack of the rule of law (although the debate between thin and thick versions of the norm colours such judgements).

As regards the link between the rule of law and (economic) development, as a specific case of this problem, there are at least three aspects to the difficulty of measurement: what is the measure of development that will be fixed on as the dependent variable; can the available data really capture the nuance and complexity of the rule of law; and even if these two issues can be resolved sufficiently to allow analysis, how do we demonstrate causality – correlation, as often reported, is not really enough (Davis 2004)? Indeed, even the correlations may not be as significant as is sometimes asserted (Haggard and Tiede 2011, p. 677). Certainly, there have been some attempts to formally link the rule of law and growth in gross domestic product, such as part of Robert Barro's overall account of the determinants of economic growth (Barro 1997), but these often use perception indexes (focused on the investment environment) rather than detailed accounts of any country's legal system. Therefore, when the rule of law is invoked it is not so much a clear empirical measurement that is being appealed to but rather a set of stories about the society being examined that comes into play. The term 'rule of law' indicates a story about the law and its contribution to the good society, and as such reflects Akerlof and Shiller's notion that stories we tell ourselves about the society (ours or others) have important implications for our confidence and trust in the future. These stories about the rule of law are central to its role as a social imaginary.

To demonstrate a plausible link between stories of the value of the rule of law and the 'animal spirits' that underpin capitalism, I will now set out how these two sets of issues interact within modern capitalist society. Taking each of Lord Bingham's eight elements of the rule of law (as set out in Chapter 2) in turn I shall suggest each is linked to one or more aspects of our 'animal spirits'. Bingham's account commences with the question of accessibility and predictability; the citizen under any particular jurisdiction must be able to access public statements of the law, and be able to understand them in such a way that their behaviour can be guided by such laws. Here, we can see a direct link to confidence in the future, refracted through what I recast above as 'legal illusion'. That is to say, knowing what the law is, I can have confidence in how society will judge my actions while also expecting such laws to continue into the future in which I undertake such actions; in legal discussions this is often rendered as predictability. Thus, economic actions that are legal remain legal and indeed given that laws should not be retrospective cannot latterly be rendered illegal. Moreover, Bingham's second element (on the limits of discretion) allows me a confidence in the stability of the law as it affects me, as it cannot be undermined by powerful actors who for one reason or another may not be supportive of my (seemingly) legal economic activity. This underpins economic behaviour (such as investment) by allowing economic actors to make calculations of benefits on the basis of a stable legal context in which they act. Indeed, the lack of discretion also acts as a guard against bad faith as regards the enforcement of laws; neither bad faith nor corruption is allowed to shape the 'legal' limits of actions.

The 'legal illusion' of stability is also served by the requirement for all to be equal under the law. This means that economic actors can assess those with whom they contract on the basis of general legal considerations, with no special knowledge of the social role or private interests, and have confidence that the law will underpin both sides' actions equally. While there may be other non-legal reasons for choice of contracting parties, the question of their legal character is thereby limited to generally available principles (perhaps based on age or whether a commercial customer is incorporated). This issue of equality under the rule of law stretches to the government and rulers of the state. The suspicion of bad faith and corruption when states (and/or ruling elites) treat their own economic transactions differently from those of others is held in check by the rule of law. States that seek to conduct their own economic relations on a legal basis do little damage to market confidence; those that seek to establish preferential legal treatment for their economic institutions can find this undermines a more general acceptance market mechanism (here again Russia's travails in the 1990s would seem to bear this out).

That there should be no impediments that limit the enjoyment of the full protection of the law, be they prior to adjudication or in the legal process itself, appeals both to an issue of fairness – if these laws obtain, then all should be protected by them – and the dislike of corruption and bad faith. Not only should we be able to ascertain the law (the first element Bingham sets out), we should have unencumbered access to the machinery of the law. This can be an argument for the continuance of an extensive pro-gramme of legal aid, and certainly a lack of ability to gain legal protection in economic relations, such as during forced nationalizations or resource 'grabs', can undermine the willingness to invest, given that the legal guarantee that the return would remain with the investor is compromised by such actions. Indeed, this story about investment in states that have a varying willingness to protect property rights has often be expressed in *The Economist* and elsewhere as an issue of the lack of respect for rule of law constraining valuable investment.

Finally, Bingham's appeal to fairness under the rule of law directly parallels Akerlof and Shiller's invocation of fairness as one of the 'animal spirits', alongside the dislike of corruption and bad faith. This appeal to fairness in its operations and prosecution reflects the desire by humans to see these values operating in the society more widely. Likewise, the issues of human rights and international obligations that Bingham seeks to include in the rule of law may appeal to our spirit of fairness and con-fidence about how society is governed more generally (adding to the more general story of the rule of law and the good society). That is to say, our general confidence about living in the good society, free from corruption and bad faith, is likely to enhance our confidence in the continuing health of market society and this confidence, as Akerlof and Shiller suggest, can be self-fulfilling and self-reinforcing. Just to make this argument clear, I have set out the comparison in Table 5.1.

If we accept the argument that it is our 'animal spirits' that drive economic relations and, more specifically, that they are best expressed through the practices and institutions of modern capitalist market society, as Akerlof and Shiller have argued, then we can also see that the rule of law plays a significant role in ensuring these 'spirits' are able to fulfil their potential to underpin beneficial economic behaviour. This also allows us to start to move beyond the assertion that capitalism is dependent on the rule of law, that successful economic development requires the

*Table 5.1    The rule of law and the animal spirits*

| Bingham's elements of the rule of law | Akerlof and Shiller's aspects of 'animal spirits' |
|---|---|
| Accessibility/predictability | Confidence; stability |
| Lack of discretion | Confidence; dislike of corruption/bad faith; stability |
| Equality under the law | Fairness; stability |
| Rulers and state apparatus held to the law | Fairness; dislike of corruption/bad faith |
| Human rights | Confidence; fairness |
| No barriers to effective enjoyment of rights | Fairness; dislike of corruption/bad faith |
| Fairness | Fairness; dislike of corruption/bad faith |
| International obligations | Fairness |

introduction of the rule of law to aspiring capitalist economies. Linking the argument about the 'animal spirits' to the rule of law allows a clearer understanding of why the relationship between the rule of law and capitalism seems to be demonstrable: it is an institutional manifestation of the human psychological drivers that lie behind economic development (under capitalism, at least). However, as I have suggested, the rule of law itself is a multifaceted and complex set of linked ideas, and as such different developed and rich states seem to have different balances between its elements. This implies that the relationship between the rule of law, 'animal spirits' and market society is likely to be more complex than this sketch has been able to convey, and linked to local cultural commitments, even if its general contours are as described above.

## CONCLUSION

Of course, this argument is much more applicable to the relationship between Anglo-Saxon capitalism and common law than other political economies. While these 'animal spirits' might remain relatively recognizable across different 'varieties of capitalism', it is plausible that in the civil law tradition some more extensive variance might be perceived in the depiction of the rule of law. Indeed, the question of the applicability of the rule of law to non-common law systems has become a major discussion in the law and development literature. This has been prompted by the fact that a number of countries where it would be difficult to suggest the rule of law obtains in a way that would be recognizable to many of the commentators mentioned in earlier chapters have nevertheless managed to expand their economies. Despite a wide range of claims for the advantages of common law in economic development as opposed to civil law, a recent historical overview conducted by Curtis Milhaupt and Katherina Pistor found little correlation between the common law and national histories of economic development (Milhaupt and Pistor 2008, pp. 23–5, *passim*), while others have linked the (supposed) advantages delivered by common law systems to colonial institutional inheritances, and then only as relates to property law (see Joireman 2004). As I will discuss later, they see a much more complex ecology of law than would be evident from the current and dominant common sense of the rule of law.

Finally, as Stephen Haggard and his co-authors warn: 'for countries at low levels of development, the types of informal institutions that generated trade early in modern Europe may be more relevant than the complex statute and demanding institutions of the American or current European legal systems' (Haggard et al. 2008, p. 221). This suggests that there may not be as great a utility in shortcutting North's stages as might be thought; a country may need to go through an evolution towards the rule of law, although it may do that more speedily than in earlier phases of history. To some extent, here the case of China is an interesting example of economic development where despite recent rhetoric many would argue that the rule of law (at least in the Westernized sense discussed here) is absent or at best underdeveloped (Tamanaha 2011, p. 229), although equally there is considerable evidence of legal development, albeit without the support of the rule of law programmes undertaken by Western states and international organizations (Tamanaha 2011, p. 243). The speed of economic development absent the presumed requirement to have the rule of law in place has been evident across East Asia (Woo-Cummings 2003), and now, of course, the experience of China looms large over analysis of these issues (Dam 2006). Certainly, the way Chinese development programmes understand the rule of law seems to be closely aligned with a thin view of the norm; approaching merely rule *by* law. Although declaring to be working within the rule of law this is largely seen by activists and others surveying Chinese engagements and/or investments in Africa and South America to merely be a rather procedural understanding that does little to further progress in aspects of the rule of law associated with thicker readings such as democracy or human rights (Cardenal and Araújo 2013, pp. 259–60). As I will discuss in Chapter 7, this is where the rule of law meets legal pluralism and the question about the essential characteristics of the (rule of) law become considerably more complex than the dominant narratives that support its role as a common sense of global politics might suggest.

# 6. Global constitutionalism: the rule of law by another name?

The constitutionalisation of international law hinges on the rule of law rather than on the rule of force. (Paulus 2009, p. 98)

Constitutional discourse is posited as a supplement, something that will supply 'more' of whatever is currently 'lacking' in transnational legality; democracy, accountability [or] legitimacy. (Buchanan 2012, p. 9)

It has become *de rigeur* to reach for constitutional language when considering postnational legal entities so long as they bear some resemblance to formal features we associate with constitutional rule. (Isiksel 2012, p. 102)

I now shift the focus of my argument to how the rule of law has played out in the discussion of global politics in the new millennium; the discussion of the possibility and actuality of a global constitution, I suggest, is merely another way of talking about the rule of law. States often use the rhetoric of the rule of law in pronouncements about other states' (political) actions, as well as using it to justify their own, but this remains largely an international issue (Watts 1993). At the supranational level the norm of the rule of law has underpinned the development of the further claim that a global constitution is both possible and beneficial, while also attracting a certain amount of criticism for the manner in which it has developed and its (legal) character.

To be clear: any move to develop a constitution depends on the strength of the rule of law, in that a constitution is impossible without some prior commitment to legality. Constitutions are primarily political instruments that may flesh out some of the political aspects of the rule of law introduced by thick discussions/definitions of the norm, while also seeking to establish settled mechanisms through which the specifics of the rule of law may be delivered or achieved. Conversely, some appeals to constitutionalism are about the (political) desire to limit the reach of the rule of law and thus render it in its thinner variety to constrain the importation of specific (unwelcome?) values. At the international level there is a further question: historically, constitutions have been related to the practices of the sovereign state and as such the lack of an analogous authority beyond the state might suggest that constitutional approaches are merely a rhetorical pretence. This may be formally true if one accepts the direct dependence between a constitution and a sovereign body (state). However, at the international level, as I suggest below, the debate about the potential of constitutional developments focuses to a large degree on functional rather than formal/legal requirements. If constitutional approaches to governance may be difficult to apply in situations lacking the (previous) sovereign grounding, the common sense of the rule of law goes some way in reducing the salience of these formal failings. Therefore, before moving to discuss global constitutionalism, it is useful to think about the relationship between the rule of law and constitutionalism. Drawing (albeit summarily) from Hans Kelsen, I want to suggest that the rule of law is the *grundnorm* that underpins constitutionalism, to the extent that arguing in favour of constitutionalization is in effect (again) arguing for the sanctity of the rule of law.

## THE RULE OF LAW: CONSTITUTIONALISM'S *GRUNDNORM*

In the debates about the character and justification of legal systems, Hans Kelsen argued that the system of law was based on a prior basic norm (or *grundnorm*): this basic norm is that the

> highest rule of law creation, establishing the unity of the entire system, is indeed on hand for the issuance of other legal norms, but it must itself be assumed to be *presupposed* as a legal norm and not *issued* in accordance with other legal norms. Its creation must therefore be seen as a material fact outside the legal system. (Kelsen 1923 [1998], p. 13, emphasis in original)

Elsewhere, Kelsen suggested that this basic norm (this highest rule) be regarded as the original constitution, the establishment of a particular social order by force, or political revolution before which time political justification relied on different norms (Kelsen 1945 [1999], pp. 115–17); the *grundnorm* is the manifestation of a political break-point. Tony Honoré has likened this metaphorically to the 'big bang'; postulated by physicists to understand subsequent developments, its own causes are not amenable to explanation based on current forms of analysis (Honoré 1998, pp. 101–3). When we seek to justify the notion of legality, the 'rule of law' is a norm that is not produced as part of the establishment and reproduction of any specific constitution but rather pre-dates it: the initial social desire for the rule of law must precede its origin.

Indeed, in Kelsen's view, there can be no legal system without a prior

assumption that a system of laws (the rule of law) will provide direction
for how those governed ought to behave (Kelsen 1982, p. 69). This tran-
scendental notion of the foundation of law suggests a depoliticization
of law as a system of governance: the content of the law comes after the
acceptance of the process of following the law itself. The basic norm/
*grundnorm* that presents the rule of law as a legitimate and effective practice prior to its actualization is essentially an act of faith, not politics (in his
later work Kelsen began to refer to the *grundnorm* as a necessary fiction).
This principle is not subject to political argument or amendment, it pre-
dates debate about the content and particulars of any specific legality; it
is apolitical, and is intended to be so in Kelsen's analysis. The belief in the
value of compliance with the law is the basis on which any system of rules
must rest for otherwise it could not be regarded as a system of regulation.
This is the crucial *a priori* step for governance and the establishment of
any constitution.

As this suggests, Kelsen's position solidified around the argument that
positive law could only exist by including as part of its character its establishing norm for which no legitimate authority could be claimed, as logi-
cally it preceded the ability to be so justified (a claim only available after
the basic norm is/was in place) (Bindreiter 2001, pp. 149–52). As Jacques
Derrida puts it in his consideration of law (which parallels Kelsen's on this
point): 'How are we to distinguish between the force of law of a legitimate
power and the supposedly original violence that must have established this
authority and that itself could not have been authorized by any anterior
legitimacy?' (Derrida 1992, p. 6). Here, the rule of law, and thus its role
as *grundnorm* is always the contemporary manifestation of some initial
(original) moment of force, or assertion of legitimate authority. Leaving
aside the continuing debates about Kelsen's analysis of the *grundnorm*,[1]
this idea has something to offer the discussion of global constitutionalism
in contemporary global political economy. The prior political move that
precedes any attempt to develop a constitution can be understood as the
establishment and (perhaps in the face of resistance) the reproduction
of the rule of law *qua grundnorm*. In this sense, the definitional debates,
the professional (re)production of the norm and the capacity building/
technical assistance discussed in earlier chapters all work to underpin a
claim that the expansion of constitutional solutions to regulatory issues
enhances the legitimacy of global governance (although many of these
practices are not explicitly focused on this end).

Once a constitution (national, international or global) is regarded as

---

[1] See, for instance, the essays in Paulson and Paulson (1998) or the discussion in Bindreiter
(2001).

problematic (that is to say, it becomes subject to critical debate), justificatory arguments track back through the hierarchy of norms, potentially leading to debate and contest about the presumption that the basic norm itself is valid (and here, for instance, Ugo Mattei and Laura Nader's claim that the 'rule of law is illegal' (Mattei and Nader 2008) is exemplary of such criticism). As the basic norm cannot be justified within the (legal) system that it precedes, this shifts the question of its validity (back) into the realm of politics. Thus, if the *grundnorm* remains uncontested, it is able to depoliticize subsequent debates about law, but when questions arise about the validity of a constitutional settlement, a political defence of its basic norm will need to be articulated. The move from acceptance to contestability of the *grundnorm* can illuminate the political activity that underpins constitutionalism. But this potential critique also reinforces the need for the continuance of normative maintenance activities around the rule of law that are the subject of this book.

The initial act of establishing a constitution also either reflects the existence of a polity to be governed or constitutes a hitherto unrecognized (or even non-existent) polity that is to be ruled. This is even more the case in the international or global legal realm, as here there is no single authority; rather (as is a commonplace observation) the law is the result of agreements between its subjects, not the provision of an order by a (formally separate) sovereign authority. The polity to be constituted is not geographic (with the partial exception of the UN) but is waiting to be identified by its function and/or practices. Thus, the political move represented by constitutionalism is the (re)definition of the legal-political realm itself, and the claim (or assertion) that this realm is subject to the rule of law. For instance, the constitution of the World Trade Organization (WTO), through its various elements, acts to define a specific set of relations as being those of international trade; in this case the WTO's inclusion of services and intellectual property widened the realm of international trade relations from a prior acceptance that this sector was limited to the exchange of 'physical' products.

As Nico Krisch has observed, global constitutionalism therefore seeks 'to tame this space, to organize it in a rational way, to hedge it in along lines we have come to know (and value) in domestic politics over centuries' (Krisch 2010, p. 67).[2] However, as there is no sovereign authority by which the legitimacy of such a move might be established, the normative

---

[2] To be clear, here the authors I cite in this chapter and myself use the term global constitutionalism to refer to the move to develop constitutions that are supranational or global. However, one could also understand the term to refer to the trend for political groups to develop constitutions for sovereign states; for a comprehensive survey of this different (if not entirely unconnected) trend see Law and Versteeg (2011).

elements of the rule of law are required to do more of the 'heavy lifting' in global constitutionalism. Indeed, the very claim to be constitutional is a claim (like that around the rule of law) of legitimacy: a constitutional regime is a legitimate regime (Klabbers 2004, p. 47). That is to say, global constitutionalism is dependent on the veracity of the common sense of the rule of law in the global political economy, although it is grounded on the rule of law in a way that is seldom explicitly acknowledged. Certainly, there have been attempts to construct (what might be called) global non-political constitutions that appeal to a connection between law and some other (non-political) aspect of the global system. Again, the WTO is exemplary; in economic constitutionalism the notion of economic relations is taken to be separate from political relations and as a result can be constitutionalized as a depoliticized regulatory structure. As this chapter will suggest, for many this is exactly the terrain over which debates about the benefits and difficulties of global constitutionalism range, and where debates over the rule of law illuminate the question of how and whether such depoliticization is possible.

As symbolic artefacts, constitutions have three main areas of effect: they put into concrete terms abstract (political) ideas; they affirm (and construct) the polity that is to be governed; and they propose a legal hierarchy to establish specific issues as worthy of significant attention and weight (Anderson 2005, p. 107). Surveying the literature of constitutionalization, Garrett Wallace Brown also notes that within the working definition(s) that can be inferred from the analyses he examines, the process of making constitutions (especially as regards the global realm) is concerned with the development of formal legal processes, with legal rights and duties clearly codified alongside settled mechanisms for adjudication. There is also the imposition of a specified judicial system; a new constitutional system's jurisdiction replaces previous legal relationships. This is allied to a dynamic of norm construction and solidification, from which more formal norms are then drawn (Brown 2012, pp. 205–6; see also Loughlin 2010, pp. 59–62). Constitutions may also prompt some common fears, of which perhaps the most notable are around the concentration of power and the problem of democratic deficits (Lawrence 2013, p. 64).

If constitutions can be seen as symbolic artefacts this also points to the difficulty of pinning down exactly what the processes of constitutionalism (or constitutionalization) actually encompass. For Jessica Lawrence, these processes include a range of largely abstract and discursive disputes that offer few concrete conditions against which actual developments might be measured to ascertain whether constitutionalism is taking place (paralleling the similar problems I have discussed with assessing the extent of the rule of law). These disputes or discussions are concerned with whether a specific institution or system is constitutional and what this judgement might mean; a set of normative questions about the appropriate form of a constitutional settlement, organization or practice; and what should be the normative substance of any constitution and how might a multiplicity of values and constitutional norms be arranged hierarchically (Lawrence 2013, pp. 70–2). As all this indicates, global constitutions are much discussed, although perhaps less easily enacted, or even recognized!

In this chapter, therefore, I suggest that the rise of the norm of the rule of law is often actualized at the global level through the discussion of constitutionalism. As the actors who are interested in, and committed to, the rule of law moved to consolidate their work in global politics, they also responded to the practical shifts in the global system. The end of the Cold War prompted a perception that there would be a political convergence around the 'winning' system, and its solidification into a putative 'international community'; for instance, in the wake of the completion of the Uruguay Round of trade negotiations, and the subsequent establishment of the WTO (of which more below), the institutionalization of a global level of governance became more pronounced (although, of course, it has a much longer history stretching back into the nineteenth century and beyond). A range of technological and political economic shifts (often brought together under the rubric of 'globalization') have also made the notion of a global space that *needs* to be governed more plausible (Krisch 2010, pp. 31–2; see also Dunoff and Trachtman 2009, pp. 5–9; Prandini 2010, pp. 312–13). So, the idea of global constitutionalism responds to ideational shifts and empirical developments, with actors comparing and contrasting their views of the possibilities of the global political space, with the physical and practical changes they confront, as well as drivers of behavioural change and new (political) actions.[3]

## THE SHAPE OF THE GLOBAL CONSTITUTION

If there is a global constitution, then it must be more than merely a contractual agreement between signatories (the treaty form common to international law); a global constitution must be supranational. In this, most (if not all) candidates for being a global constitution fall short, although the expansion of constitutional proposals seems intended (by its agents)

---

[3] Riccardo Prandini (2010) also assembles an account of global constitutionalism using analytical tools derived from Margaret Archer's work in a way parallel to my discussion in Chapter 2 (although presented very differently).

to move legal arrangements nearer this state of affairs. It is less clear whether this should indicate that we have nothing approaching a global constitution because we have nothing that is completely supranational yet, or because the threshold for identifying such a constitution (by drawing parallels from domestic political constitutions) has been set in a way that does not recognize the particularities of the global system. Thus, on one side of this argument,[4] Michael Doyle (2009) argues that the UN Charter falls short of this threshold due to what he has referred to as 'sovereign pushback' that results in the Charter remaining constrained by its own recognition of state sovereignty, and the continued assertion by states of such sovereignty. Conversely, Bardo Fassbender (2009) adopts a more pragmatic (and functional) approach to suggest that while it might not be fully constitutional, nevertheless the UN Charter is treated as such most of the time and is nearer constitutionality than not. Therefore, it makes some sense to think about how a global constitution built on the foundations of the acceptance of the rule of law across (a putative) global society might be recognized or identified. The supremacy of a (global) constitution is not a matter of assertion (stating that it is) but rather is the practical acceptance by the global community (however defined) of its legitimacy and applicability.

One place to start is with the self-avowedly functional approach to constitutionalization presented by Jeffrey Dunoff and Joel Trachtman (at the same workshop where Fassbender and Doyle presented their views), which usefully summarizes three functions that a global constitution needs to fulfil. Constitutions are meant to:

1.  Enable or regularize processes for making ordinary international law under circumstances where more efficient production of law seems desirable (enabling constitutionalization).
2.  Constrain the production of ordinary international law, preserving a sphere of autonomy for the state or other actors (constraining constitutionalization).
3.  Supplement domestic constitutional protections (supplemental constitutionalization) (Dunoff and Trachtman 2009, pp. 17–18).

It will be no surprise that there are many other lists one could appeal to. Here, I will just add one further set of functions; Riccardo Prandini suggests there are four more general functions performed by constitutions. Constitutions:

---

[4] As played out in a workshop whose papers are collected in Dunoff and Trachtman (2009).

1. Establish a legitimacy principle for political power.
2. Regulate the conditions for the real exercise of power (that is, they establish the basic legal norms that comprehensively regulate the social and political life of a polity and usually impose special impediments over unwarranted transformations).
3. Institute the boundaries between the political system and the other subsystems (for example, civil society).
4. Determine the ultimate goals of the polity (Prandini 2010, p. 312).

Drawing on these functional accounts, a constitution encompasses a set of principles of which the most basic is the rule of law, but which also includes the definition of legitimate lawmaking (and reforming) capacity, the limits to this capacity and the bodies (or organizations) within whom such capacity is vested.

If the legal system is the collection of laws established by a specific polity, the constitution is the law of that system's operation, the manner by which political norms and principles are turned into government. Most importantly, the constitution is independent of the government of the day and as such is understood (politically) as a neutral (and to some extent effectively external) force that constrains the actions of any particular government. Thus, as Tűrkűler Isiksel points out, the

> most frequently cited signs of constitutionalism include the hierarchical organisation of norms, the authority to produce binding rules, direct applicability, binding mechanisms of dispute resolution, systems of precedent, schedules of fundamental rights, and rudimentary channels of democratic accountability. (Isiksel 2012, p. 103)

Mostly, these will be familiar from the earlier discussions of the rule of law, and are intended to limit the scope of radical action to reshape governance. The allocation of authority over the rule of law is achieved by establishing a stable mechanism of overarching authority that can be appealed to adjudge tensions and conflicts within the legal system. Focusing on the EU, we might follow Neil MacCormick's depiction of its constitutional order, to suggest the more specific functions that the constitutional order (at a global level) would need to fulfil:

> [The EU's] legal order has direct effect to create rights and obligations for citizens and corporations *as well as* for the states themselves. Its laws have primacy over the laws of the member states within the areas of competence transferred to the organs of the Community or Union by the states in the treaties (as interpreted by the [European] Court [of Justice]). There is a self-referential quality about all of this – the treaties as interpreted by the Court gave the authority for

the Court to interpret the treaties as a new legal order distinct from international law and from the laws of the member states. *Self-reference of this kind is
typical of independent constitutional orders.* (MacCormick 2007, p. 48, emphasis
added)

Once functional in a legal sense, then the constitution (albeit based on a
self-referential moment) becomes the manner in which the rule of law can
be maintained.

This leads us to the distinction between constituent power and constituted power, which is especially fraught at the global level; the former is
the power that (once) establishes the constitution for a specified jurisdiction (by revolution, coup d'état or other political 'earthquake'), while the
latter is the power limited by the terms of the constitution so established.
At the global level there is no consensus about the character and legitimacy of any constituent power; there may be regional authorities (such as
the EU) that approach some acceptable level of constituent authority (at
least partly derived from the better grounded national constituent authority of state members), but at the global level only the UN might be said
to enjoy something even approaching the required levels of legitimacy.
Conversely, the establishing constituent moment at the global level might
be regarded as being so disruptive (if of a similar character to domestic
'earthquakes') that no existing global authority could hope to successfully
initiate such a disruption.[5] However, as will be discussed in the section on
the WTO (below), sector agreements allied with specialized knowledge
and a powerful set of supporters have enabled the development of a claim
towards constitutionalism in the realm of global trade, reflecting a different idea of how the expansion of constitutional settlements might proceed.

One key question posed by global constitutionalism therefore is: can a
constitution lack a single constituent power and/or constituting revolutionary moment?[6] As noted above, for Fassbender, the UN Charter has
become the constitution of the international community; it was drafted
with the intent to look in some ways like a (putative) constitution but
most importantly in the over half century since its founding, the Charter

---

[5] This is Hedley Bull's famous argument that it would require a world war of such devasta-
tion to establish a world government in the face of state sovereignty and the balance of
power that no state or alliance could be successful in establishing a state-like structure
at the global level – see Bull (2012), which includes an essay on Bull's work's continuing
contemporary relevance.

[6] These issues as regard the EU are explored in Walker (2007) and more generally the issue
of the constitutionalization of the EU are covered at some length in the three chapters in
part II of Dobner and Loughlin (2010). In this chapter, I will focus (in a section below)
on the WTO rather than the EU, partly due to space constraints and partly to deal with
an institution that has global pretentions rather than being an (albeit very important)
regional case.

has increasingly been referred to, and treated as, a constitution. Here, while there is a founding moment it is not necessarily fully constitutive, but a process of political engagement and accretion of legal precedent has allowed the Charter to become (something akin to) a constitution (Fassbender 2007, p. 281). Fassbender argues that the 'Peoples of the United Nations' cited in the Charter are the constituent power (organized through the state parties in 1945) with the ascendance of the democratic norm in global politics buttressing that position (Fassbender 2007, p. 289). Indeed, in constitutional politics the shift from territory and statehood to the 'people' as the political grounding for a constitution has (at least potentially) freed constitutions to be established by non-territorially defined groups, and at the limit a global demos/community (Preuss 2010). In self-reflexive terms this potentiality is also carried forward as the 'people' are then constituted *by* the (globalized) constitutional settlement.

However, if the community from which a constitution might be developed must in itself be self-constituted in the moment of constitutional assertion, then this can hardly be said to be the case of the plural, multi-faceted, multi-civilization global system (Besson 2009, p. 398). As Gunther Teubner (perhaps rather acidly) concludes: 'While the UN has itself undergone a constitutionalisation process, the result was certainly not a world constitution, but rather the more limited constitution of a formal organisation' (Teubner 2012, p. 46). This reflects Martin Loughlin's argument that the expansion of constitutions has been primarily to build (what he terms) liberal-legal constitutions that are concerned to centralize and formalize authority (Loughlin 2010, p. 61). Those developing constitutions seek to (re)constitute society as one governed by market-facilitating regulations and protections. This is a project not to recognize previously existing local norms but to install a 'new order' as part of the neoliberalization of (global) society (as discussed later in this chapter). Moreover, especially in its supranational form, the process of establishing constitutions has not been driven by popular demand from a wide polity but rather by elite institutions; here the example of the work of the central EU institutions to further develop the constitutional elements of the EU (Loughlin 2012, p. 66), or the driving forces behind the establishment of the WTO, are particularly noteworthy. The question of the legitimacy of constituent power remains fraught and timely.

Moving to constituted power, national constitutions usually (although not always) now include some invocation of a range of socio-economic rights (of which the right to education seems the most widespread, and health care the next most popular) (Hirschl and Rosevear 2011). The developing global constitution is more fragmented, but includes limits to political power linked to assertions of human rights through the Universal

Declaration of Human Rights, and (more locally for Europeans) the
European Convention on Human Rights, the latter of which has considerable enforcement capacity linked to its Articles. However, the question of
adjudication is crucial for such a linkage; to whom does one appeal when
your human rights have been abused? As Andreas Paulus points out, there
is an argument that the

> deficiency of the rule of law in international affairs is, in the first place, not
> due to a lack of rules, but to a lack of adjudication of those rules. Progress of
> constitutionalisation would thus be tied to a rise of adjudication. (Paulus 2009,
> p. 99)

This suggests that the global constitutional project will be carried forward
through the expansion of globally focused courts (as suggested earlier,
also a possible measurement of the extent of legalization). Indeed, one
of the key effects of a written constitution is the empowerment of the
(related) judiciary over and above political actors, as the judiciary is able
to claim the legitimacy of the constitution as their own (Pek 2008). Unlike
domestic systems where the rule of law might be argued to obtain, there is
less of a clear link between the courts at this level and any putative (global)
demos for whose benefit constituted power is acting. These difficulties
with global constitutionalism are to some extent typified by the problems
of the EU's democratic deficit. As Ulrich Haltern observed (quoting from
an EU White Paper): 'While the Union's competences and responsibilities
closely resemble those of most nation-states, its institutions do not have
a relationship with the general public "that remotely compares with that
of national institutions"' (Haltern 2003, p. 30). Certainly, the EU's diplomats and bureaucrats have been working to address this problem, and
many see the EU Parliament's extension of powers and profile as a move
towards better public engagement with the European polity.

As this implies, global constitutionalism cannot just be seen as constitutionalism read up to the global level but rather has to be understood
differently for both practical and historical reasons. It also includes a
shift in global political perceptions that Martti Koskenniemi has referred
to as a 'constitutional mindset'. Here, lawyers and policy makers utilize
constitutional vocabularies (such as 'self-determination', 'fundamental
rights', 'division and accountability of power') to criticize and seek to
modify contemporary political settlements (Koskenniemi 2007b, p. 34).
Instrumental governance and universal norms are brought together to
engage with the realities of politics, and therefore Koskenniemi argues
that the constitutional mindset is not a set of solutions, but a method for
finding a political solution on the terrain of the rule of law. Indeed, given

their perfectly understandable preference for the regulation of international society through legal instruments, it should be no surprise that (international) lawyers are often drawn towards constitutional solutions (Schwöbel 2012). So, for instance, if one of the key difficulties confronted by any putative global constitution is the manner in which its regulatory intent is perceived, those analysts advocating the recognition and expansion of global administrative law believe they have a solution: global administrative law bootstraps global governance and is drawn into its operation by the recognition of the need to ensure the global constitution's practices are legitimate and acceptable to those that it seeks to regulate, and this is achieved by its relationship with the norm of the rule of law.

This is a dialectical relationship: developments in global administrative law contribute to the consolidation of global constitutionalism while these moves to solidify (global) constitutional elements serve to draw more global administrative legal practices into the regulatory realm so constituted (Kuo 2011, pp. 70–1). Thus, as Ming-Sung Kuo concludes:

> global administrative law functionally provides the fundamental normative principles underpinning the operation of global governance. Specifically, the fundamental principles at the core of global administrative law are aimed at bolstering the values of due process transparency and accountability which are central to the relationship between modern administration and citizens in a constitutional order. (Kuo 2011, p. 79)

The practices and norms of the rule of law that underpin the idea of global constitutionalism are provided not directly through the (global) constitutional settlement itself but rather through the development of a global administrative law. That is to say,

> [global constitutionalism] underpinned by global administrative law rests on the routine operation of functional systems and *the everyday adoption of traditional rule-of-law virtues by players in the process of global governance without reference to another external source of ultimate authority such as the people.* (Kuo 2011, p. 93, emphasis added)

These 'traditional rule-of-law virtues' are the aspects of the global common sense of the rule of law I have been concerned with, and provide a non-politicized legitimization of the practices of administrative law in and about the constitutionalized elements of global governance. If what is evident in the global system is a series of parallel constitutions for different global institutions, then the common acceptance of the rule of law as articulated through global administrative law underpins any claim for the general benefit of expanding the scope and reach of constitutional forms of regulation.

Once established, any supranational constitution may become more than the sum of its parts (as the EU has become); while deriving its initial moment of establishment from a treaty agreement, the politico-legal principles encompassed in the constitution are responsive to the wider normative values it encompasses *qua* constitution (including the notion of the rule of law at its centre) (Kumm 2010, p. 214). The question remains whether such a practice-based conception of constitutionalism is sufficient to maintain its political justification as a mechanism/system of global governance. Certainly, in the end any account of constitutionalism (or the process of constitutionalization) requires there to be some minimum level of organization of the political realm by legal means; there needs to be some level of 'accumulated facts'. However, Isiksel warns that the 'easy resort to constitutional terminology . . . can result in dignifying every legal and quasi-legal entity in the supranational context with the constitutional label' (Isiksel 2012, p. 103). Thus, it should be of little surprise that the WTO is presented as a key case of the role and importance of global constitutionalism both by supporters and critics, given both its legal pretensions and its lack of any developed system of democratic legitimation that one might demand of a 'normal' constitutional body; it is to this case we now turn.

## THE WTO AND GLOBAL CONSTITUTIONALIZATION

It is generally accepted in studies of global political economy that the international trade regime is among the most legalized realms of global politics, if not *the* most legalized, due to the establishment of the WTO in 1995. What makes the WTO such an important innovation is that unlike its predecessor (the General Agreement on Tariffs and Trade – GATT), which was essentially a treaty and a secretariat with little or no enforcement capacity, the WTO through its powerful and non-sectorally specific dispute settlement mechanism (DSM) has the capacity to facilitate sanctions where its rules have been broken. The mechanism allows sanctions to be enacted in different sectors from that which the complaint has been made (although limited in scale by the amount of 'damage' claimed) once the Appellate Body has decided a case. Moreover, unlike the GATT, members of the WTO make a 'single undertaking' that means they cannot pick and choose which elements of international trade regulation they will abide by (Bernauer et al. 2012, p. 487). It is these innovations, the result of the Uruguay Round of trade negotiations, that have led to such interest in the manner in which the WTO has shaped (and continues to shape) the global system of trade.

Within the WTO's governance structure three councils – for goods, for intellectual property and for services – are spaces where the norms encompassed in the agreement can be both communicated and elaborated (or refined), allowing discussion of diversity in understanding among members' trade diplomats and the (attempted) resolution of tensions between differing interpretations of the basic principles of the overall trade agreement(s). Alongside these general councils, around 35 other committees are constantly working to develop understandings, norms and sub-agreements to facilitate the practice of trade relations overseen by the WTO. Andrew Lang and Joanne Scott (2009) have referred to this network of meetings and interactions as the 'hidden world of WTO governance'; hidden in the sense that accounts of the WTO tend to assume much greater unity and centralization at the organization, and often seek to present its rules as a (singular) constitution for world trade. Given that the negotiators during the Uruguay Round clearly intended the WTO to encompass some constitutional practices, key among which is the notion of the organization having 'something like' a judiciary (Matsushita 2012, p. 527), this relatively common approach is hardly outlandish nor completely mistaken (whatever views one might have about the application of such constitutional perspectives to a sectoral organization).

Debates about whether the WTO is developing a global constitution therefore often hinge on whether proponents wish to defend the global (technical) role of the organization or argue that it is a membership organization at least formally controlled by (and serving the needs of) its members (Lawrence 2013, p. 75). Significant debates are also concerned with the constitutional character (or otherwise) of the international trade law overseen by the organization, and as such whether it is equal to or above other elements of international law (Lawrence 2013, p. 85). An appeal to constitutionalism also reflects the desire of those who support the WTO's work in furthering free trade to provide the organization with a more solid legal and non-political basis for its interventions in the global political economy (Buchanan 2012, p. 8). Nevertheless, Jeffrey Dunoff has argued that while the WTO might potentially become a constitutional body, in its current form it falls too short of what would normally be required. For Dunoff, the discourse of constitutionalism has proved attractive to those working on WTO politics due to an anxiety about the place and legitimacy of international law in international (or global) politics in general (Dunoff 2009). Indeed, the counter-posing of constitution (the WTO) with pluralism (continued sovereignty over trade relations) is a reflection of common enough trope of unity against fragmentation (Buchanan 2012, p. 14), and as such reflects the implicit unitary logic of the rule of law.

The use of constitutional language may create a positive feedback loop when the analytical standpoint further entrenches constitutional-like interpretation and practice, which is then (re)identified to further buttress the constitutional claim (Kill 2011, p. 69). By appealing to the idea of constitutionalism, supporters of the WTO are seeking to link the WTO to a more general political commitment to the rule of law by states who have joined the organization and thus might be regarded as the constituent powers who have through the agreement constrained their actions. Thus, there is considerable narrative power in the presentation of the WTO as a constitutional organization reflecting (implicitly or explicitly) the norm(s) of the rule of law. There is also considerable value to the WTO in presenting itself as constitutional and thereby distancing itself from political debates about the application of its regulations and litigation. In Jens Mortensen's terms, when the WTO looks in the mirror (Mortensen 2012), it sees itself as a constitutional body encompassing not politics or ideologies about free trade but rather a neutral arbiter over a settled and legitimate constitution furthering the transcendent value of free trade via technical support for the constitutional principles it has not settled for itself.

The relationship between WTO law and the rest of international law is another vexed issue in the WTO's claimed constitutional character, and is certainly more complex than some attempts to privilege the WTO's rules might imply through claims of constitutionalism. Joost Pauwelyn has argued at some length that the law that can be applied in WTO dispute panels and in the Appellate Body is not limited to intra-WTO law. Rather, by virtue of the WTO legal regime's place within the complex of international law, 'a defendant should be allowed to invoke non-WTO rules as justification for breach of WTO rules, even if the WTO treaty itself does not offer such justification (say, with respect to human rights) . . . [and more importantly] non-WTO rules may actually apply before a WTO panel and overrule WTO rules' (Pauwelyn 2001, p. 577, 2003, *passim*). The assumption that WTO law should be privileged is therefore a misconception of the WTO's relation with the general body of international law but one that is sometimes asserted by the WTO's legal representatives and those wishing to stress the legitimacy of the promotion of free trade as a global value. In fact, a wide range of other international law finds its way into judgments and litigation so that the impact of these legal instruments is sometimes widened and enhanced by their inclusion in WTO litigation (Flett 2012). International trade litigation is part of a complex and dynamic relationship with other aspects of international law and other treaties/undertakings. Therefore, it would seem clear that the WTO agreement(s) cannot be taken as a global constitution, as perhaps the UN Charter might be. However, this is not to say that it may not operate in a constitutional manner, and indeed this is how its work is often understood.

It is the narrow focus on trade that may actually allow the organization to be regarded as constitutional. Isiksel, in defending the term 'constitutional' from the political dilution that he identifies across global politics, proposes a relaxed (and less fully constitutional) definition; a 'functional constitutionalism'. This characterizes legal regimes as functional constitutions when they have a limited scope, and clear purpose (or telos in his terms), but lack the wider political aspects expected of modern constitutions (primarily universalism and democratic structures), while clearly exhibiting the technical forms often adopted by constitutional entities (Isiksel 2012; cf. Marks 2000). This separates the argument about the constitutionalization of international trade from the usual appeals to state or municipal constitutionalism that either find the WTO wanting or conclude by recommending a line of future convergence with such forms (Buchanan 2012, p. 6). This (thinner) notion of constitutionalism has some parallels with the procedural or thin norm of the rule of law discussed in Chapter 2. Moreover, this more 'moderate' position on constitutionalization avoids the implication of any uniform world constitution or putative world state (Peters 2009b, p. 404). In this sense, by removing some of the more 'political' elements a 'thin constitutionalism' can be formulated allowing the WTO to be regarded as fulfilling the (reduced) criteria for recognition.

Looking at these thinner elements, the establishment of the WTO specifically reoriented international trade politics from a realm of negotiated treaty making (legislative politics) to the realm of the court (judicial politics). To a large extent, this is due to the legislative deadlock that has followed on from the initial moment of constitutional settlement represented by the final act of the Uruguay Round. In this, we can see a form of constitutionalism: the WTO's Appellate Body (a court-like arrangement by which judges review cases submitted by WTO members) now makes law through filing gaps (by interpretation of the WTO's statutes or, we might say, constitution) and clarifying ambiguities in the agreement itself. This lawmaking goes as far as formalizing and settling issues where the language of the original agreement(s) had been left vague precisely because agreement could not be reached (Goldstein and Steinberg 2009, pp. 228–30; Matsushita 2012, pp. 528–9). As might be expected, in the majority of cases the Appellate Body decides in favour of moves towards freer trade (Goldstein and Steinberg 2009, p. 235). Nevertheless, although there have been at least two major attempts to revise the DSM, partly focused on reducing the ability of the Appellate Body to continue to fill the gaps it perceives in the WTO's agreement(s), and also an attempt to reduce the relative autonomy of the judges themselves, the overall mechanism retains substantial support from WTO members and as such reform is unlikely soon (Bernauer et al. 2012, p. 502). This process appeals to the rule of law (a judicial process linked to a constitutional settlement) and is dependent on the use of sanctions through the DSM to enforce decisions. However, the Appellate Body, on some analyses, has almost unlimited power, with a lack within the WTO of constitutional check mechanisms that might constrain an activist group of judges in a similar domestic constitutional system (Matsushita 2012, p. 530), not least of all due to the need for consensus among the members to overthrow a decision (unlikely as this would have to include the 'winner' in any specific case).

This becomes increasingly important to members if the (claimed) constitutional character of the WTO means that its decisions and law may seek to overrule domestic legislation. Certainly, the ECJ has repeatedly maintained that the laws of the WTO and judgements within the DSM have no direct effect on European states (Cottier 2012, p. 616). Likewise, elsewhere (for example, in China or the USA) the direct effect of the legal practices of the WTO and the Appellate Body have been legislatively constrained. Other countries (for example, Switzerland) have been more flexible, allowing direct effect in some circumstances but still regarding a general undertaking to allow judgements at the WTO to take a direct effect on national practices as untenable (Cottier 2012, p. 619). The denial of direct effect (that is to say, any laws and decisions are not self-executing, and need to be enacted by domestic legislatures and/or courts) marks the key limit of any constitutional pretensions that analysts and commentators may have for the WTO.

This also means that unlike other (true?) constitutions there can be no WTO-based judicial review of law or actions in members' states and as such the claim for a constitutional character is further undermined, but also returns the argument to the issue of whether a functional constitutionalism produces legal arrangements that are properly constitutional.[7] Interestingly, William Magnuson, having reviewed the Appellate Body's rulings, argues that the resort to narrowly textural approaches to interpreting and applying WTO provisions, alongside the attempt to engage and change domestic political decisions and conversely an increasingly permissive attitude to how infringing measures might be brought into compliance, can all be understood as a response by the judges to claims that the WTO is developing a (global) constitution. That is to say, the Appellate Body 'has developed an interpretive approach that hews closely to the text

---

[7] This is, however, less easily asserted in the realm of intellectual property rights, where the WTO's Appellate Body can reach into the state to assess the acceptability of domestic legislation (rather than only those rules applicable to cross-border trade) – see May (2010).

of the treaty with little reference to its context or structure in conscious repudiation of constitutional understandings of the treaty' (Magnuson 2010, p. 152). As this suggests, the question of the constitutional character of the WTO's agreements is by no means settled nor accepted even within the organization. While the Appellate Body continues to draw on narrowly textural interpretations, it lessens its reliance on the rule of law (in constitutional terms), relying rather on the general understanding that states will keep the agreements they have made in the international arena (*pacta sunt servanda*). In the terms that I have been using, this exhibits a preference for a thinner reading of the rule of law than those who stress a more developed constitutional character of the WTO.

Finally, the debates about the constitutional character of the WTO are directly related to how the organization can be seen to reflect the commitment to the rule of law. If it is effectively constitutional, then there is an interesting issue about whose rights might be protected; reflecting the rule of law (constitutionalism's founding norm) the WTO is at least partly seeking to establish individual rights to market freedom at the global level. Eva Hartmann argues that the WTO, and its DSM specifically, is

> not a simple device in the hands of the powerful. It establishes a new mode of societalisation [*sic*] at [the] global level, providing individuals the opportunity to claim their rights and by doing so to inscribe themselves into the global hegemonic order. (Hartmann 2011, p. 567)

That is to say, the DSM by opening up trade relations to complaints by those that international trade affects (albeit mediated through state trade teams) constitutes complainants as part of the globalized regulatory realm that the WTO has established. As Kill describes it, this 'rights-based' constitutionalism has the impact of reducing (if enacted) the ability of states to respond to democratic accountability, by removing certain norms (around the individual economic actor) from national deliberation and making them part of the (trade) constitution's key values it is intended to protect and foster (Kill 2011, p. 117). It is this direction of critical analysis that has prompted a very different approach to understanding global constitutionalism at the WTO and more widely.

## GLOBAL CONSTITUTIONALISM AS NEOLIBERALIZATION

The above discussion suggests that in many ways the notion of constitutionalism that is invoked in much of the 'positive' literature has a relatively thin notion of its political value and its attendant place in the rule of law. This has led to a preference in some quarters for the term 'constitutionalization', suggesting not so much the establishment of a fully political constitution, but a continuing process of approach towards such a political value (Krisch 2010, p. 58). It is exactly the thinness of the constitutional norms in these developments that has attracted a critique that seeks to unmask the 'real' motives behind these developments. For instance, in David Schneiderman's interpretation of this 'new constitutionalism', the purpose of these legal moves is to 'freeze politics and inhibit the imagination of alternative futures . . . [it] inhibits the possibilities for political action by enacting binding constraints, in the form of general legal principles, on the ability of states to intervene in the market' (Schneiderman 2008, p. 208). Here, the constitution is intended to appeal to the technical status of the rule of law and by doing so depoliticize its shaping of the range of available economic policy. Likewise, Rachel Turner has suggested that neoliberals have 'attempted to construct a constitutional discourse that places strict limitations on politics', although in itself this is a political move (Turner 2008, p. 54). Only those controls and regulations that are directly related to market activity are fully enacted, and thus at the global level, as Michael Allen points out:

> To the extent that the framework of rules for the protection and governance of investment and trade are more coherent, universal and enforceable through market sanctions, this is tantamount to a privileging of property rights over human and ecological rights in the emerging globalist constitutionalism. (Allen 2004, p. 347)

For its critics, therefore, this form of constitutionalism does not fulfil the requirements to be regarded as constitutional that obtain in the domestic political arena.

Stephen Gill has developed one of the most influential critical accounts of this form of constitutionalism. At the centre of his analysis of the 'new constitutionalism' is the suggestion that globalization has involved the establishment of a globalized 'market civilization'. This is the latest phase of the expansion of a neoliberal capitalism that finds its origins in the nineteenth-century international system, or (domestically) further back with the nascent liberal state that emerged in Britain in the seventeenth century (Gill 1998, pp. 27–9, 2003, p. 118). Although this is a complex process that has a number of important facets, one of its central elements is the increasing marketization of social relations. Furthermore, drawing from Foucault, Gill sees this process as being furthered and supported by a set of 'disciplinary practices' (Gill 2003, p. 130), of which a key element is the use of legal institutions to structure and shape both state and international political forms of regulation and governance. Gill defines this 'new constitutionalism' as

> a macro-political dimension of the process whereby the nature and purpose of the public sphere in the OECD has been redefined in a more globalized and abstract frame of reference . . . [It is] the political project of attempting to make transnational liberalism, and if possible liberal democratic, the sole model for future development. (Gill 2003, pp. 131–2)
>
> It mandates a particular set of state policies geared to maintaining business confidence through the delivery of a consistent and credible climate for investment and thus for the accumulation of capital . . . It stresses the rule of law . . . [and expands] state activity to provide greater legal and other protections for business. (Gill 1998, p. 38)
>
> [and] involves *pre-commitment mechanisms* to lock in not only present governments and citizens into the reforms, but more fundamentally to prevent *future* governments from undoing the reforms. In this way its central purpose is to reconstruct the political and legal terms through which governance and accountability operate not only in the near term, but also in the longer run. (Bakker and Gill 2003, p. 30, emphasis in original)

Emphasizing 'market efficiency; discipline and confidence; economic policy credibility and consistency; and limitation[s] on democratic decision-making processes' this new discipline establishes 'binding constraints' on fiscal and economic policy (Gill 2003, p. 132). Crucially, this 'new constitutionalism' seeks to confer privileged rights of citizenship on global corporate capital, and establish mechanisms by which the commitment to these values is embedded in current and future political practice.

As Gill notes, 'traditional notions of constitutionalism are associated with political rights, obligations and freedoms, and procedures that give an institutional form to the state' (Gill 2003, p. 132). Although this new constitutionalism is progressed at the global level, rather than focusing on the rights and obligations of the global citizenry as relating to some form of globalized governing body (or bodies), it is concerned with a much smaller group: global capital and its operating agents, corporations (both national and multinational). A key aspect of this constitutionalism is to hold the political and economic realms separate for the purposes of (globalized) governance, ensuring that the economic remains uncontaminated by the political. Here, the rule of law stands between the political and the economic: markets are facilitated by the legal structures of property, contract and other laws. Politics can add to these laws but their basic components represent the rule of law not of politics, the latter of which is limited to amending laws that deal with the effects of these rules: problems such as 'market failure'. In this sense, the 'pre-commitment' to the rule of law limits and shapes any subsequent reformist dynamic.

The national governance practices that are promoted as 'benchmarks' or 'best practice' by the World Bank, as discussed earlier, support this constitutional settlement in favour of property rights, contract law and other constitutional elements by constraining political impulses against such laws as undermining the rule of law (Gill 1998, pp. 32ff.). Although the World Bank emphasizes both judicial independence and the separation of powers as good constitutional practice, the Bank also identifies a key third 'external' 'mechanism of restraint'. As Gill notes, the Bank suggests that international agreements help states 'strengthen commitments' by raising the (international) political costs of policy reversal; states risk international censure for breaking international law, and domestic laws that are part of the standard legal structures of liberal democracy.

At the centre of this notion of 'new constitutionalism', therefore, is the manner in which specific forms of capitalist social relations are normalized through multilateral agreements on the rights of property owners and investors, and the institutionalization in domestic legislation of these rights. Although requiring the recognition and protection of non-national property, requiring unrestricted access to national markets and establishing compensation ('damages') for state actions that impede these rights, such benefits are all set out in supposedly neutral, technical, trading and investment agreements, most obviously those associated with the WTO. These are then presented as local manifestations of the norm of the rule of law: these rights have been established via a legitimate constitutional/ legislative process, and as such are tied up with a commitment to the rule of law, and are abstracted out of the political realm, if not totally then to a large extent.

It is also interesting to note that this notion of constitutionalization is not limited to Gill's critique; as I have already indicated, a number of scholars have set out the current political economy of the WTO as a mode of constitutionalism (in addition to those cited above, see also Cass 2005; Petersman 2002).[8] Here, unlike Gill's critique, the rule of law and its consolidation through a formal constitution are presented not as the operations of power to shape the political economy but rather as a legal arena in which conflicts can be helpfully ameliorated and adjudicated. However, this use of the notion of law reflects structural power (to use Strange's term) in the political economy, as political power is not actuated through direct political influence or force, but rather appeals to the norm of the rule of law: how could expropriation of property be just (it is after all

---

[8] Neither should Gill's approach to 'constitutionalism' be confused with the sort of constitutional political economy that draws its inspiration from James Buchanan and Frederick Hayek. For a discussion of this approach see Vanberg (2005).

theft!)? Opening markets allows competition to bring efficiency which, by definition, is socially valuable, and indeed in Petersman's case is directly linked to a putative human right to trade. However, Deborah Cass concludes her study of constitutional developments at the WTO by arguing for an approach she terms 'trading democracy', which would put development at the forefront of the concerns of the WTO (Cass 2005, pp. 242–3). Here, the notion of constitutions as potentially empowering a democratic polity is foregrounded, rather than Gill's argument that the constitution of the WTO can only be an artefact of sectional political economic power.

However, for Gill, these legal mechanisms (and these arguments made to support them) are intended to shield global capital from local, popular democracy (threats 'from below'), to insulate property rights from either democratic or oligarchic interference (Gill 1998, pp. 25, 30). What is hidden by the appeal and commitment to the rule of law is the manner in which powerful (class) interests shape the forms of political economic relations that *can* be established. His approach recognizes that the more general legal context underpins political economic power and hegemony, even as disputes and conflicts play out within the limited field this legal system maps out within the scope of the rule of law and its constitutional articulation. If hegemony in Gill's analysis (following Antonio Gramsci) is about the construction of a common sense as uncontroversial (at the very same time that it serves and privileges the interests of a specific class or interest), then 'new constitutionalism' by establishing a 'pre-commitment' to the rule of law (in its Western particularity) as the *sine qua non* of development at the global level (or a 'killer ap' of 'civilization' in Niall Ferguson's account) achieves the normalization of a skewered and exploitative global system.

In this critical perspective, the new constitutionalism not only shapes and develops political structures to advantage certain groups/interests, it also limits the modes of political engagement to the 'constitutional' and seeks to limit the ability of national governments to make laws unwelcome to global corporations and investors in the economic realm (Turner 2008, p. 54). Criticism and resistance are channelled into the forms of amendment and accountability that are established within the constitution(s). Those forms of political engagement that fall outside are rendered illegal or at least illegitimate, while those that conform to the rule of law's strictures about process and legality may be constrained in the range of alternatives that can be offered: hence, an alternative settlement that seeks not to respect certain classes of property rights (based perhaps on the basis of nationality of owner) falls foul of the well-established (sub-)norm of equal treatment by the law.

Gavin Anderson suggests that the key difference between these two discussions of constitutionalism is that while mainstream constitutional-ism seeks to

> put the constitutional framework out of the bounds of political debate, with the effect of further insulating its protection of private power, new constitutional-ism puts the framework itself in the spotlight with a view to stimulating debate on the legitimacy of private power. In other words, new constitutionalism gives 'constitution' the political charge which [the former approach] seeks to diffuse. (Anderson 2005, p. 115)

The critical approach to constitutionalism sees it as an elite project (Hartmann 2011, p. 565), and certainly for Gill this reflects the processes of neoliberalization that are driven forward by interests that he would define as related to a transnational capital class.

Thus, the point of constitutionalism is to freeze politics as it is, and commit future generations to our judgements about the acceptable shape of legality, ensuring they are less able to transcend politics than we are/were. Of course, this then means that efforts to adapt to political and social change are moved to the margins, leading not to the consolida-tion of law envisaged by constitutionalists but rather to the potential for politics (responding to new needs) having to work around the existing constitution, paradoxically producing the very fragmentation of law the constitution was intended to curtail in the first place (Klabbers 2004)! Andrei Marmor suggests that this is the 'Ulysses strategy'; as is well known in the myth, Ulysses

> commanded that he be tied to the ship's mast, and crucially, commanded his subordinates to *disregard his commands in the future*, when the sirens' influence might curtail his judgment, knowing in advance that his judgment at that future time, under the influence of the sirens, was not to be trusted. (Marmor 2007, p. 97)

Here, the sirens represent democratic pressures and influences that would be unwelcome to the political project of the constitution's drafters. The problem of course is that given its longevity it is not themselves the draft-ers are tying to the mast but rather their political successors, and secondly, unlike Ulysses, the drafter cannot be sure of what the future holds.

However, even this critique may miss a significant aspect of the deploy-ment of the rule of law; the rule of law itself, whatever its shortcomings, still offers structure and at least a patina of values that can be appealed to by non-elites when seeking justice or recompense. Thus, Judy Fudge has argued from a position broadly sympathetic to Gill's that it remains pos-sible, however, to see positive good from the process of making constitu-tions; for her, the example of the moves towards a European constitutional settlement for labour rights (albeit faltering and at times unbalanced) suggest that this can be a dialectical process (Fudge deploys Karl Polanyi's notion of the 'double movement'). Here, pressures on labour have been refracted through a judicial process protecting human rights to ensure that a more constitutional approach to labour rights has (at least, partially) protected labour (workers) in key transnational disputes (Fudge 2011). Indeed, one of the key questions prompted by the discussion of the political project of cosmopolitan democracy has been how such non-state political groupings can influence or shape international law; how is democratic inclusion achieved in the international realm (Marks 2000, pp. 101–20)? If the rule of law at the global level requires a global constitution, then given the link to democracy, the need for a form of cosmopolitan democracy to be developed may be crucial to its legitimacy.

Moreover, if as many argue participatory democracy is not feasible at a global scale, nevertheless 'contestatory democracy' is (Peters 2009a, p. 270). Here, those outside states' governments and international structures of governance must have available to them the open and clear mechanisms of contestation. Although global civil society's engagement with global governance and international law has been mostly contestatory in character, their democratic credentials are not firmly established (even if their political heft is increasing). Making these mechanisms available, however, does not require their institutionalization; rather, it requires the recognition and acceptance of their legitimacy. Interestingly, as Anne Peters has pointed out, the discussion of 'constitutionalization'

> unveils precisely those deficits by introducing the constitutional vocabulary [and] although constitutionalism is a value-loaded concept, it is nevertheless a legal approach in which consideration for the rule of law in a formal sense, for legal stability and predictability, plays a part and which acknowledges that legality itself can engender a type of legitimacy. (Peters 2009b, p. 409)

And by introducing this particular discourse, these claims also highlight the history of constitutional elements that have promoted democratic involvement in governance. Given the difficulty of scale for international constitution(s) one of the ways that the claim that there is a formal lack of (direct) democratic deliberation can be resolved is to suggest that instead of focusing on legitimacy derived from electoral process, for pragmatic reasons, global constitutional politics needs to be more concerned with ensuring an enhanced representation by (global) civil societal actors and groups (Kumm 2009, p. 296). If these 'representatives' are limited (as they frequently are) to insider groups, then we must be clear about what mechanisms of influence remain for those with non-mainstream positions to articulate.

Conversely, Petra Dobner suggests that responses to the democratic shortcomings of global constitutionalism that argue that there is sufficient agreement on the basics (here including most importantly the rule of law and human rights) for the demos' support to be invoked cannot legitimately replace direct involvement with such inferences of support and remain legitimately constitutional in their politics (Dobner 2010, p. 150). If democracy remains the means through which legal systems are ultimately rendered legitimate (and thereby most effective), the shortcomings of democracy at the global level are likely to prove a major problem for any global constitutional settlement (Dobner 2010, p. 155) even if the underpinning norm of the rule of law is accepted and widely held (in itself and an issue that requires some discussion – see next chapter). For Dobner, the 'neglect of democracy does not come as a natural force; it is a consequence of a shift in attention and valuation from legitimacy to efficiency, from political to legal constitutionalism, from democracy to legal technocracy' (Dobner 2010, p. 161). Thus, the question of a global constitution cannot avoid the question of constituent power noted at the start of this chapter. Certainly, an appeal to the rule of law allows the process and structures to gain legitimacy, but although this is buttressed by the rule of law's ability to act as a common sense of global politics, this is only likely to be an acceptable ground for expanding the scope and reach of constitutions if it is a thicker understanding of the norm that is used. However, as Gill's critique makes clear, any normative cluster around the thicker rule of law that is utilized is also likely to encounter the argument that the values so freighted are partial and favour specific politics, elites or interests.

## CONCLUSION

Any discussion of constitutionalism in global politics can at the very least be inferred to be taking a position on the manner in which social relations are constituted by the regulatory and governance structures that are being constitutionalized by the processes and actors identified in such analyses. That is to say, before there can be any move to develop a constitution there must be some commitment to the more general norm of the rule of law. Any society that encompasses the rule of law also constitutes social relations in certain ways and whether these are acceptable (or legitimate) at a specific point in time is a political (or perhaps political-ethical) issue of some importance. Certainly, some might argue that the EU has in the last decades increasingly constituted Europeans as consumers rather than citizens (Chadwick and May 2003; Haltern 2003) and indeed this would be broadly one aspect of the more general criticism set out by Gill. Others have suggested that the global system is far too varied, multifaceted and complex to support in any meaningful manner a single constitutional settlement and as such only a pluralist alternative can be legitimate if the system is to move beyond a history of domination and hegemony of external norms. However, this then suggests that the norm of the rule of law is compromised, or rendered problematic, by a pluralist rather than constitutionalist settlement within global politics (Krisch 2010, pp. 276–85). Thus, in the pluralist critique of (global) constitutionalism, the rule of law is rendered not a founding norm but a political value that competes (contests) with others in the governance of a plural society. This view of the rule of law works against its characteristic common sense depiction, and this rejection of essentialism – the dismissal of the position that there is just one rule of law – is the subject of the next chapter.

# 7. One rule of law or many? Internal and external challenges to the rule of law

[L]aws will be self-defeating when they undermine social norms whose maintenance turns out to be necessary to make those very laws effective. (Pildes 1996, p. 2058)

[F]oreign national concepts may be inconsistent with the pre-existing legal and social concepts in the law-receiving country. (Pistor 2002, pp. 106, 109)

Between 1988 and 1998 the Chinese economy went from half the size of Russia's to twice its size, Russia of course being a country famous for largely following the advice of American economists. (Upham 2009, p. 591)

In the previous chapter's discussion, the question of the plurality of perceptions of the rule of law and the impact this would have on a global constitution lay behind much of the discussion even if this was not always explicit. I now take up this issue to examine the challenges presented to the dominant (Westernized) idea of the rule of law by different perceptions of what the norm might entail (or include), or indeed whether there can be a single norm of the rule of law in a global society made up of widely varying societies with very different histories. Challenges to the rule of law might be broadly seen as coming from within the particular rule of law system itself – which I will discuss as civil disobedience – or from the tension between different rule(s) of law, with their own norms of legality, which is often identified as 'legal pluralism'. For ease, I call these 'internal' and 'external' challenges to the rule of law. Let me also be clear: these forms of challenge are different not least of all as civil disobedience (as conceived below) is directly and positively focused on the rule of law, while the challenge that stems from legal pluralism is a form of structural tension between contending 'understandings' of the very character, practice(s) and promise of systems that we might collectively recognize as (some sort of) law.

Given this book's overall focus on common sense and the ideational drivers to political change, in the discussion of civil disobedience that I develop below, I am also seeking to explore some of the everyday behavioural aspects of the (re)production of the rule of law, which parallel the discussion of the 'animal spirits' in Chapter 5. Following Leonard Seabrooke, and focusing on the role of legitimation, I am looking at 'how actors, often non-elite actors, generate the social sources of change rather than waiting for elites to tell them what to do' (Seabrooke 2010, p. 78; see also Ewick and Silbey 1998). In what Seabrooke calls 'everyday politics', 'non-elites are able to decide incrementally to participate or withdraw from institutions, providing either confirmation or challenges to elites who have designed and created institutions through material or ideational power games' (Seabrooke 2010, p. 88). My analysis of the rule of law, focused as it is on perception of the norms as a common sense and thereby its political legitimacy, therefore, is directly concerned with such everyday politics of the rule of law. These everyday politics are patterned either by an acceptance of the rule of law as a legitimate norm of (social) behavioural guidance, as it is presented under its own terms (Archer's commonality), or as a site of argument and dispute, ranging from the individual to the collective (Archer's contestation). To some extent it is difficult to capture the individual as critic of the rule of law, but contestation becomes visible when (even relatively small) groups embark on campaigns of civil disobedience, and therefore this chapter starts with this issue. Afterwards, I examine whether legal pluralism helps us understand the contested character of the rule of law in the global realm and where the differences over the term (and its normative enaction) might lie. Thus, while the two parts of this chapter are very differently focused, they come together through my concern to recognize challenges to the rule of law and how these engage its common sense.

As we have seen, the rule of law is generally presented in contemporary political discourse as a social and public good: it is commonly seen as in itself (partly) constitutive of the good society. This means that any claim that a particular political practice is bounded by the rule of law is an attempt to legitimate and justify political action(s), even though the term's continuing indeterminacy allows it to be claimed (often) by all sides in disputes. Indeed, political disagreements frequently involve the depiction of a tension between an (imagined) rule of law and the practice of the rule of law as found: the notion of the rule of law is therefore a value against which actual governance may be compared for political reasons. While the rule of law has established legislative modes of review and reform, there are also extra-legal practices that help amend the rule of law on the basis of identifying a problem with the current legal settlement, and it to these 'internal' challenges that I turn first.

# CONTESTING THE RULE OF LAW FROM WITHIN: CIVIL DISOBEDIENCE

To develop my argument, I am going to use a relatively narrow definition of civil disobedience, one focused on activity directed at changing the law, and where its justification is based on either the appeal to a higher law (natural law, justice or some other politico-legal value) or by utilitarian arguments of the greater or common good in the cause of amending laws themselves.[1] Civil disobedience is directly related to the rule of law as the challenge it presents is seldom to the whole legal system, but rather seeks to hold the rule of law (in its everyday practice) to the standards that a (perhaps) idealized perception of the rule of law expects. Thus, individuals taking part in acts of civil disobedience often have their own view of the rule of law, frequently an instinctive notion rather than one informed by an extensive knowledge of jurisprudence, against which they hold the actual legal practices of society and find them wanting.

Certainly, the argument that recognizing *any* justification for civil disobedience may sap the strength of the rule of law more generally is not without its adherents,[2] but public or collective (and symbolic) illegality is widely regarded as exhibiting a political character when self-defined as principled behaviour, even if private illegality is less easily so characterized. The question of the 'quality of opinion' may also be important in making this assessment (Arendt 1973, p. 62): who are those conducting civil disobedience, and can their politico-legal demands be safely ignored or not? There might be some shading here of course: the robbing of banks might be taken by extreme anti-capitalists to be civil disobedience (to fund their righteous activity) rather than merely criminal activity, although it is unlikely the wider population, the police or courts would agree. Likewise, private refusal to pay taxes may indicate disobedience related to governmental spending policy, although again such judgement may depend on the character of those refusing to pay, and the manner in which such refusal is articulated. A principled refusal to pay tax is (politically) not the same as tax evasion; the intent is different, even if the actions are similar.

Leaving aside these potential grey areas, I will follow John Brenkman's useful characterization: civil disobedience is 'a temporary, disciplined crossing of the boundary of lawfulness for the purpose of achieving something *on behalf of* the rule of law, that cannot, in the judgment of those taking action, be accomplished by merely obeying the law' (Brenkman

---

[1] See Acton (1956 [1969]) for a discussion of these various forms of justification.
[2] See Singer (1974, part one) for an examination of this position.

2007, p. 75, fn 23, emphasis in original). This is a common trope of opposition movements: formal legal rules may need to be broken or ignored, to serve a different conception of legality; *a universal legality can be served by particular illegality*. The justification of politically focused illegality, however, can never be finally settled and thus codified: there can be no legal 'right' to civil disobedience as this itself renders civil disobediences non-disobedient (Raz 1979b [1991], p. 168). Civil disobedience is always exceptional in legal terms even when seen as an acceptable mode of making a political point.[3]

Although there can be no legal 'right' to civil disobedience, Ronald Dworkin suggested that most commentators on legal affairs accept to various degrees the notion that while we have a moral duty to obey and follow the law, 'this duty cannot be an absolute duty, because even a society that is in principle just may produce unjust laws and policies, and a man [*sic*] has duties other than his duties to the state' (Dworkin 1978, p. 186). Individuals may hold beliefs as regards an acceptable morality that are contradicted by specific laws, and where personal (in Dworkin's term: 'honest') convictions are strongly held, there is a recognition that people may act on these beliefs but face the (legal) consequences. However, a confusion arises when the word 'right' is introduced: in its strong sense, a right to act on these convictions would imply that the state does not have a right to halt such actions (where they are driven by honestly held convictions); conversely, in the sense of 'right' as acceptable or correct, we might conclude that while the state is right to prosecute the illegality, the individual is right to draw public attention to the contradiction between a law and their strongly held moral position (Dworkin 1978, p. 190). This issue may be easier to resolve where formal constitutions are in place, as an appeal to a particular interpretation of 'fundamental rights' encapsulated by a general legal document (a Bill of Rights, for instance) is a key aspect of breaking the law in support of the wider rule of law (Dworkin 1978, pp. 206–22). Where there is no Bill of Rights or formal constitution any wider conception of the moral content of the rule of law may be subject to some disagreement. That said, in the UK the Human Rights Act (1998) has made the argument that such principles are a key element of the rule of law much easier (as the European Convention has done so across the EU) (Bingham 2010, pp. 66–84), and has ensured that any appeal to such principles is considerably easier to maintain as a defence for action.

---

[3] There is a significant debate about a 'moral' right of civil disobedience, with the question of the form of regime in which disobedience is acted playing a major role in differentiating the legitimacy of such a right – see the overview in Brownlee (2009). Here, as I am more interested in the role civil disobedience plays vis-à-vis the rule of law, I leave this issue to one side and merely follow Dworkin's argument (see next paragraph).

This suggests two questions. Firstly, what overriding moral rights might be regarded as an acceptable basis for civil disobedience? Secondly, once the law has been broken how does the state decide between recognizing illegality as a prompt to re-examine the particular law(s) subject to such political actions and merely dismissing such actions as criminal? A constitution may help resolve the first question, but more generally human rights and wider (or substantive) definitions of the requirements of the rule of law are often appealed to when formal law and moral-political convictions are in tension. For instance, justification for some acts of civil disobedience can involve an appeal to the 'Nuremberg principles'. Under Article 6 of the London Charter, through which the notion of war crimes was introduced into international law, and enacted at Nuremberg in the first instance, individuals as well as policy makers are held responsible for the planning and waging of war in contravention of specific treaties or international law more generally (Cohan 2007, p. 166). Here, civil disobedience may break local laws, but in the service of preventing the contravention of international laws, or the commission of an international crime by the governments, companies or groups the protestors' actions target. If not always successful as a defence of actions, this appeal can serve a communicative end, and acts to identify a potential lack of alignment with the rule of law by the organization(s) or state(s) concerned.

However, what is a reasonable justification for civil disobedience, and what is not, may change over time and between groups; so, while religious conviction was seen as an acceptable reason for civil disobedience in the past, with the increasing secularization of many societies, such justification is not necessarily so readily nor widely accepted, although appeals to faith have revived in the new millennium. Indeed, social attitudes are often affected by the civil disobedience campaign itself (key examples being the anti-slavery campaign in the nineteenth century and the US civil rights movement in the last century). Campaigns are often explicitly intended to both protest an unjust law and build a socially accepted position that the state and/or government must respond to.

Kimberley Brownlee argues that 'civil disobedience actually can seem most justifiable when the situation appears hopeless and when the government refuses to listen to conventional forms of communication' (Brownlee 2009, section 2:1). One of the most powerful justifications for civil disobedience, therefore, is frequently social communication, which seeks to draw the maximum publicity to a particular social problem, not least as illegal actions have news value in a competitive news environment. Civil disobedience also communicates the commitment and strength of political opinion of those who are involved as well as directing the government *qua* audience to the changes in the law required to ameliorate the 'problem' identified (Brownlee 2007). This commitment is indicated to observers by the willingness of participants to pay the price for acting illegally; from being assaulted to imprisonment. In many campaigns the role of the legal system has been used in a sort of jujitsu politics, where the politico-legal weight bearing down on the committed activist can be turned around and depicted as unreasonable or disproportionate, as a way of seeking further support for the campaign. When civil disobedience becomes widespread, states have been forced to consider whether a specific law still reflects the mores of society and whether enforcement continues to garner societal support. Conversely, where prohibitions are regarded as being for the social good, even if popular views offer little support, governments may ask whether the specific (collective) good is still worth the time and expense of enforcement; successive campaigns in the UK by organized ramblers are an interesting example of establishing a shift in the manner in which a key legal right can be exercised (here a right to property).

When civil disobedience is only carried out by an individual (or a small number of campaigners) and there is adjudged to be little support, a state (and its government) is likely to prosecute on the basis of criminality. Moreover, it is difficult to coherently account for civil disobedience as anything other than a collective action (Arendt 1973, pp. 45–7); individual acts, even if prompted by political concerns, are only really politically coherent when they are part of collective action (which would include individual actions as part of an organized campaign). Furthermore, for civil disobedience to be regarded as legitimate in a democratic society, Peter Singer argues there must have been a prior, and ongoing, legal political campaign (Singer 1974, p. 84); previous channels of democratic deliberation and influence must be seen to have failed for political reasons (not merely because the cause was extensively aired and gained little support). However, this is a dynamic issue: civil disobedience and its prosecution may lead to changing social attitudes that in themselves may both encourage expanded civil disobedience and shifts in courts' attitudes to the 'crimes' and may eventually lead to amendments of legislation. This process (which is far from unusual) may see a progression from prosecution of vocal individuals, to leniency of sentencing (adjudication accepting political mitigation),[4] to calls for legal change through the actions of larger groups, and finally legislatures accepting democratic pressure to change the law.

For Hannah Arendt, this process indicates that civil disobedience should be institutionalized and its authors given access to the centres

---

[4] See Brownlee (2007) for a discussion of the justification of the legal punishment of civil disobedience.

of legislative power (Arendt 1973; Smith 2010), but this would serve to remove the distinction between legal and non-legal protest, and as such bring civil disobedience within the 'normal' rule of law. This would likely lead to the emergence of groups that were not recognized as legitimate in Arendt's institutionalized order of disobedience, and who would then still find themselves protesting what they saw as legitimate concerns outside the law.[5] Thus, for the purposes of the argument herein the definition with which I started seems to remain salient: civil disobedience is a *particular illegality* to promote a *more universal legality* through communicative collective action.

For Dworkin particularly, the crucial arguments about civil disobedience rest on the question of political conscience; law-abiding citizens still need to consider the strengths and weaknesses of the legal system as regards their own 'political' beliefs. Where they have reasonable grounds for doubting the validity of a law on moral grounds (judged against some justified system of values) they are at liberty to disobey. Where their actions are followed and supported, then this is part of the 'development and testing of the law through experimentation by citizens and through the adversary process' (Dworkin 1978, pp. 216–17). As Catherine Valcke puts it, civil disobedience is 'part of a collective lawmaking enterprise . . . [through which] laws are enacted by the officials as tentative statements of morality and/or efficiency and turned over to the citizens for their approval' (Valcke 1994, p. 58). This presents lawmaking as a social iterative process in which civil disobedience serves to identify the limits of the (legitimate) rule of law. Civil disobedience can reflect a failure of the judicial function in specific circumstances to realign the law with socially accepted views of morality (Arendt 1973, pp. 81–2). Assessing the influence of Gandhi, Tolstoy, Thoreau, King and others on the politics of dissent, Roland Bleiker argues that they helped shift 'foci from individual to collective action and from rejecting society to engaging with it' (Bleiker 2000, p. 95).[6] Most importantly, civil disobedience is not a rejection of any society and its rule of law; rather, it is an engagement with such a society, with the explicit intent of improvement or progress towards a better (fairer) rule of law. Democracy certainly rests on consent, but it cannot compel consent, and it is this duality that resonates with discussions of the manner in which the rule of law (and a constitution) might be legitimated. In this sense, I have called this an 'internal' challenge to the rule of law,

---

[5] See Hakimi (2007, p. 684) for a similar argument as regards 'tolerated deviations' from international law.

[6] There is a canon of writings on civil disobedience that is frequently anthologized: see Bedau (1991) and Murphy (1971) for representative examples, where the authors assessed by Bleiker are given pride of place.

although it might initially be regarded as coming from outside, given the appeal to norms that seem absent from the local articulation of the rule of law, but it is only a temporary externalization of political interest that seeks resolution by reincorporation into the existing legitimate rule of law.

Civil disobedience must, by virtue of the judgement about people's *own* actions that it entails (albeit often enacted collectively through political organization), work within an individualized understanding of the rule of law. This position is clearly and succinctly summarized by T.R.S. Allan:

> [T]he rule of law is most persuasively understood as an ideal of consent to just laws, freely given by all those to whom they apply . . . An illegitimate demand, that violates moral precepts taken to be fundamental limits on the state's authority, imposes no genuine legal duty of obedience; and the state cannot be permitted to enlarge its legitimate jurisdiction by curtailing the citizen's ability to judge whether or not its power have been exceeded. (Allan 2001, pp. 90–1)

Here, it is the rule of law's potential to appeal to values external to the positively enacted law that opens a space for the articulation of the notion that universal legality can be served by particular illegality, where universal legality is a higher politico-legal norm or morality.

Particular illegality reflects not the wholesale disregard of the law but rather a tacit acceptance of the rule of law in general. However, it is also a way of articulating a popular sovereignty that in any Lockean political system is the root of the state's legitimacy. By disrupting the product of the state's legislating, the citizens reassert their (retained) sovereignty over the governance of society. Moreover, as Loughlin glosses Locke, it 'is precisely this threat of legitimate rebellion . . . which will ensure that those in power are not tempted to abuse it' (Loughlin 2000, p. 169). Thus if, as Locke maintained, politics is built on the (implied) foundations of a prior social contract between individuals, and from which the state derives its legitimacy, then it must also include a potentially legitimate practice of civil disobedience (at particular times) as the manifestation of the wrestling back of popular sovereignty from its (normally accepted) political location within the state. This implies that for civil disobedience to be effective there has to be, at least some, rhetorical claim on behalf of the state and its government to the rule of law and (a form) of democracy. Without these appeals, demonstrations may be politically powerful but are unlikely to take the political form of civil disobedience.

Civil disobedience, by maintaining an ability to recognize social pressures towards principled reform, acts not to compromise the rule of law but rather to demonstrate its overall robustness; civil disobedience is actually a process of reconnecting civil and political society (Habermas 1996, p. 382) *through* the common sense of the rule of law. Therefore, Jürgen

Habermas argues that its legitimation relies on a dynamic understanding of the constitutional state, 'whose purpose is to realize the system of rights *anew* in changing circumstances, that is, to interpret the system of rights better, to institutionalize it more appropriately, and to draw out its contents more radically' (Habermas 1996, p. 384, emphasis in original). It is a process of improvement of fit between contemporary society and the inherited constitution, or general sense of the rule of law that is judged to be widely accepted in the polity. Those who are joined together in civil disobedience regard themselves as a constituent power (albeit closely focused), sovereign to form a view about the law's content and act 'illegally' to change the current constellation of laws so that the new law is better constituted as regards the 'will of the people'. From their point of view, in Rajeev Dhavan's words:

> The answers do not necessarily lie with the constitution or legal institutions, but in civil society's capacity to find justice before it is forced to wholly abandon the law. In this, the image of 'law as struggle' should not conjure anarchy but a creative initiative by the oppressed to re-structure society. (Dhavan 1994, p. 47)

In developed states the focus may be narrower, but the process of engaging with the law through a struggle to rework the law differs more by foci than by intent, although, as noted earlier, the memory of law as struggle in the most developed countries has often been dissipated or forgotten when rule of law programmes are conceived and delivered around the world.

In campaigns of civil disobedience, legal and social arrangements around governance are tested and the rule of law is flexed due to perceptions of social or political need, justice or fairness. This form of political boundary testing does not necessarily undermine the rule of law as such; rather, it is part of the mechanism by which it develops. Clearly, this is not the only way the rule of law changes over time, but unlike legislative change and precedent in common law legal systems, this form of testing the rule of law is conducted outside its formal institutions, requiring these institutions to react when political necessity is established.

Returning to the focus of the previous chapter, one of the key questions prompted by the political project of cosmopolitan democracy has been how non-state political groupings can influence or shape international law and its associated constitution(s); how is democratic inclusion achieved in the international realm if it is to be regarded as moving towards a more extensive utilization of constitutional mechanisms (Marks 2000, pp. 101–20)? If the rule of law at the global level requires a global constitution for some form of cosmopolitan democracy to be developed, then these mechanisms of inclusion are crucial to its legitimacy. If, as many argue, participatory democracy is not feasible at a global scale, nevertheless as noted earlier, 'contestatory democracy is' (Peters 2009a, p. 270). Thus, one of the ways that we might deal with the claim that there is a formal lack of (direct) democratic deliberation at the international level is to suggest that instead of focusing on legitimacy derived from electoral process, for pragmatic reasons, global constitutional politics needs to be more concerned with ensuring an enhanced representation by (global) civil societal actors and groups (Kumm 2009, p. 296). If these 'representatives' are limited (as they frequently are) to insider groups, then we must be clear about what mechanisms of influence remain for those with non-mainstream positions to articulate. Here, the role of civil disobedience can immediately be seen as both relevant and directly related to a legitimate process for engaging with the rule of law from 'outside' while retaining an internal (reformist) logic.

As Allen Buchanan has observed, changes in international law 'through the creation of new customary norms often includes illegalities in the initial stages, yet this has not resulted in the destruction of the international legal system' (Buchanan 2004, p. 461). The position that the international legal realm is a seamless whole, whose integrity is devastated by any particular illegal action, does not accord with the historical record. As with the domestic situations discussed above, the (international) rule of law is at least partly developed by states' governments pushing the boundaries of what is legal and by such testing either international norms are shifted through acquiescence or the status quo is defended leaving the particular actions illegal and (broadly) unsupported. States may act in consort through regional organizations to emphasize the order/justice-supporting ends of a specific 'illegal' intervention (Hakimi 2007, p. 682, *passim*), and by doing so seek, as do domestic campaigns of civil disobedience, to add weight to their concerns through collective action. Indeed, Buchanan himself makes an explicit link in his argumentation to civil disobedience (Buchanan 2004, pp. 464–8) but, as above, rejects the stretching of the institutionalization of reform to include a 'legalized' disobedience, arguing that this blurs the notion of illegality unnecessarily, when the real judgement of the justification of illegal acts in the furtherance of reform must be an assessment of their morality.

So, when we expand the analysis of civil disobedience into the realm of global constitutionalism, it suggests further ways that the international rule of law can be subject to legitimate political amendment even where there is a clear democratic deficit in the legislative deliberation around any global constitutional settlement. At the domestic level civil disobedience is a practice by which the rule of law is developed through an iterative process of boundary testing, while states themselves may sometimes also act against the (international) rule of law while claiming legitimacy based on 'higher values'. However, what is important is that these processes are able to gain political legitimacy outside the formal processes of the rule of law, even if they are clearly focused on the rule of law. Absent directly deliberative processes at the global level, the democratic deficit is a political problem for global constitutionalism. The recognition of the legitimacy of these non-legal processes of engagement with the rule of law, offering a long history of legitimization, suggests that even without the formal democratic element, global constitutionalism can offer avenues of political engagement that do not need to wait for (perhaps illusive) extensive participatory apparatus to be built. Moreover, if the international rule of law is to endure (at least in its thicker conceptions, linked, for instance, to human rights), then mechanisms by which legitimate interests can be articulated and encompassed within the political processes of review and renewal will likely need to be both recognized (analytically and politically) and deployed by groups seeking to influence and shape the further iterative development of a global constitutionalism.

## CONTESTING THE RULE OF LAW FROM OUTSIDE: LEGAL PLURALISM AND THE RULE OF LAW

The previous section has dealt with what I have called 'internal' challenges to the rule of law; these essentially accept the dominant depiction of the rule of law as legitimate (with all its difficulties of definition) and seek to amend or 'improve' it. I now move to examine challenges that are 'external' to the rule of law. Recognizing that the global system is multi-cultural and multi-polar, much of the discussion of the rule of law so far might be regarded as having adopted a Westernized and universalist reading of its character as the common sense of global politics. To some extent this is true, but reflects much of the academic and media commentary on the subject. However, an important challenge to this common sense comes from the recognition and acceptance that there is considerable variance and indeed tension between different (cultural) understandings of the rule of law. Thus, Yasuaki Onuma in setting out an 'inter-civilizational' or 'trans-civilizational' understanding of the rule of law in the global system argues that:

> For any education, research, discussion and dialogue [about international legal affairs] to become legitimate on a global scale, they must be conducted in such a way as to listen to the voices of people all over the world, and to understand the values, virtues, assumptions, and views embraced by these people. (Onuma 2012, p. 180)

He identifies the virtual disappearance of a 'counter ideology' to 'liberal/capitalist democracy' as a major impediment to this recognition and inclusion of further perspectives on the (rule of) law. This is not merely about understanding differences in conception, it is about challenges to the dominant understanding of the rule of law from other (that is to say, non-Western) perspectives about what it might actually mean. Therefore, having examined how the rule of law could be challenged from within societies whose populations broadly support the norm, I now turn to legal pluralism as a challenge to the universalist (or even essentialist) understanding of the rule of law in global politics.

Firstly, there are two dimensions in which legal pluralism might be recognized; for ease I'll call these the 'vertical' and the 'horizontal'. The former is the sort of legal pluralism that is identified in debates about the varying levels of sovereign legal authority in a global system with institutions of global governance seeking to shape the actions of (still sovereign) states. This vertical legal pluralism focuses on issues such as subsidiarity and transfers of powers from states to international organizations of one sort or another. The vertical pluralist question has (unsurprisingly) been explored in most detail, and with considerable political impact in the EU (see, for instance, de Búrca and Weiler 2012). I am not seeking to downplay the importance of this dimension of legal pluralism, but it strikes me that while there is competition between the levels working out of legitimate authority, this echoes and is built upon previous hierarchies of law (and judicial review) that are essentially part of the common sense of the rule of law (as already discussed). However, the horizontal dimension, where there are competing legalities at the same level of social relations, seems to me to be much more problematic for the rule of law norm. This horizontal debate is not about identifying the difference between law and non-law but rather seeks to understand the normative commitments of a community and how interactions between various norms produce such commitments and thereby social rules and their legal orders (Berman 2009, p. 237). This may open the possibility that these different legal orders still can be understood as the rule of law, but only if the norm is slimmed down, made thinner: the question is, can *different* rule(s) of law be recognized as legitimate, and indeed should they?

In Chapter 2 I mentioned that Boaventura de Sousa Santos sees the thicker approach to the rule of law as a central aspect of the contemporary counter-hegemonic resistance that seeks to criticize and resist contemporary neoliberal (globalized) capitalism (de Sousa Santos 2002, pp. 278–311). This can be seen (albeit at a global scale) in similar terms to the sorts of resistance set out above; the appeal to a universal legality to contest a particular (perceived) illegality. Interestingly, and to further underline a point made earlier, David Dyzenhaus has detailed how those who had a substantive view of the rule of law worked in the courts of Apartheid South Africa to try and force judges to recognize the (universal) rule of law standards that seemed to have been obscured by the thin (and proceduralist) view that the courts worked with when applying Apartheid to ethnic groups in South Africa (Dyzenhaus 2007). Albeit, not that successful, these lawyers' harrying of the legal system never allowed Apartheid to settle as a fully legitimate legality. Likewise, Stuart Scheingold suggests that even in autocratic and unstable states some cause lawyers still try to push for minimal rights, even if to claim human rights is seen a 'confrontational and *hostile* political act' (Scheingold 2001, p. 400, *passim*, emphasis in original). In this, they are conducting the sort of critique de Sousa Santos identifies, albeit with a different target and usually at the national level. This suggests that the common sense of the rule of law is something from which (political) sustenance can be drawn by those seeking to contest specific legal settlements or practices.

Thus, in one depiction of legal pluralism, the plurality is in the values and policies that the (or perhaps 'a') rule of law underpins rather than in the rule of law itself. Here, it retains its character as a universalized norm albeit one that is not the terrain over which multiple legal 'authorities' may contest their jurisdiction or efficacy. The thin rule of law norm, with its emphasis on formalism and procedure, can fulfil this role relatively well and indeed one might presume that for contending authorities to compete there would need to be some shared appreciation of these elements of the norm. Competition between states, international organizations and other institutions making claims to rule through legal instruments clash not on how the rule of law should be operated but rather on the legitimate site of authority, and claims about hierarchy and subsidiarity in regulation. Thus, like Francesco Viola, one might stress that the rule of law is about the 'general diffusion of legal practice in the government of human affairs' and by doing so, 'observe that it is enacted in varying degrees depending on the situation of the social context' (Viola 2007, p. 130). The rule of law as a (perhaps slightly more vague) common sense is retained and rendered as a flexible standard that specific legal systems and arrangements may approach or be relatively distanced from; this retains the rule of law as a benchmark, albeit more relaxed. Alternatively, we might call this a rule of law mindset, an approach awaiting (moral and normative) content to be given it by the community taking it forward.

Before coming back to this issue of the shared thin view of the rule of law, I want to explore more incommensurable perspectives on the rule of law; perspectives that cannot merely be easily subsumed within the thicker reading of the rule of law but rather are in some important aspects not able to be understood as conforming with any global common sense depiction of the norm at all. The rule of law is not always understood outside Europe or the West more generally as it is within these regions, although in states that emerged from colonialism with common law-like systems still in place, the appeal to the Westernized rule of law can remain a significant underpinning for their legal culture; a key example here would be India.[7] If we accept this, are there any forms of legality (socially justified locally) that would be so far distant from a flexible or relaxed norm that we would regard them as competing norms of the rule of law within a global milieu of competing social norms? This consideration leads Viola to conclude:

> We can well consider the traditional formula of the rule of law as the *virtue of a legal system* already existing but we now have to consider the rule of law at work in contemporary law in all its extension as the legal becoming of social and political orders that progressively submit in their own way to the dominion of law i.e. a living rule of law in progress, and in this way also succeed in conversing with one another, which is necessary to reconstructing a political identity in the world of fragmentation. (Viola 2007, p. 131, emphasis in original)

Here, the rule of law confronts other rule(s) of law and rather than merely dominating them, seeks some sort of accommodation with local understandings of legality and regulatory practices, or more accurately legal (and political) actors seek to bring into some sort of local alignment the common sense of the rule of law as diffused across the global system.

As discussed in Chapters 4 and 5, during the introduction of the rule of law by external agencies and organizations – in post-conflict situations and in programmes focused on economic development – one of the abiding issues regarded as a problem is the retention of local or traditional laws and customs of legality in 'targeted' populations. Local laws are depicted as scapegoats for the (relative) failure of the (new) rule of law to take hold but actually what may happen on the ground is the slow interaction between local understandings of the law (and its normative purposes) with the Westernized rule of law. However, equally, Franz von Benda-Beckmann (1989) has suggested that sometimes local laws are interpreted more robustly when confronted with the incoming (new) legality as a defensive measure or move, and although they might be flexible enough in their everyday use to accommodate at least some of the (new) law(s), they are used politically to resist external imposition. If this is the case, then

---

[7] For example, in Menon (2008) a range of Indian writers from academia and the legal system all utilize in their discussions an understanding of the rule of law that sits well with that described in Chapter 2.

legal reform (and the importation of new types of laws and institutions) is likely only to be successful when a strong demand exists among influential groups in the 'receiving' society (Pistor 2002, p. 126), because otherwise such resistance will be fatal to any legal transplant. Thus, the recognition of legal pluralism includes an understanding that the rule of (local) law is no less weighted down by normative commitments than the norm that reflects the Westernized common sense of legality. Interestingly, as the rule of law 'exported' from developed countries is often less flexible and more stringent than that which actually operates in their own domestic legal systems, we might say this defensiveness appears on both sides of many legal pluralist interactions; two idealized and more strident legal norms confront each other when both in their more flexible (domestic) modes might offer more chances for accommodation.

When the norms and values encompassed by the generalized (global) rule of law confront their local counterparts, is the only way of understanding the outcome, either as a move to adopt the common sense of the rule of law or as the failure of this attempt with the retention of a localized legal system reflecting different norms, regarded by outsiders as an impediment? It certainly might be advisable for those seeking to introduce the rule of law into new societies to be more modest about what advantages the Westernized norm (and its attendant practices) can achieve. The most appropriate legal reference points for any developing country may not be those of the major developed countries but rather the legal systems of other countries that share important aspects of their history, social and cultural traditions (Davis and Trebilcock 2008). Thus, modesty about the rule of law as a solution requires some recognition that there may be other rule(s) of law that might be as, or even more, suitable as models for countries and societies seeking to (re)build their legal system.

One way to demonstrate this modesty might be to develop a 'basic' universal principle of the rule of law (to develop a different 'thin' norm), which is Ricardo Gosalbo-Bono's project. He summarizes his exploration of other ways that legality is treated outside the 'Western World' by noting that for some states (primarily those governed by a 'socialist' political system) law is merely a means to achieve the transformation of society, and thus 'cannot bind the state' or where states are organized through a religious system, the theocratic courts must be able to trump law by virtue of their direct line to the deity. Thus,

> States that rely on the law to govern, but do not accept the basic requirement that law binds the state, state actors and states in transition to a democratic form of government, cannot be identified as states governed by the 'rule of law', but rather are best described as states 'ruled by law'. (Gosalbo-Bono 2010, p. 289)

Although Gosalbo-Bono is using the common sense notion of the rule of law as a benchmark, his project is not to exclude such legal regimes but to try to find a basic norm that they would be able to adopt/accept. This leads him to suggest that a basic (universal) norm of the rule of law would need to (only) include: a rejection of arbitrary rule (including prospective, accessible and clear law); supremacy of the law, that the law is a applicable to all and independent; and that all are equal in front of the law (Gosalbo-Bono 2010, p. 290). In one sense, this is a very thin version of the rule of law, right at the end of the continuum discussed in Chapter 2, and is an attempt to deal with pluralism by denying the rule of law encompasses fundamental values central to liberal perceptions of the value of the rule of law.

This analysis can be complemented by deploying Ugo Mattei's classification system for the plurality of legal systems that presents three elements that are always present but differently weighted in specific legal systems: the 'rule of professional law'; the 'rule of political law'; and the 'rule of traditional law'. Each pattern of 'social incentives (or social constraints) [is] at play in all legal systems simultaneously. The only difference is in terms of quantity, acceptability and, most importantly, hegemony' (Mattei 1997, p. 16). This leads him to argue that all legal systems can be recognized as belonging to one or other of these groups of families (where their defining aspect is hegemonic). Thus, once there is something that might be recognized as a system of (legal-like) rules, then what captures that extent and character of the pluralism in the global system is the balance between these three aspects of rule. Most explicitly, he seeks to reject a classificatory scheme that privileges the 'Western Legal Tradition' (Mattei 1997, p. 19). This classification is concerned with the normative grounds for a legal system not the specific institutionalization of those norms (Mattei 1997, p. 20). For Mattei, these three interpenetrated rule of law types are not absolutes but points on a triangle between which actual legal systems (the real rule of law) can be located.

The 'rule of professional law' is broadly coterminous with the Western legal tradition (where the distinction between common and civil law is treated as a variation within the type). Key aspects of this type of legal system are that: it is clearly distinguishable from the political arena; the legal process is essentially secular; and therefore decisions are taken on their technical and legal merits as interpreted by (legal) professionals, and (rhetorically at least) claim legitimacy through democracy (Mattei 1997, pp. 23–7). As one would expect, much of Mattei's characterization of the 'rule of professional law' is familiar from the discussion in Chapter 2 and I will not repeat it here. The 'rule of political law' is typified by the lack of separation between law and politics, with the legal process often determined by political relationships and as such the notion of limiting government's actions through the legal system is inconsistent with how the purpose of law is understood. Certainly, most of the time the government and its agencies may rule *by* law but this is not regarded as a strong limitation on their activity. As Mattei points out, for those looking at this system from the perspective of the 'rule of professional law', 'many aspects of the *rule of political law* are labelled "corruption", are considered a pathology, and in general are not accepted or regarded by the social actors as structural elements of the social order' (Mattei 1997, p. 29). However, these concerns are less important within these systems as they are formally focused on a 'political target, be it free market and privatisation, be it self sufficiency, or be it development [which] determines, justifies and makes socially acceptable the outcome of most decision making' (Mattei 1997, p. 31). The 'rule of political law' is often self-defined as being part of a transitional phase; at some point the legal and political structures may change (more democracy may be allowed), but only when the political goals have been reached (Mattei 1997, p. 35). From outside there may be a question about how and when the assessment of the completion might be made, but this of course emphasizes that it is the rule of 'political' law.

The third type that Mattei identifies is the 'rule of traditional law'. Here, there is no separation between the system of law and a society's religious system, and as such the 'individual's internal dimension and the societal dimension are not separated' (Mattei 1997, p. 36). To stress the religious and philosophical/transcendental beliefs that might govern such a legal system, he labels this the Eastern Legal Tradition. While the role of religious and other values plays an important role here, nevertheless there is also often considerable structural similarity between this group and societies where 'professional law' obtains. Thus, he stresses that

> one should not confuse the *rule of traditional law* with the absence of law or even the absence of formal legal institutions. In the *rule of traditional law* formal legal institutions do exist, but the working rule is different from what we are used to in Western societies. (Mattei 1997, p. 39)

Rather than seeking to justify the system by appeals to democracy, in the 'rule of traditional law' hierarchy, including deference to religious opinion (and elders), is crucial for the making of decisions with the 'strong, very ancient and respected rhetoric' of supernatural legitimization playing a major role (Mattei 1997, p. 40). Most importantly, Mattei's argument stresses that while systems may tend towards one or other of these points (on a taxonomic triangle) no system completely excludes the characteristic aspects of the other two. This suggests why it may be possible, as Gosalbo-Bono suggests, that a very basic (very thin) form of the rule of law can support a claim that there is a universally accepted idea of the rule of law, even if it is only a sliver of what those who propose a thicker reading of the norm would accept. However, one of the key insights of pluralism is that law, in Paul Schiff Berman's words, is 'an ongoing process of articulation, adaptation, rearticulation, absorption, resistance, deployment and on and on. It is a process that never ends' (Berman 2009, p. 239). As such, the interaction and interpenetration of Mattei's three 'families' of law may indicate how new forms of the rule of law may emerge. This, of course, assumes some toleration towards difference and an acceptance of varying stories about the rule of law and its value.

This question of different forms of the rule of law can be illustrated by the political discussions around the rule of law in China.[8] Partly due to the increasing influence (and practical engagement) of China in the global political economy (Cardenal and Araújo 2013), the Chinese view of the rule of law is often seen as a challenge to the dominant common sense of the rule of law as expounded and understood by Western legal practitioners. This might also be seen as a counter-move to the form of 'legalization' often identified in the global political economy (as discussed in Chapter 3). Writing at the end of the 1990s, Richard Appelbaum could already see in the rise of the Chinese economy a shift in the manner in which the rule of law patterned business relations. In these new relations between Chinese economic organizations (private and state-owned) themselves, and between those organizations and others, he detected a move away from law and the (re)ascendance of business relations built on personal connections and non-legally defined relationships, reflecting traditional 'Chinese' ways of doing business (Appelbaum 1998). In the first decade of the millennium this shift had had little real impact on the character of the legal reform programmes at the Asian Development Bank (ADB), which still relied on models of judicial and other legal reform derived from the broadly defined rule of law used by Western institutions (Armytage 2011). While the ADB seems to have been broadly immune from any potential process of modification and adaption between contending legalities, it is far from the case that the norm of the rule of law (in its common sense form) has carried all before it in Asia, nor that other cultures of legality (here the Chinese) are necessary non-functional for economic relations (as is often presupposed by the mainstream depiction of the norm).

The history of the rule of law in China has been tied up with the recognition and legitimacy of non-legal, moral forms of conflict resolution, sometimes referred to as the 'rule of men', which has run parallel

---

[8] Such is intellectual fashion and political economic reality that a quarter of a century ago Japan would have likely been the subject of the next paragraphs.

to the long-term development of a Chinese tradition of legal thought. Although here is not the space to develop a historical treatment of the Chinese legal system, generally approaches that stress conciliation and forbearance, and even injustice for the good of stability have confronted a legal perspective that while nearer Western notions of the rule of law still retained the authority of the ruler whose discretion was only limited by his own morality or understanding of social expectations (Gosalbo-Bono 2010, pp. 280–1). The Chinese Imperial system attempted to combine these two traditions, but successive modernizations and the revolution of 1949 further (re)shaped the rule of law, to the point now where the chief difficulty the system confronts is how to reconcile the leading role of the Chinese Communist Party with the principle of the supremacy of the law (Gosalbo-Bono 2010, p. 283). Additionally, as Ji Weidong has suggested,

> In terms of contemporary China's reality, the main characteristic of the principle of order is that facts have precedence compared to norms, and reciprocity to rights; in the view of the rule of law being established before or above interpersonal relationships, even if it is not completely absent, it is extremely weak. Rather than ignorance of or failure to abide by the law, the cause of this situation is according to people's understanding of or bias towards fairness, and draw[s] on the widespread influence of state power to arbitrarily explain rules, manipulating clauses according to utilitarian goals. (Weidong 2008, p. 41)

In Mattei's taxonomy this would place the Chinese legal system nearest the 'rule of political law' axis (side of the triangle) even as reformers struggle to move further towards the 'rule of professional law'. Thus, Prime Minister Lee Kuan Yew's famous championing of Asian Values as a way of dealing with criticisms around human rights can be seen as an articulation of this (Chinese) view; even if there is no single Asian approach to the rule of law, many states can be located in the political 'family' of systems alongside China.

It is possible that as China continues to globalize its economy, with increasing interaction with global legal practices and international law firms, there may be some convergence in understanding of the rule of law; conversely, Chinese practices may remain influential, drawing other understandings towards them (Appelbaum 1998, p. 176), and as such this does not necessarily mean that it is a foregone conclusion that at some point the Chinese legal system will shift from a political to professional rule of law. At present it seems likely that the business (and social) culture of *guanxi* is still a stronger influence on economic (and social) organization than legal considerations. *Guanxi*'s mix of social interactions, personal relationships, obligations and indebtedness remains strongly shaped by traditions of morality and sociality that have millennia or longer histories in the region.

This in turn reflects the political character of Chinese (and more generally Asian) capitalism, which rather than being built on an understanding that economic relations are contractual often depends more on the crucial role of non-market relations, horizontally between economic actors and vertically between them and the state (Jayasuriya 1999, p. 7). However, as Mattei makes clear, his 'families' are not exclusive; in any specific instance (here China) we will find elements of all three rule(s) of law.

Indeed, discussions of the rule of law in China are frequently related to the Western norm, even if (especially post-1949) legal developments are then defined against a depiction of bourgeois legal systems (Turner 1992, p. 2). This led Randall Peerenboom to explore how low the threshold for the rule of law would need to be lowered to allow China to be accorded the recognition of being governed by an (albeit 'imperfect') rule of law (Peerenboom 2002, pp. 510–26). This parallels Gosalbo-Bono's analysis, but again is perhaps better developed using Mattei's approach, recognizing not an imperfect rule of law but rather that the Chinese rule of law is currently one in which the 'political' element/family is dominant, even if the mix of families is dynamic and (potentially) moving more towards the 'professional' without any necessary teleology. However, these questions about whether the rule of law can be said to obtain has led to significant additional debates about what this might indicate for the posited link between the rule of law and economic development.

Kenneth Dam, for instance, argues that the absence of an institution that looks like the Western liberal rule of law suggests that while China may have been able to work with a different model of economic development until now, the country will not be able to make this a sustainable trajectory without the development of liberal-like legal norms and institutions. Regarding this as a test case for the relationship between law and development, he concludes that it 'is certainly too early to accept the notion that the recent Chinese experience is a counter example to the need to focus on [liberal] institutions in the developing world, and indeed the rule of law in China itself' (Dam 2006, p. 277). However, Frank Upham observes that Dam's

> conclusion represents the popular view that China may have done all right without [the rule of] law up to the present, but is likely to crash if it does not quickly create an effective legal system.
> Dam's recognition that China has grown rapidly without law is important, but he refuses to take the logical next step and conclude that the Chinese experience should lead to reconsideration of the conventional wisdom of law and development. (Upham 2009, p. 573)

However, the value of Mattei's approach to the taxonomy of the rule of law is that much of the conventional wisdom (or common sense in my terms) of the rule of law can be retained, but a more pluralistic treatment enables it to recognize that the common sense of the rule of law actually also applies to such a difficult case. Again, as Upham has suggested, this common sense can lead to the ignoring of important contrary evidence; 'it is as if the World Bank's focus on China's less than satisfactory legal system has rendered its remarkable growth invisible' (Upham 2009, p. 569). While China may require us to modify our understanding of the rule of law and the manner in which it interacts with the political economy, using Mattei's 'families' the common sense of the rule of law can reach beyond its liberal origins and allows us to understand that moves towards the 'professional rule of law' do not necessarily require a legal rupture in China or elsewhere. More importantly, adopting this plural idea of the rule of law allows us to recognize where there are similarities and commonalities between legal systems and their normative underpinnings (even if these are relatively thin in the terms of the rule of law continuum I set out in Chapter 2, and which is self-avowedly broadly Western in origin).

This mixture of rule of law 'families' is also evident across East Asia: hence, to give one further example, in the late twentieth century Kanishka Jayasuriya notes that while there was a move towards increasing professionalization of the judiciary in many countries across Asia, and a centralization of courts, these (local and supreme) courts remained subject to political influence and control, even as they were developing a stronger practice of judicial 'professional' mission (Jayasuriya 1999, p. 22). While elements of judicial autonomy were being established, the state still controlled the courts in the final analysis and this has shaped/shapes judicial deliberation.[9] It should therefore not be surprising that an equally long history can be found for Chinese valorization of the rule of law (as understood in the 'professional' family) with, for instance, Han Fei Tzu in the third century BC praising the clarity, unyielding and non-arbitrary nature of law (Bouloukos and Dakin 2001, p. 147).[10] Nevertheless, the formal distinction between private and public power that is accomplished (albeit incompletely) through the 'professional rule of law' is not evident in the 'political' variant of the rule of law and this is often the focus of criticisms that suggest China does not in fact benefit from the rule of law at all.

Finally, in contemporary China the debate about the rule of law, drawing on its own national history as well as the debates in the West, has led some observers to suggest that China may be moving towards legal reform (partly as a response to a series of scandals that have unfolded in the

---

[9] For a detailed comparative analysis of variations in the rule of law across Asia see Peerenboom (2004) and for a shorter summary evaluation see Woo-Cummings (2003).

[10] For an extended survey of early Chinese discussion of the rule of law see Turner (1992).

newly emergent Chinese social media). Cheng Li and Chen Guangcheng have recently argued that the social unrest linked to these scandals as well as an increasingly vocal and critical legal profession within the universities is leading the Communist Party towards the development of a more 'credible legal system' (Li and Guangcheng 2013), perhaps reflecting the sorts of political processes identified in the first half of this chapter. However, Carl Minzner sees this recent move as part of series of swings between the consolidation of political power over the legal system in China, and legal reform prompted by specific scandals about court decisions or changes of leadership. In his view, and contrasted to Li and Guangcheng, the Chinese Communist Party is again seeking to consolidate power, and not to develop more open legal and political channels for reform towards a more 'professional rule of law' (Minzner 2013). Adopting the pluralist approach detailed above, however, allows this political oscillation to be rendered as internal to the norm of the rule of law rather than be seen as an external threat.

As will now be clear, taking such a pluralist approach to the rule of law can lead to a relaxation of its threshold requirements, with a focus on the general aspects of the norm and a more permissive approach to the details (of delivery). Indeed, for Nico Krisch (2012), it becomes more an issue of accepted and predictable social practice rather than necessarily shared wider normative elements. Legal pluralism requires the notion of the rule of law to become a more abstract set of principles about procedural similarities that while requiring some social recognition of the value of lawfulness does not require this to be articulated in a way that sits within Westernized notions of the rule of law state or society. Thus, as von Benda-Beckmann puts it, here legal pluralism 'treats all laws according to the same analytical standard. It does not postulate any concrete empirical form or social and political significance of any law' (von Benda-Beckmann 2001, p. 49). Taking this argument into a debate about constitutionalism, James Tully has argued that only by recognizing these cultural differences and varied customary practices, reflecting the original liberal notions of neutrality and autonomy, can constitutions (and thereby the rule of law) survive in an age of cultural diversity. However, and perhaps this is the crucial point, this requires a mutual recognition of legitimacy: both the rule of law and the other local customs and practices must proceed with an allowance for the legitimacy of the other (Tully 1995). That is to say, beyond some very basic facilitative mechanisms and protections for effective (individual) autonomy, the mainstream rule of law needs to encompass difference, allowing it to be articulated *within* the norm, while alternative systems equally must accept their interactivity with forms of legality that are in line with the common sense of the rule of law.

The difficulty is that this sort of agnosticism may not survive the trials and tribulations of political debate outside the academy. Because many claim that the rule of law has important socio-political effects, even with a relatively permissive notion of the rule of law, the issue will remain highly political. Even if the rule of law will always be related to state-like structures of governance, its significance will always be linked to (and often co-dependent on) 'non-state normative and institutional orders for the same practices' (von Benda-Beckmann 2001, p. 53). Von Benda-Beckmann is also very firm that evaluations must be 'critical':

> If 'access to justice', in the sense of having access to the court system, may actually mean access to injustice, we should say so. If 'equity' is interpreted as meaning that changes be proportional to the present distribution of rights to resources, we should say that it reproduces existing unjust distributions. (von Benda-Beckmann 2001, p. 54)

This of course leads back to the issue (exercised at some length earlier) about how one defines the rule of law norm and its core elements; a very thin notion of the rule of law may indeed be able to encompass such plurality but by trying (politically) to satisfy a wider range of traditions would it in the end lose its appeal as political value altogether? However, and conversely, the continued appeal of other rule of law norms may be accomplished by the acceptance of a relaxed (less absolute) understanding of the Westernized rule of law itself; an acceptance that it provides less certainty and predictability than its (often) mythical characterization suggests (Krisch 2010, pp. 280–5). We should be wary of depicting other rule(s) of law as failing to meet an absolute standard; by foregoing such forms of critique, any two opposing depictions may be able to move nearer to each other, supporting a more pluralist standpoint on the issue. While this might shift the range of threshold(s) that could be identified for the acceptance by anyone that a specific claim that the rule of law obtains is justified, it does not remove a threshold condition of some sort completely. And as such, this approach to legal pluralism returns to the issue of universal claims, merely changing the level of abstraction or generality at which such discussion might take place.

## CONCLUSION

That there might be a plurality of systems of legality that can be regarded as conforming in one way or another to the broad brush notion of the rule of law (which still reflects its common sense usage) should not be taken as a problem for economic development, as might be inferred from some analyses of law and development. As already noted, the link between common law and accelerated economic development is far from proven (although there may be a closer correlation with the recognition of forms of property rights), and as such we might say that the rule of law (when related to economic development) can easily accommodate a mixed ecology of legality. Although legal systems must (if they are to promote economic development) be supportive of market mechanisms, this does not indicate that there is only one type of rule of law that will foster economic growth (Milhaupt and Pistor 2008). Rather, a pluralist, and permissive, approach to the rule of law, an inclusive imaginary, may not undermine development in the real world of economic relations and indeed with sensitivity to other (local) legalities may well enhance the social acceptance and conformity to the rule of law more generally and related to other non-economic priorities. However, as de Sousa Santos warns, neither should we automatically conclude because we can insert a particular legal order into a notion of legal pluralism that these orders are necessarily politically (or ethically) acceptable; for instance, legal orders established by military groups in areas under their control may conform to some pluralist thinner reading of the rule of law yet offer little that might be recognized as the rule of law by others seeking some relation to a wider set of human rights (de Sousa Santos 2002, p. 89). Thus, despite its contestability and the potential plurality of legal orders that we might accept as approximating in some way to the rule of law, there is something quite robust about the common sense of the rule of law. Even in this inclusive and flexible form of the social imaginary, the common sense of the rule of law retains some of the value that E.P. Thompson's depiction of it as an unqualified social good was intended to capture.

# 8. Concluding thoughts

> Although legal history has not provided us with a phrase equivalent to Smith's 'invisible hand,' the law[,] like the market, is seen as operating without human agency and hence without the vices of bureaucracies and politicians, two of our time's least favourite institutions. Just as a market needs only clear property rights and freedom of exchange, the rule of law needs only the correct rules and institutions. (Upham 2004, p. 313)[1]

In this book I have been arguing that it makes sense to think of the rule of law as a common sense of global politics, or as a global social imaginary. Although I started with a rather top-down, legalistic view of the common sense character of the rule of law, as the book has progressed I have tried to leaven that view by introducing further and different perspectives. These perspectives are not alternatives but rather complement each other to give a fuller understanding of the rule of law's place in (global) politics. The strength of this common sense is indicated by the difficulty of thinking of any alternative to the rule of law, although some on the Marxist left would argue that an interest in human emancipation must include the notion of a society with no need for the law as a mediator of political economic relations (Taiwo 1999). However, for most of the rest of us, imagining an alternative to the rule of law is a challenge. Indeed, Andrei Marmor notes:

> [I]f we maintain that the ideal of the rule of law is premised on the basic assumption that it is good to be governed by law, the obvious question arises: as opposed to what? How else can a population be governed if not by law? . . . [T]he idea that if we are to be governed, we should be governed by law, amounts to a tautology that it if it is good to be governed it is good to be governed. (Marmor 2010, p. 667)

This may indeed be a common contemporary tautology, but if we accept Marmor's description of the discussion, the question remains: why *this* tautology *now*? If like gravity the rule of law had always been with us, then definitions might be sufficient (and indeed progressive, in that they would get us closer to realizing the 'truth' of the rule of law). However,

---

[1] Just to be on the safe side, Upham is here (in the last sentence) being ironic; he recognizes that both the market and the rule of law need more than these depoliticized descriptions!

the expansion of appeals to the rule of law as a common sense proposition for the practice of (global) politics actually alerts us to the fact that it was not always this way. To be clear: this is not to say that there is not a long history of modes of governance we might refer to as rule *by* law. However, the deployment of a normative evaluation acting as an albeit contested threshold for the political legitimation of particular legal systems as passing a political test defined as the rule of law is relatively recent. If we are, as I believe we should be, interested in the reasons for social change not just its contours, then the rise of the rule of law bears investigation, alongside any debates about what it actually is (or can be).

While much of the discussion of the rule of law in legal studies is concerned with a rich and nuanced debate about the definition of the rule of law and its possible threshold conditions, beyond these (specialized) discussions the rule of law has a rather different existence. Across global politics the term (and by implication its normative heft or weight) has become a mantra of political judgement; a criterion against which political actions are judged. There is an increasingly generalized perception that the rule of law is both possible and meaningful, but as I stressed at the end of the last chapter, to argue convincingly that it is truly a global common sense, the definition of the norm needs to approach the thinnest end of the continuum that I set out in Chapter 2. What is notable is that even so, a shared understanding of the rule of law can be said to exist as a value most if not all societies will accede to in one way or another (even if such a term/ conclusion hides significant divergence).

The question of whether an international (or global) rule of law is possible continues to exercise international lawyers and others interested in politics beyond the confines of the sovereign state.[2] As the discussion in Chapter 6 set out, there has been considerable debate about the existence and character of a global (legal-like) constitution, and certainly one can map the rise (in global politics) of the rhetoric of the rule of law onto the expansion of political interest in global governance. If we need governing then we end up with a system of law (although this may be differently constructed and legitimated depending on social developments and values); if we have a system of law (however characterized) we start to think about how that system might be understood practically, and we end up thinking about the rule of law (not least as a necessary pre-commitment), even if this is at the thin end of the array of definitions that might be available.

---

[2] See Watts (1993) for one frequently cited exploration of the question of the possibility of the international rule of law, or Chesterman (2008b) for a more recent attempt to answer this question by offering an acceptable definition of the rule of law.

Understanding the rule of law as a social imaginary rather than mere rhetorical flourish or in David Kennedy's terms 'policy vernacular' (Kennedy 2001) depends on how seriously we take the under-determined character of the rule of law as placed along the continuum of normative definition I have been working with. For the rule of law to be considered a social imaginary there is no need for a fully agreed definition, as long as there are a set of key attributes that can be understood to be shared and acted upon in various combinations and weightings; a shared repertoire that might include courts, written laws, trials and so on. This is where the pluralist triangular taxonomy set out at the end of the previous chapter has some value: the rule of law as common sense encompasses a field of meaning bounded by the rule of professional, the political and traditional law. As this emphasizes, a thinner version of the rule of law norm (focused largely on procedure) is widely enough accepted in global politics to establish that a version of the rule of law can be regarded as exhibiting many of Taylor's posited characteristics of a social imaginary.

The lack of consensus around the rule of law norm also explains why the social imaginary remains the subject of continued political activity despite its seeming ascendance as a global common sense. While the neoliberal/ new right agenda saw the rule of law (to simplify a little) as merely a thin procedural mechanism to deliver the order required for the expansion of capitalist markets, for those seeking to advance liberal-democratic values thicker readings of the norm are preferred as conceptions of legal development that support human rights, social justice and fairness, which are values that continue to lie at the heart of the self-conception of most developed countries. In the Western tradition the contemporary rule of law was the product of two well-known historical and cultural transitions, the move from a religious to a secular appreciation of political order and the move from a monarchical (or authoritarian) mode of sovereignty to the popular (or democratic) (Kahn 1999, p. 41). Other political systems have not completely traversed these changes (or even started), but the social imaginary of the rule of law offers a way to think about how such transitions might progress. Understanding the rule of law not as an artefact of jurisprudence but rather as a social imaginary or common sense offers a way of setting the rule *by* law in the context of the rule *of* law, and by doing so offers the possibility for societies whose conception of the rule of law remain at the thin end of the continuum to nevertheless see their connection with thicker conceptions. This pluralist grounding offers further support for understanding both the appeal and widespread use of the norm, even if there remain significant disagreements about what it means. That there are disagreements indicates not the rule of law's vacuity but rather the strength of the social imaginary it encompasses.

Furthermore, the establishment of the rule of law as a (global) social imaginary is not a natural phenomenon; it cannot merely have happened spontaneously across the world. Here, Margaret Archer's analysis is informative: the dynamic development of the rule of law is the product of the interaction between commonality and contradiction in understandings of the rule of law and the social facts of its practice(s). Thus, the (claimed) lack of the rule of law is a prompt for social action, a contradiction in Archer's sense: there is a contradiction between how actors or agents normatively understand good governance and its actuality in a given situation. The norm prompts behaviour meant to close the gap, address the lack, and this is expressed as introducing the rule of law, even in realms that are governed by law, just not the right law! It is also worth noting that in parallel to Samuel Moyn's revisionist history of human rights (Moyn 2010), it is not necessarily the case that the call for the rule of law always originates with lawyers. Certainly they may shape what is (formally) possible, but often social movements, political actors and others are at the forefront of demanding the benefits that the epistemic community of law(yers) has claimed for its favoured technology. Moreover, although in one sense the seeming impossibility of resolving debates between thick and thin conceptions of the rule of law leads some to regard it is a rhetorical flourish, equally, seeing the rule of law as a social imaginary suggests that its flexibility of meaning is what allows a wide range of agents (including lawyers and their familiars) to reinforce the ascendance of the social imaginary itself by offering convincing arguments for commonality between various practices and beliefs about the law.

The rule of law may be the common sense of global politics but this is not to say that this has merely been a narrative of political discovery, an emergent norm becoming recognized as self-evidently 'true'. Indeed, we might regard the rule of law as one in a line of successive universalisms that have been invoked by the powerful when seeking to legitimize their rule; it would therefore follow Christianity, civilization, modernization and development (Koskenniemi 2012, p. 311; Upham 2004, p. 280), and as such it should be no surprise that the idea itself remains often contentious. For others, thinking about imperialism and the utilization of the law by dominant social forces, the rule of law is about the legitimization of power and therefore is a tool (or practice) of political domination. However, as Eugene Genovese pointed out some years ago, 'no class in the modern Western world could rule long without some ability to present itself as the guardian of the interests and sentiments of those being ruled' (Genovese 1975, p. 25). Therefore, as E.P. Thompson (1975) famously suggested, the rule of law has to fulfil (on a reasonably regular basis) the normative function claimed for it, if it is to effectively replace the rule of force, and to be accepted as legitimate and thereby be broadly acceded to by the polity at large. Just to give one recent example of why this might be important: Václav Havel has been clear that the success of Charter 77 in working to transform communist bloc politics in the 1970s and 1980s was reliant on communist governments 'pretend[ing] to respect human rights' while their appeal to legalism allowed dissidents to prosper through 'persistent and never-ending appeal to the laws' so enacted (quoted in Moyn 2010, p. 163). Of course, this form of resistance through the law may have been available for centuries (which is Thompson's point), but what interests me is why the political technology of the rule of law is no longer something that is in the background (practised but mainly unarticulated) and has become a political value celebrated by those with little knowledge of or interest in the jurisprudential debates that pattern the more specialized consid- erations of the issue. Is this because this claim can no longer be taken for granted? Does the very fact of its increasingly explicit articulation indicate that like other universalisms its grounds are becoming politically suspect, or does the pluralist triangle suggest that there is a clear basic human value accorded to the rule of law (albeit in a thin sense)?

In this book I have tried to answer these questions but make no claims to have come to a comprehensive conclusion. I can only claim to have sug- gested a number of contributory and potentially interesting explanations to a conundrum that has puzzled me for a while: why is it that the rule of law is now just taken as a social good in political discussion without much dissent? This is not to say that I want to launch a major critique of the rule of law (and indeed have not done so in the previous chapters), only that I want to unpack a social process that seems to me to be central to modern global politics but which has not been examined at any great length outside the discipline of law.

The claims for the rule of law that have had a reasonable salience in domestic, liberal politics for a century or more have now entered the global political realm due partly to structural changes linked to the process(es) of globalization, and the practices and interests of the epistemic community of law(yers) alongside a wider political demand for order and (good) governance. Across the world the availability of technical expertise in the law, and the increasingly complex character of global political-economic relations has prompted interest in forms of regulation that rely less on coercion and more on shared understandings of the normativity of law. The rule of law has been deployed by certain powerful groups to narrow the forms of governance that might be regarded as legitimate in the global political economy, although such claims, by virtue of the rule of law's normative elements, have also allowed some engagement with the stric- tures thereby implied. Nevertheless, the rule of law as social imaginary, or common sense, is about shaping the manner in which we all see the world's possibilities for governance and order.

There are, as I have indicated, all sorts of problems and issues with the rule of law that have vexed commentators, analysts, practitioners, citizens and legislators across the world, but what is notable is that the debates now are about the rule of law and seldom about any alternative. But again, I would stress: the rule of law does not automatically favour the strong and powerful; it is a set of possible norms, mechanisms and practices that balance social interest and power with considerations of justice and social equity. Critics may see this as merely a cynical ploy to make governance cheaper, but like E.P. Thompson I remain convinced that the rule of law is a social good, albeit compromised and incomplete in any particular manifestation. Moreover, as I hope to have demonstrated, the rise of the rule of law needs to be understood as the result of social interactions, the mobilization of interest through professionalization and as a response to material changes in the global political economy, not merely as a story of the triumph of jurisprudential good sense. There is much more to say on the rule of law, but I hope by now at the very least you agree that we cannot merely take the veracity of claims around the ascendance of the rule of law at face value or for granted, even if we think the rule of law is broadly a good thing.

# Bibliography

Abbott, Andrew (1988), *The System of Professions: An Essay on the Division of Expert Labour*, Chicago, IL: University of Chicago Press.

Abel, Richard (2003), *English Lawyers Between Market and State: The Politics of Professionalism*, Oxford: Oxford University Press.

Acemoglu, Daron and James A. Robinson (2012), *Why Nations Fail: The Origins of Power, Prosperity and Poverty*, London: Profile Books.

Acharya, Amitav (2004), 'How ideas spread: whose norms matter? Norm localisation and institutional change in Asian regionalism', *International Organisation*, **58** (2), April, 239–75.

Acton, H.B. (1956), 'Political justification', reprinted in H.A. Bedau (ed.) (1969), *Civil Disobedience: Theory and Practice*, Indianapolis: Pegasus.

Adler, Emanuel and Steven Bernstein (2005), 'Knowledge in power: the epistemic construction of global governance', in M. Barnett and R. Duvall (eds), *Power in Global Governance*, Cambridge: Cambridge University Press.

Agrast, Mark David, Juan Carlos Botero, Joel Martinez, Alejandro Ponce and Christine S. Pratt (2012), *The World Justice Project: Rule of Law Index*, Washington, DC: World Justice Project.

Akerlof, George A. and Robert J. Shiller (2010), *Animal Spirits: How Human Psychology Drives the Economy, and Why It Matters for Global Capitalism* (updated paperback edn), Princeton, NJ: Princeton University Press.

Albert, Michel (1993), *Capitalism vs. Capitalism*, New York: Four Walls Eight Windows.

Allan, T.R.S. (2001), *Constitutional Justice: A Liberal Theory of the Rule of Law*, Oxford: Oxford University Press.

Allen, Michael H. (2004), 'Globalization and pre-emptory norms in international law: from Westphalian to global constitutionalism?', *International Politics*, **41** (3), 341–55.

Almqvist, Jessica and Carlos Esposito (eds) (2012), *The Role of Courts in Transitional Justice: Voices from Latin America and Spain*, London: Routledge.

Alter, Karen J. (2001), *Establishing the Supremacy of European Law: The*

*Making of an International Rule of Law in Europe*, Oxford: Oxford University Press.

Alter, Karen J. (2012), 'The global spread of European style international courts', *West European Politics*, **35** (1), 135–54.

Anderson, Gavin W. (2005), *Constitutional Rights After Globalisation*, Oxford: Hart Publishing.

An-Na'im, Abdullahi (1999), 'The cultural mediation of human rights: the Al-Arqam case in Malaysia', in J.R. Bauer and D.A. Bell (eds), *The East Asian Challenge for Human Rights*, Cambridge: Cambridge University Press.

Appelbaum, Richard P. (1998), 'The future of law in a global economy', *Social and Legal Studies*, **7** (2), 171–92.

Archer, Margaret (1982), 'Morphogenesis versus structuration: on combining structure and action', *British Journal of Sociology*, **33** (4), 455–83.

Archer, Margaret (1995), *Realist Social Theory: The Morphogenetic Approach*, Cambridge: Cambridge University Press.

Archer, Margaret (2007), *Making Our Way Through the World: Human Reflexivity and Social Mobility*, Cambridge: Cambridge University Press.

Archer, Margaret (2012), *The Reflexive Imperative in Late Modernity*, Cambridge: Cambridge University Press.

Archibugi, Daniele, Mathias Koenig-Archibugi and Raffaele Marchetti (2012), 'Introduction: mapping global democracy', in D. Archibugi, M. Koenig-Archibugi and R. Marchetti (eds), *Global Democracy: Normative and Empirical Perspectives*, Cambridge: Cambridge University Press.

Arendt, Hannah (1973), *Crises of the Republic*, Harmondsworth: Penguin Books.

Ariens, Michael (1992), 'Modern legal times: making a professional legal culture', *Journal of American Culture*, **15** (1), 15–25.

Armytage, Livingston (2011), 'Judicial reform in Asia: case study of ADB's experience 1990–2007', *Hague Journal on the Rule of Law*, **3** (1), 70–105.

Arts, Bas and Dieter Kerwer (2007), 'Beyond legalisation? How global standards work', in C. Brütsch and D. Lehmkhul (eds), *Law and Legalization in Transnational Relations*, Abingdon: Routledge.

Astrada, Sebastian R. (2009), 'Exporting the rule of law to Mongolia: post-socialist legal and judicial reforms', *Berkeley Electronic Press: Selected Works*, available at http://works.bepress/sebastian_astrada/4/ (accessed 24 June 2010).

Bakker, Isabella and Stephen Gill (2003), 'Ontology, method, and hypotheses', in I. Bakker and S. Gill (eds), *Power, Production and Social Reproduction*, Basingstoke: Palgrave Macmillan.

Barad, Elizabeth (2005), 'Export and import of the rule of law in the global era', *International Law Students Association Journal of International and Comparative Law*, **11**, Spring, 323–9.

Barber, N.W. (2004), 'Must legalistic conceptions of the rule of law have a social dimension?', *Ratio Juris*, **17** (4), December, 474–88.

Barnett, Michael and Raymond Duvall (2005), 'Power in global governance', in M. Barnett and R. Duvall (eds), *Power in Global Governance*, Cambridge: Cambridge University Press.

Barro, Robert J. (1997), *Determinants of Economic Growth: A Cross-country Empirical Study*, Cambridge, MA: MIT Press.

Barros, D. Benjamin (ed.) (2010), *Hernando de Soto and Property in a Market Society*, Farnham: Ashgate.

Barry, Brian (1970), *Sociologists, Economists and Democracy*, London: Collier-Macmillan.

Bartelson, Jens (2009), *Visions of World Community*, Cambridge: Cambridge University Press.

Bassu, Giovanni (2008), 'Law overruled: strengthening the rule of law in postconflict states', *Global Governance*, **14** (1), 21–38.

Beard, Jennifer (2006), 'The confessional framework of rule of law development: how to offer salvation to willing legal subjects', *Nordic Journal of International Law*, **75**, 409–49.

Bedau, Hugo Adam (ed.) (1991), *Civil Disobedience in Focus*, London: Routledge.

Bedner, Adriaan (2010), 'An elementary approach to the rule of law', *Hague Journal on the Rule of Law*, **2** (1), 48–74.

Berling, Per (2006), *Rule of Law on the International Agenda: International Support to Legal and Judicial Reform in International Administration, Transition and Development Co-operation*, Antwerp: Intersentia.

Berman, Harold J. (1983), *Law and Revolution: The Formation of the Western Legal Tradition*, Cambridge, MA: Harvard University Press.

Berman, Harold J. and Charles J. Reid (2000), 'Max Weber as legal historian', in S. Turner (ed.), *The Cambridge Companion to Weber*, Cambridge: Cambridge University Press.

Berman, Paul Schiff (2005), 'From international law to law and globalisation', *Columbia Journal of Transnational Law*, **43**, 485–556.

Berman, Paul Schiff (2009), 'The new legal pluralism', *Annual Review of Law and Social Science*, **5**, 225–42.

Bernauer, Thomas, Manfred Elsig and Joost Pauwelyn (2012), 'Dispute settlement mechanism: analysis and problems', in A. Narlikar, M. Daunton and R. Stern (eds), *The Oxford Handbook on the World Trade Organization*, Oxford: Oxford University Press.

Besson, Samantha (2009), 'Whose Constitution(s)? International law, constitutionalism and democracy', in J.L. Dunoff and J.P. Trachtman (eds), *Ruling the World? Constitutionalism, International Law and Global Governance*, Cambridge: Cambridge University Press.

Bessy, Christian (2012), 'Law, forms of organisation and the market for legal services', *Economic Sociology: The European Electronic Newsletter*, **14** (1), November, 20–30.

Bevir, Mark (1999), *The Logic of the History of Ideas*, Cambridge: Cambridge University Press.

Bevir, Mark and R.A.W. Rhodes (2010), *The State as Cultural Practice*, Oxford: Oxford University Press.

Billig, Michael (2013), *How to Write Badly: How to Succeed in the Social Sciences*, Cambridge: Cambridge University Press.

Bingham, Tom (2010), *The Rule of Law*, London: Allen Lane.

Bindreiter, Uta U. (2001), 'Presupposing the basic norm', *Ratio Juris*, **14** (2), 143–75.

Bleiker, Roland (2000), *Popular Dissent, Human Agency and Global Politics*, Cambridge: Cambridge University Press.

Blyth, Mark (1997), '"Any more bright ideas?": the ideational turn in comparative political economy (review article)', *Comparative Politics*, **29** (2), January, 229–50.

Blyth, Mark (2002), *Great Transformations: Economic Ideas and Institutional Change in the Twentieth Century*, Cambridge: Cambridge University Press.

Boon, Kristen E. (2007), '"Open for business": international financial institutions, post-conflict economic reform and the rule of law', *New York University Journal of International Law and Politics*, **39** (3), 513–81.

Botero, Juan Carlos, Robert L. Nelson and Christine Pratt (2011), *Measuring the Rule of Law*, Special Issue of the *Hague Journal on the Rule of Law*, **3** (2), The Hague: TMC Asser Press and Cambridge University Press.

Boulier, Abbé (1958), *The Law Above the Rule of Law: A Criticism of an Enterprise of the Cold War*, Brussels: International Association of Democratic Lawyers.

Bouloukos, Adam C. and Brett Dakin (2001), 'Toward a universal declaration of the rule of law: implications for criminal justice and sustainable development', *International Journal of Comparative Sociology*, **42** (1–2), 145–62.

Bourdieu, Pierre (1987), 'The force of law: toward a sociology of the juridical field', *Hastings Law Journal*, **38**, July, 805–53.

Braithwaite, John and Peter Drahos (2000), *Global Business Regulation*, Cambridge: Cambridge University Press.

Brenkman, John (2007), *The Cultural Contradictions of Democracy: Political Thought since September 11th*, Princeton, NJ: Princeton University Press.

Brooks, Rosa Ehrenreich (2003), 'The new imperialism: violence, norms and the "rule of law"', *Michigan Law Review*, **101** (7), June, 2275–340.

Brøther, Mona Elizabeth (2008), 'Legal empowerment as a new concept in development: translating good ideas into action', in D. Banik (ed.), *Rights and Legal Empowerment in Eradicating Poverty*, Farnham: Ashgate.

Brown, Garrett Wallace (2012), 'The constitutionalisation of what?', *Global Constitutionalism*, **1** (2), July, 201–28.

Brownlee, Kimberley (2007), 'The communicative aspects of civil disobedience and lawful punishment', *Criminal Law and Philosophy*, **1**, 179–92.

Brownlee, Kimberley (2009), 'Civil disobedience', *Stanford Encyclopaedia of Philosophy*, online version, available at http://plato.stanford.edu/entries/civil-disobedience (accessed 17 August 2010).

Brunnée, Jutta and Stephen J. Toope (2010), *Legitimacy and Legality in International Law: An Interactional Account*, Cambridge: Cambridge University Press.

Brunnée, Jutta and Stephen J. Toope (2011), 'Interactional international law and the practice of legality', in E. Adler and V. Pouliot (eds), *International Practices*, Cambridge: Cambridge University Press.

Brunnée, Jutta and Stephen J. Toope (2013), 'Constructivism and international law', in J.L. Dunoff and M.A. Pollack (eds), *Interdisciplinary Perspectives on International Law and International Relations: The State of the Art*, Cambridge: Cambridge University Press.

Brütsch, Christian and Dirk Lehmkhul (2007), 'Complex legalization and the many moves to law', in C. Brütsch and D. Lehmkhul (eds), *Law and Legalization in Transnational Relations*, Abingdon: Routledge.

Buchanan, Allen (2004), *Justice, Legitimacy and Self-Determination: Moral Foundations for International Law*, Oxford: Oxford University Press.

Buchanan, Ruth (2012), 'Legitimating global trade governance: constitutional and legal pluralist approaches', *Northern Ireland Legal Quarterly*, **57** (4), 1–19.

Bull, Carolyn (2008), *No Entry Without Strategy: Building the Rule of Law Under UN Transitional Administration*, Tokyo: United Nations University Press.

Bull, Hedley (2012), *The Anarchical Society: A Study of Order in World Politics* (fourth edn), Basingstoke: Palgrave Macmillan.

Burley, Anne-Marie (1993), 'Regulating the world: multilateralism, international law and the projection of the New Deal regulatory state', in

J.G. Ruggie (ed.), *Multilateralism Matters: The Theory and Praxis of an International Form*, New York: Columbia University Press.
Cammack, Paul (1997), *Capitalism and Democracy in the Third World: The Doctrine of Political Development*, London: Leicester University Press.
Campbell, John L. (2002), 'Ideas, politics and public policy', *Annual Review of Sociology*, **28**, 21–38.
Cardenal, Juan Pablo and Heriberto Araújo (2013), *China's Secret Army: The Pioneers, Traders, Fixers and Workers Who are Remaking the World in Beijing's Image*, London: Allen Lane.
Carfield, Maggi (2011), 'Participatory law and development: remapping the locus of authority', *University of Colorado Law Review*, **82** (3–4), 739–91.
Carothers, Thomas (1999), *Aiding Democracy Abroad: The Learning Curve*, Washington, DC: Carnegies Endowment for International Peace.
Carothers, Thomas (2006), 'The rule-of-law revival', in T. Carothers (ed.), *Promoting the Rule of Law Abroad: In Search of Knowledge*, Washington, DC: Carnegie Endowment for International Peace.
Carothers, Thomas (2007), 'The "sequencing" fallacy', *Journal of Democracy*, **18** (1), 12–27.
Carothers, Thomas (2009), 'Rule of law temptations', *Fletcher Forum of World Affairs*, **33** (1), Winter/Spring, 49–61.
Cass, Deborah Z. (2005), *The Constitutionalisation of the World Trade Organization: Legitimacy, Democracy and Community in the International Trading System*, Oxford: Oxford University Press.
Cassese, Sabino (2005), 'The globalization of law', *New York University Journal of International Law and Politics*, **37**, Summer, 973–92.
CEO (Corporate European Observatory) (2012), *Profiting from Injustice: How Law Firms, Arbitrators and Financiers are Fuelling an Investment Arbitration Boom*, Brussels: Corporate European Observatory.
CGG (Commission on Global Governance) (1995), *Our Global Neighbourhood*, Oxford: Oxford University Press.
Chabbott, Collette (1999), 'Development INGOs', in J. Boli and G.M. Thomas (eds), *Constructing World Culture: International Non-governmental Organisations Since 1875*, Stanford, CA: Stanford University Press.
Chadwick, Andrew and Christopher May (2003), 'Interaction between states and citizens in the age of the internet: "e-government" in the Unites States, Britain and the European Union', *Governance: An International Journal of Policy, Administration and Institutions*, **16** (2), April, 271–300.
Chandler, David (2006), 'Back to the future? The limits of neo-Wilsonian

ideals of exporting democracy', *Review of International Studies*, **32**, 475–94.

Charlesworth, Hilary (2010), 'Human rights and the rule of law after conflict', in P. Cane (ed.), *The Hart-Fuller Debate in the Twentieth Century*, Oxford: Hart Publishing.

Chayes, Abram and Antonia Handler Chayes (1995), *The New Sovereignty: Compliance with International Regulatory Agreements*, Cambridge, MA: Harvard University Press.

Chesterman, Simon (2008a), *The UN Security Council and the Rule of Law: The Role of the Security Council in Strengthening a Rules-based International System*, Final Report and Recommendations from the Austrian Initiative, 2004–2008, Vienna: Federal Ministry for European and International Affairs.

Chesterman, Simon (2008b), 'An international rule of law', *American Journal of Comparative Law*, **56** (3), Spring, 331–61.

CLEP (Commission on Legal Empowerment of the Poor) (2008), *Making the Law Work for Everyone*, New York: CLEP and United Nations Development Programme.

Cohan, John Alan (2007), 'Civil disobedience and the necessity defence', *Pierce Law Review*, **6**, September, 111–75.

Cohen, Amy J. (2009), 'Thinking with culture in law and development', *Buffalo Law Review*, **57**, April, 511–86.

Cohen, Benjamin J. (2008), *International Political Economy: An Intellectual History*, Princeton, NJ: Princeton University Press.

Cohen, Edward S. (2007), 'The harmonization of private commercial law: the case of secured finance', in C. Brütsch and D. Lehmkhul (eds), *Law and Legalization in Transnational Relations*, Abingdon: Routledge.

Cole, Daniel H. (2001), '"An unqualified human good": E.P. Thompson and the rule of law', *Journal of Law and Society*, **28** (2), June, 177–203.

Comaroff, John L. and Jean Comaroff (2009), 'Reflections on the anthropology of law, governance and sovereignty', in F. von Benda-Beckmann, K. von Benda-Beckmann and J. Eckert (eds), *Rule of Law and Laws of Ruling: On the Governance of Law*, Farnham: Ashgate.

Cooley, Alexander (2010), 'Outsourcing authority: how project contracts transform global governance networks', in D.D. Avant, M. Finnemore and S.K. Sell (eds), *Who Governs the Globe?*, Cambridge: Cambridge University Press.

Corell, Hans (2001), 'The visible college of international law: "towards the rule of law in international relations"', *American Society of International Law Proceedings 2001*, 262–70.

Corrigan, Phillip and Derek Sayer (1981), 'How the law rules: variations on some themes in Karl Marx', in B. Fryer, A. Hunt, D. McBarnet and B. Moorhouse (eds), *Law, State and Society*, London: Croom Helm.

Cortell, Andrew P. and James W. Davis (2000), 'Understanding the domestic impact of international norms: a research agenda', *International Studies Review*, **2** (1), Spring, 65–87.

Cosgrove, Richard A. (1980), *The Rule of Law: Albert Venn Dicey, Victorian Jurist*, Chapel Hill, NC: University of North Carolina Press.

Costa, Pietro and Danilo Zolo (eds) (2007), *The Rule of Law: History, Theory and Criticism*, Dordrecht: Springer.

Cottier, Thomas (2012), 'The rise of domestic courts in the implementation of WTO law: the political economy of separation of powers and checks and balances in international trade regulation', in A. Narlikar, M. Daunton and R. Stern (eds), *The Oxford Handbook of the World Trade Organization*, Oxford: Oxford University Press.

Council of Europe (2008), *The Council of Europe and the Rule of Law: An Overview*, Document GR-J(2008)11, Strasbourg: Council of Europe.

Cover, Robert (1995), 'The folktales of justice: tales of jurisdiction', in M. Minow, M. Ryan and A. Sarat (eds), *Narrative, Violence and the Law: The Essays of Robert Cover*, Ann Arbor, MI: University of Michigan Press.

Cox, Robert W. (1996) (with Timothy J. Sinclair), *Approaches to World Order*, Cambridge: Cambridge University Press.

Craig, Paul (1997), 'Formal and substantive conceptions of the rule of law: an analytical framework', *Public Law*, **3**, Autumn, 467–87.

Cross, Frank B. (2002), 'Law and economic growth', *Texas Law Review*, **80**, 1737–75.

Cumming, Gordon D. (2008), 'French NGOs in the global era: professionalization "without borders"', *Voluntas*, **19**, 372–94.

Dam, Kenneth W. (2006), *The Law-Growth Nexus: The Rule of Law and Economic Development*, Washington, DC: The Brookings Institution.

Davidson, Nestor M. (2010), 'The bell jar and the bullhorn: Hernando de Soto and communication through title', in D.B. Barros (ed.), *Hernando de Soto and Property in a Market Society*, Farnham: Ashgate.

Davis, Kevin E. and Michael J. Trebilcock (2008), 'The relationship between law and development: optimists versus skeptics', *American Journal of Comparative Law*, **56**, 895–946.

Davis, Kevin E. (2004), 'What can the rule of law variable tell us about rule of law reforms?', *Michigan Journal of International Law*, **26**, Fall, 141–61.

Davis Cross, Mai'a K. (2013), 'Rethinking epistemic communities twenty years later', *Review of International Studies*, **39** (1), January, 137–60.

de Búrca, Gráinne and J.H.H. Weiler (eds) (2012), *The Worlds of European Constitutionalism*, Cambridge: Cambridge University Press.

de Soto, Hernando (2000), *The Mystery of Capital: Why Capitalism Triumphs in the West and Fails Everywhere Else*, London: Transworld Publishers.

de Soto, Hernando (2008), 'Are Africans culturally unsuited to property rights and the rule of law? Some reflections based on the Tanzanian case', in D. Banik (ed.), *Rights and Legal Empowerment in Eradicating Poverty*, Farnham: Ashgate.

de Sousa Santos, Boaventura (2002), *Towards a New Legal Common Sense* (second edn), London: Butterworths/LexisNexis.

de Sousa Santos, Boaventura and César Rodríguez-Garavito (2005), 'Law, politics, and the subaltern in counter-hegemonic globalisation', in B. de Sousa Santos and C. Rodríguez-Garavito (eds), *Law and Globalisation from Below: Towards a Cosmopolitan Legality*, Cambridge: Cambridge University Press.

Decker, Klaus (2010), 'World Bank rule-of-law assistance in fragile states: development and perspectives', in A. Perry-Kessaris (ed.), *Law in the Pursuit of Development: Principles into Practice?*, Abingdon: Routledge.

Deitelhoff, Nicole (2009), 'The discursive process of legalization: charting islands of persuasion in the ICC case', *International Organisation*, **63** (91), 33–65.

Delacroix, Sylvie (2009), 'You'd better be committed: legal norms and normativity', *American Journal of Jurisprudence*, **54** (1), 117–32.

Delacroix, Sylvie (2011), 'Tracing a genealogy of legal normativity: responsibility, authorship and contingency', in S. Bertea and G. Pavlakos (eds), *New Essays in the Normativity of the Law*, Oxford: Hart Publishing.

Demsetz, Harold (1967), 'Towards a theory of property rights', *American Economic Review*, **57** (2), May, 347–59.

Demsorean, Ana, Sorana Parvulsecu and Bogdan Vetrici-Soimu (2009), 'Romania: vetoed reforms, skewed results', in A. Magen and L. Morlino (eds), *International Actors, Democratization and the Rule of Law: Anchoring Democracy?*, London: Routledge.

Derrida, Jacques (1992), 'Force of law: the "mystical foundation of authority"', in D. Cornell, M. Rosenfeld and D.G. Carlson (eds), *Deconstruction and the Possibility of Justice*, New York: Routledge.

Dezalay, Yves and Bryant G. Garth (1996), *Dealing in Virtue: International Commercial Arbitration and the Construction of a Transnational Legal Order*, Chicago, IL: University of Chicago Press.

Dezalay, Yves and Bryant G. Garth (2002), *The Internationalisation of Palace Wars: Lawyers, Economists and the Contest to Transform Latin American States*, Chicago, IL: University of Chicago Press.

Dezalay, Yves and Bryant G. Garth (2010), *Asian Legal Revivals: Lawyers in the Shadow of Empire*, Chicago, IL: University of Chicago Press.

Dezalay, Yves and Bryant G. Garth (2011a), 'Introduction: lawyers, law and society', in Y. Dezalay and B.G. Garth (eds), *Lawyers and the Rule of Law in an Era of Globalisation*, Abingdon: Routledge and GlassHouse.

Dezalay, Yves and Bryant G. Garth (2011b), 'Conclusion: how to convert social capital into legal capital and transfer legitimacy across the major practice divide', in Y. Dezalay and B.G. Garth (eds), *Lawyers and the Rule of Law in an Era of Globalisation*, Abingdon: Routledge and GlassHouse.

Dhagamwar, Vasudha (1998), 'Rule of law: squaring the circle', in S. Saberwal and H. Sievers (eds), *Rules, Laws, Constitutions*, New Delhi: Sage Publications.

Dhavan, Rajeev (1994), 'Law as concern: reflecting on law and development', in Y. Vyvas, K. Kibwana, O. Owati and S. Wanjála (eds), *Law and Development in the Third World*, Nairobi: Faculty of Law, University of Nairobi.

Dicey, Albert Venn (1915), *Introduction to the Study of the Law of the Constitution*, reprinted in 1982, Indianapolis: Liberty Classics.

Dobbins, James, Seth G. Jones, Keith Crane and Beth Cole DeGrasse (2007), *The Beginner's Guide to Nation-building*, Santa Monica: RAND Corporation, National Security Research Division.

Dobner, Petra (2010), 'More law, less democracy? Democracy and transnational constitutionalism', in P. Dobner and M. Loughlin (eds), *The Twilight of Constitutionalism?*, Oxford: Oxford University Press.

Dobner, Petra and Martin Loughlin (eds) (2010), *The Twilight of Constitutionalism?*, Oxford: Oxford University Press.

Domingo, Pilar and Rachel Sieder (2001), 'Conclusions: promoting the rule of law in Latin America', in P. Domingo and R. Sieder (eds), *Rule of Law in Latin America: The International Promotion of Judicial Reform*, London: Institute of Latin American Studies.

Doyle, Michael (2009), 'The UN Charter – a global constitution?', in J.L. Dunoff and J.P. Trachtman (eds), *Ruling the World? Constitutionalism, International Law and Global Governance*, Cambridge: Cambridge University Press.

Dunoff, Jeffrey L. (2009), 'The politics of international constitutions: the curious case of the World Trade Organization', in J.L. Dunoff and J.P. Trachtman (eds), *Ruling the World? Constitutionalism, International Law and Global Governance*, Cambridge: Cambridge University Press.

Dunoff, Jeffrey L. and Joel P. Trachtman (eds) (2009), *Ruling the*

*World? Constitutionalism, International Law and Global Governance*, Cambridge: Cambridge University Press.

Dworkin, Ronald (1978), *Taking Rights Seriously* (New Impression with a Reply to Critics), London: Duckworth.

Dworkin, Ronald (1985), 'Political judges and the rule of law', in R. Dworkin, *A Matter of Principle*, Cambridge, MA: Harvard University Press.

Dyzenhaus, David (2006), *The Constitution of the Law: Legality in a Time of Emergency*, Cambridge: Cambridge University Press.

Dyzenhaus, David (2007), 'The past and future of the rule of law in South Africa', *South African Law Journal*, **124** (4), 734–61.

Dyzenhaus, David (2010), 'The very idea of a judge', *University of Toronto Law Journal*, **60**, 61–80.

Ellerman, David (2008), 'Pushing into a pipeline or pushing on a string? Duelling representations in development and educational theories', in D.F. Ruccio (ed.), *Economic Representations: Academic and Everyday*, London: Routledge.

Ellmann, Stephen (1998), 'Cause lawyering in the Third World', in A. Sarat and S. Scheingold (eds), *Cause Lawyering: Political Commitments and Professional Responsibilities*, New York: Oxford University Press.

Elster, Jon (2004), *Closing the Books: Transitional Justice in Historical Perspective*, Cambridge: Cambridge University Press.

Ewick, Patricia and Susan S. Silbey (1998), *The Common Place of Law: Stories from Everyday Life*, Chicago, IL: University of Chicago Press.

Fallon, Richard (1997), '"The rule of law" as a concept in constitutional discourse', *Columbia Law Review*, **97** (1), January, 1–56.

Farrall, Jeremy M. (2007), *United Nations Sanctions and the Rule of Law*, Cambridge: Cambridge University Press.

Fassbender, Bardo (2007), '"We the peoples of the United Nations": constituent power and constitutional form in international law', in M. Loughlin and N. Walker (eds), *The Paradox of Constitutionalism: Constituent Power and Constitutional Form*, Oxford: Oxford University Press.

Fassbender, Bardo (2009), 'Rediscovering a forgotten constitution: notes on the place of the UN Charter in the international legal order', in J.L. Dunoff and J.P. Trachtman (eds), *Ruling the World? Constitutionalism, International Law and Global Governance*, Cambridge: Cambridge University Press.

Faundez, Julio (2005), 'The rule of law enterprise: promoting a dialogue between practitioners and academics', *Democratization*, **12** (4), 567–86.

Faundez, Julio (2009), 'Empowering workers in the informal economy', *Hague Journal on the Rule of Law*, **1** (1), 156–72.

Feldman, Stephen M. (1991), 'An interpretation of Max Weber's theory of law: metaphysics, economics and the iron cage of constitutional Law', *Law and Social Enquiry*, **16** (2), Spring, 205–48.

Ferguson, Niall (2003), *Empire: How Britain Made the Modern World*, London: Allen Lane.

Ferguson, Niall (2011), *Civilisation: The Six Ways the West Beat the Rest*, London: Allen Lane.

Fine, Ben (2002), 'Economics imperialism and the new development economics as Kuhnian paradigm shift?', *World Development*, **30** (12), 2057–70.

Finnemore, Martha and Kathryn Sikkink (1998), 'International norm dynamics and political change', *International Organisation*, **52** (4), 887–917.

Finnemore, Martha and Stephen J. Toope (2001), 'Alternatives to "legalization": Richer views of law and politics', *International Organisation*, **55** (3), Summer, 743–58.

Fletcher, George P. (1996), *Basic Concepts of Legal Thought*, New York: Oxford University Press.

Flett, James (2012), 'Importing other international regimes into World Trade Organization litigation', in M.A. Young (ed.), *Regime Interaction in International Law: Facing Fragmentation*, Cambridge: Cambridge University Press.

Flood, John (2007), 'Lawyers as sanctifiers: the role of elite law firms in international business transactions', *Indiana Journal of Global Legal Studies*, **14** (1), Spring, 35–66.

Fogelklou, Anders (1997), 'Principles of rule of law and legal development', in P. Sevastik (ed.), *Legal Assistance in Developing Countries: Swedish Perspectives on the Rule of Law*, Dordrecht: Kluwer Law International.

Folbre, Nancy (2009), *Greed, Lust and Gender: A History of Economic Ideas*, Oxford: Oxford University Press.

Friedman, Lawrence M. (1969), 'On legal development', *Rutgers Law Review*, **24**, 11–64.

Friedman, Lawrence M. (1994), 'Is there a modern legal culture?', *Ratio Juris*, **7** (2), 117–31.

Friedmann, Wolfgang (1971), *The State and the Rule of Law in a Mixed Economy*, London: Stevens & Sons.

Friman, H. Richard (ed.) (2009), *Crime and the Global Political Economy, IPE Yearbook Vol. 16*, Boulder, CO: Lynne Rienner Publishers.

Fudge, Judy (2011), 'Constitutionalising labour rights in Europe', in T. Campbell, K.D. Ewing and A. Tomkins (eds), *The Legal Protection of Human Rights: Sceptical Essays*, Oxford: Oxford University Press.

Fukuyama, Francis (2004), *State Building: Governance and World Order in the Twenty-first Century*, London: Profile Books.

Fukuyama, Francis (2010), 'Transitions to the rule of law', *Journal of Democracy*, **21** (1), January, 33–44.

Fukuyama, Francis, Thomas Carothers, Edward D. Mansfield, Jack Snyder and Sheri Berman (2007), 'The debate on "sequencing" (exchange)', *Journal of Democracy*, **18** (3), 5–22.

Fuller, Lon L. (1969), *The Morality of Law* (revised edn), New Haven, CT: Yale University Press.

Gabel, Peter (1980), 'Reification in legal reasoning', in S. Spitzer (ed.), *Research in Law and Sociology*, Vol. 3, Greenwich, CT: JAI Press.

Ganev, Venelin I. (2009), 'The rule of law as institutionalized wager: constitutions, courts and transformative social dynamics in Eastern Europe', *Hague Journal on the Rule of Law*, **1** (2), 263–83.

Gardner, James A. (1980), *Legal Imperialism: American Lawyers and Foreign Aid in Latin America*, Madison, WI: University of Wisconsin Press.

Garth, Bryant G. (2008), 'The globalization of law', in K.E. Whittington, R.D. Keleman and G.A. Caldeira (eds), *The Oxford Handbook of Law and Politics*, Oxford: Oxford University Press.

Garth, Bryant G. and Yves Dezalay (2002), 'Introduction', in Y. Dezalay and B.G. Garth (eds), *Global Prescriptions: The Production, Exportation and Importation of a New Legal Orthodoxy*, Ann Arbor, MI: University of Michigan Press.

Genovese, Eugene D. (1975), *Roll Jordan Roll: The World Slaves Made*, London: Andre Deutsch.

Gilbert, Alan (2012), 'Viewpoint: De Soto's *The Mystery of Capital*: reflections on the book's public impact', *International Development Planning Review*, **34** (3), v–xvii.

Gill, Stephen (1998), 'New constitutionalism, democratisation and global political economy', *Pacifica Review*, **10** (1), February, 23–38.

Gill, Stephen (2003), *Power and Resistance in the New World Order*, Basingstoke: Palgrave Macmillan.

Gilman, Nils, Jesse Goldhammer and Steven Weber (2011), *Deviant Globalization: Black Market Economy in the 21st Century*, New York: Continuum.

Goldman, Michael (2005), *Imperial Knowledge: The World Bank and Struggles for Social Justice in the Age of Globalization*, New Haven, CT: Yale University Press.

Goldsmith, Lord (2006), 'Government and the rule of law in the modern age', London School of Economics Law Department and Clifford Chance Lecture Series on Rule of Law, available at http://www2.

lse.ac.uk/PublicEvents/pdf/20060222-Goldsmith.pdf (accessed 16 May 2013).

Goldstein, Judith L. and Richard H. Steinberg (2009), 'Regulatory shift: the rise of judicial liberalisation at the WTO', in W. Mattli and N. Woods (eds), *The Politics of Global Regulation*, Princeton, NJ: Princeton University Press.

Goldstein, Judith L., Miles Kahler, Robert Keohane and Anne-Marie Slaughter (eds) (2001), *Legalization and World Politics*, Cambridge, MA: MIT Press.

Golub, Stephen (2006), 'A house without a foundation', in T. Carothers (ed.), *Promoting the Rule of Law Abroad: In Search of Knowledge*, Washington, DC: Carnegie Endowment for International Peace.

Golub, Stephen (2009), 'The Commission on Legal Empowerment of the Poor: one big step forward and a few steps back for development policy and practice', *Hague Journal on the Rule of Law*, **1** (1), 101–16.

Golub, Stephen (2010), *Legal Empowerment: Practitioners' Perspectives (Legal and Governance Reforms: Lessons Learned – No. 2)*, Rome: International Development Law Organization.

Goodpaster, Gary (2003), 'Law reform in developing countries', *Transnational Law and Contemporary Problems*, **13**, Fall, 659–97.

Gosalbo-Bono, Ricardo (2010), 'The significance of the rule of law and its implications for the European Union and the United States', *University of Pittsburgh Law Review*, **72**, 231–360.

Graubart, Jonathan (2004), '"Legalizing" politics, "politicizing" law: transnational activism and international law', *International Politics*, **41**, 319–40.

Guilhot, Nicolas (2005), *The Democracy Makers: Human Rights and the Politics of Global Order*, New York: Columbia University Press.

Habermas, Jürgen (1996), *Between Facts and Norms: Contributions to a Discourse Theory of Law and Democracy*, Cambridge, MA: MIT Press.

Habermas, Jürgen (2001), *The Postnational Constellation: Political Essays* (trans., edited and with an introduction by Max Pensky), Cambridge: Polity Press.

Hager, L. Michael (1986), 'Training lawyers for development: the IDLI Experience', *Third World Legal Studies – 1986*, 57–62.

Haggard, Stephen and Lydia Tiede (2011), 'The rule of law and economic growth: where are we?', *World Development*, **39** (5), 673–85.

Haggard, Stephen, Andrew MacIntyre and Lydia Tiede (2008), 'The rule of law and economic development', *Annual Review of Political Science*, **11**, 205–34.

Hakimi, Monica (2007), 'To condone or condemn? Regional enforcement actions in the absence of Security Council authorisation', *Vanderbilt Journal of Transnational Law*, **40**, 643–85.

Hall, Rodney Bruce (2008), *Central Banking as Global Governance: Constructing Financial Credibility*, Cambridge: Cambridge University Press.

Haltern, Ulrich (2003), 'Pathos and patina: the failure and promise of constitutionalism in the European imagination', *European Law Journal*, **9** (1), February, 14–44.

Hammergren, Linn (2010), 'With friends like these: can multilateral development banks promote institutional development to strengthen the rule of law?', in A. Perry-Kessaris (ed.), *Law in the Pursuit of Development: Principles into Practice*, Abingdon: Routledge and GlassHouse.

Hammerslev, Ole (2011), 'The European Union and the United States in Eastern Europe: two ways of exporting law, expertise and state power', in Y. Dezalay and B.G. Garth (eds), *Lawyers and the Rule of Law in an Era of Globalisation*, Abingdon: Routledge and GlassHouse.

Hartmann, Eva (2011), 'The difficult relation between international law and politics: the legal turn from a critical IPE perspective', *New Political Economy*, **16** (5), 561–84.

Hay, Colin (2011), 'Ideas and the construction of interests', in D. Béland and R.H. Cox (eds), *Ideas and Politics in Social Science Research*, Oxford: Oxford University Press.

Hayek, Friedrich A. (1944), *The Road to Serfdom*, reprinted in 1993, London: Routledge.

Hayek, Friedrich A. (1973), *Law, Legislation and Liberty, Volume One: Rules and Order*, London: Routledge & Kegan Paul.

Hayek, Friedrich A. (1988), 'The origins of liberty, property and justice', in F.A. Hayek, *The Fatal Conceit: The Errors of Socialism*, Vol. 1 of The Collected World of F.A. Hayek, ed. W.W. Bartley, London: Routledge.

Henkin, Louis (1979), *How Nations Behave: Law and Foreign Policy* (second edn), New York: Columbia University Press and Council on Foreign Relations.

HiiL (Hague Institute for the Internationalisation of Law) (2007), *Rule of Law Inventory Report: Academic Part*, The Hague: Hague Institute for the Internationalisation of Law.

Hillbom, Ellen (2011), 'The right to water: an inquiry into legal empowerment and property rights formation in Tanzania', in D. Banik (ed.), *The Legal Empowerment Agenda: Poverty, Labour and the Informal Economy in Africa*, Farnham: Ashgate.

Hirschl, Ran and Evan Rosevear (2011), 'Constitutional law meets comparative politics: socio-economic rights and political realities', in

T. Campbell, K.D. Ewing and A. Tomkins (eds), *The Legal Protection of Human Rights: Sceptical Essays*, Oxford: Oxford University Press.

Hobson, John M. (2012), *The Eurocentric Conception of World Politics: Western International Theory, 1760–2010*, Cambridge: Cambridge University Press.

Holderness, Clifford (1985), 'A Legal Foundation for Exchange', *Journal of Legal Studies*, **14**, June, 321–44.

Holmes, Stephen (2010), *Theatre of the Rule of Law: Transnational Legal Intervention in Theory and Practice*, Cambridge: Cambridge University Press.

Honoré, Tony (1998), 'The basic norm of society', in S.L. Paulson and B.L. Paulson (eds), *Normativity and Norms: Critical Perspectives on Kelsenian Themes*, Oxford: Clarendon Press.

Horton, Scott (2007), 'State of exception: Bush's war on the rule of law', *Harpers Magazine*, July, 74–81.

Houtzager, Peter P. (2001), 'We make the law and the law makes us: some ideas on a law in development research agenda', *IDS Bulletin*, **32** (1), 8–18.

Huang, Reyko (2008), 'Counterterrorism and the rule of law', in A. Hurwitz and R. Huang (eds), *Civil War and the Rule of Law: Security, Development, Human Rights*, Boulder, CO: Lynne Rienner Publishers.

Hudson, David and Mary Martin (2010), 'Narratives of neoliberalism: the role of everyday media practices and the reproduction of dominant ideas', in A. Gofas and C. Hay (eds), *The Role of Ideas in Political Analysis: A Portrait of Contemporary Debates*, Abingdon: Routledge.

Humphreys, Stephen (2010), *Theatre of the Rule of Law: Transnational Legal Intervention in Theory and Practice*, Cambridge: Cambridge University Press.

Huntington, Samuel P. (1991), *The Third Wave: Democratization in the Late Twentieth Century*, Norman, OK: University of Oklahoma Press.

Huntington, Samuel P. (2002), *The Clash of Civilisations and the Remaking of the World Order*, London: Simon & Schuster and The Free Press.

Hutchinson, Allan C. and Patrick Monahan (1987), 'Democracy and the rule of law', in A.C. Hutchinson and P. Monahan (eds), *The Rule of Law: Ideal or Ideology*, Toronto: Carswell.

Hutton, Will (2010), *Them and Us: Changing Britain – Why We Need a Fair Society*, London: Little Brown.

ICJ (International Commission of Jurists) (1959), *The Rule of Law in a Free Society. A Report on the International Congress of Jurists, New Delhi, India 1959*, Geneva: International Commission of Jurists.

ICJ (International Commission of Jurists) (1965), *The Dynamic Aspects of the Rule of Law in the Modern Age. Report on the Proceedings of the South-East Asian and Pacific Conference of Jurists*, Geneva: International Commission of Jurists.

ICJ (International Commission of Jurists) (1966), *The Rule of Law and Human Rights: Principles and Definitions as Elaborated at the Congresses and Conferences Held Under the Auspices of the International Commission of Jurists, 1955–1966*, Geneva: International Commission of Jurists.

Isiksel, Tŭrkŭler (2012), 'On Europe's functional constitutionalism: towards a constitutional theory of specialized international regimes', *Constellations*, **19** (1), 102–20.

Jayakumar, S. (2009), 'The meaning and importance of the rule of law', reproduced in F. Neate (ed.), *The Rule of Law: Perspectives from Around the Globe*, London: LexisNexis and International Bar Association.

Jayasuriya, Kanishka (1999), 'Introduction: a framework for the analysis of legal institutions in East Asia', in K. Jayasuriya (ed.), *Law, Capitalism and Power in Asia: The Rule of Law and Legal Institutions*, London: Routledge.

Jenkins, Kate and William Plowden (2006), *Governance and Nation-building: The Failure of International Intervention*, Cheltenham, UK and Northampton, MA, USA: Edward Elgar.

Johnson, Paul (1999), 'Laying down the law', in the series The Millennium That Was, *Wall Street Journal*, 10 March, available at http://wwwhsc.usc.edu/~hrkaslow/Governance/MFA/Laying%20Down%20the%20Law.pdf (accessed 13 February 2013).

Johnstone, Ian (2005), 'The power of interpretive communities', in M. Barnett and R. Duvall (eds), *Power in Global Governance*, Cambridge: Cambridge University Press.

Johnstone, Ian (2010), 'Legal deliberation and argumentation in international decision making', in H. Charlesworth and J.-M. Coicaud (eds), *Fault Lines of International Legitimacy*, Cambridge: Cambridge University Press.

Joireman, Sandra F. (2004), 'Colonization and the rule of law: comparing the effectiveness of common law and civil law countries', *Constitutional Political Economy*, **15**, 315–38.

Joseph, Andrew (2012), 'Legitimacy norms as change agents: examining the role of the public voice', in R. Falk, M. Juergensmeyer and V. Popoovoski (eds), *Legality and Legitimacy in Global Affairs*, Oxford University Press.

Jowell, Jeffrey (2004), 'The rule of law today', in J. Jowell and D. Oliver (eds), *The Changing Constitution* (fifth edn), Oxford: Oxford University Press.

Kahler, Miles (2001), 'Conclusion: the causes and consequences of legalisation', in J. Goldstein, M. Kahler, R. Keohane and A.-M. Slaughter (eds), *Legalization and World Politics*, Cambridge, MA: MIT Press.

Kahn, Jeffrey (2008), 'Vladimir Putin and the rule of law in Russia', *Georgia Journal of International and Comparative Law*, **36**, Spring, 511–58.

Kahn, Paul W. (1999), *The Cultural Study of Law: Reconstructing Legal Scholarship*, Chicago, IL: University of Chicago Press.

Kahn, Paul W. (2011), *Political Theology: Four New Chapters on the Concept of Sovereignty*, New York: Columbia University Press.

Kaufman, Ted (2010), 'Another view: a victory for the rule of law', *New York Times*, 16 July, available at http://dealbook.nytimes.com/2010/07/16/another-view-a-victory-for-the-rule-of-law/ (accessed 13 May 2013).

Keck, Margaret and Kathryn Sikkink (1998), *Activists Beyond Borders*, Ithaca, NY: Cornell University Press.

Kelman, Mark (1987), *A Guide to Critical Legal Studies*, Cambridge, MA: Harvard University Press.

Kelsen, Hans (1923), 'Forward to the second printing of main problems in the theory of public law', reprinted in S.L. Paulson and B.L. Paulson (eds) (1998), *Normativity and Norms: Critical Perspectives on Kelsenian Themes*, Oxford: Clarendon Press.

Kelsen, Hans (1945), *General Theory of Law and State*, trans. Anders Wedberg (1999), Clark, NJ: The Lawbook Exchange.

Kelsen, Hans (1982), 'The concept of the legal order', *American Journal of Jurisprudence*, **27**, 64–84.

Kennedy, David (2001), 'The politics of the invisible college: international governance and the politics of expertise', *European Human Rights Law Review*, **5**, 463–97.

Kennedy, David (2004), *The Dark Sides of Virtue: Reassessing International Humanitarianism*, Princeton, NJ: Princeton University Press.

Kennedy, David (2006), 'The "rule of aw," political choices and development common sense', in D.M. Trubek and A. Santos (eds), *The New Law and Economic Development*, Cambridge: Cambridge University Press.

Kettle, Martin (2006), 'We need leaders who better understand the rule of law', *Guardian*, 25 November, 33.

Khagram, Sanjeev, James V. Riker and Kathryn Sikkink (eds) (2002), *Restructuring World Politics: Transnational Social Movements, Networks and Norms*, Minneapolis: University of Minnesota Press.

Khan, Abdullah Freed (2010), 'The Pakistani Lawyers' Movement and the popular currency of judicial power', *Harvard Law Review*, **123** (7), 1705–26.

Kill, Theodore (2011), 'The evidence for constitutionalization of the WTO: revisiting the *Telmex Report*', *Minnesota Journal of International Law*, **20** (1), 65–122.

Klabbers, Jan (2004), 'Constitutionalism lite', *International Organizations Law Review*, **1** (1), 31–58.

Klare, Karl (1979), 'Law making as praxis', *Telos*, **40**, Summer, 124–35.

Kleinfeld, Rachel (2006), 'Competing definitions of the rule of law', in T. Carothers (ed.), *Promoting the Rule of Law Abroad: In Search of Knowledge*, Washington, DC: Carnegie Endowment for International Peace.

Kleinfeld, Rachel (2012), *Advancing the Rule of Law Abroad: Next Generation Reform*, Washington, DC: Carnegie Endowment for International Peace.

Kleinfeld, Rachel and Kalypso Nicolaïdis (2009), 'Can a post-colonial power export the rule of law?', in G. Palombella and N. Walker (eds), *Relocating the Rule of Law*, Oxford: Hart Publishing.

Kornhauser, Lewis A. (1999), 'The normativity of law', *American Law and Economics Review*, **1** (1–2), 3–24.

Koskenniemi, Martti (2005), *From Apology to Utopia: The Structure of International Legal Argument* (Reissue with new epilogue), Cambridge: Cambridge University Press.

Koskenniemi, Martti (2007a), 'The fate of public international law: between technique and politics', *Modern Law Review*, **70** (1), January, 1–30.

Koskenniemi, Martti (2007b), 'Constitutionalism as mindset: reflections on Kantian themes about international law and globalization', *Theoretical Enquires in Law*, **8**, 9–36.

Koskenniemi, Martti (2012), 'Hegemonic regimes', in M.A. Young (ed.), *Regime Interaction in International Law: Facing Fragmentation*, Cambridge: Cambridge University Press.

Kothari, Uma (2005), 'Authority and expertise: the professionalization of international development and the ordering of dissent', in N. Laurie and L. Bondi (eds), *Working the Spaces of Neoliberalism: Activism, Professionalization and Incorporation*, Malden, MA: Blackwell Publishing.

Kramer, Matthew H. (1991), *Legal Theory, Political Theory and Deconstruction: Against Rhadamanthus*, Bloomington, IN: Indiana University Press.

Kratochwil, Friedrich (2009), 'Has the "rule of law" become the "rule of lawyers"?: an inquiry into the use and abuse of an ancient *Topos* in contemporary debates', in G. Palombella and N. Walker (eds), *Relocating the Rule of Law*, Oxford: Hart Publishing.

Krebs, Ronald R. and Patrick Thaddeus Jackson (2007), 'Twisting tongues and twisting arms: the power of political rhetoric', *European Journal of International Relations*, **13** (1), 35–66.

Krever, Tor (2011), 'The legal turn in late development theory: the rule of law and the World Bank's development model', *Harvard International Law Journal*, **52** (1), Winter, 287–319.

Krever, Tor (2013), 'Quantifying law: legal indicator projects and the reproduction of neo-liberal common sense', *Third World Quarterly*, **34** (1), 131–50.

Krisch, Nico (2010), *Beyond Constitutionalism: The Pluralist Structure of Postnational Law*, Oxford: Oxford University Press.

Krisch, Nico (2012), 'The case for pluralism in postnational law', in G. de Búrca and J.H.H. Weiler (eds), *The Worlds of European Constitutionalism*, Cambridge: Cambridge University Press.

Krygier, Martin (1999), 'Institutional optimism, cultural pessimism and the rule of law', in M. Krygier and A. Czarnota (eds), *The Rule of Law after Communism: Problems and Prospects in East-Central Europe*, Aldershot: Ashgate and Dartmouth.

Krygier, Martin (2001), 'Transitional questions about the rule of law: why, what and how?', *East Central Europe*, **28** (1), 1–34.

Krygier, Martin (2004), 'False dichotomies, true perplexities and the rule of law', in A. Sajó (ed.), *Human Rights With Modesty: The Problem of Universalism*, Leiden: Martinus Nijhoff Publishers.

Krygier, Martin (2006), 'The rule of law: an abuser's guide', in A. Sajó (ed.), *Abuse: The Dark Side of Fundamental Rights*, Utrecht: Eleven International Publishing.

Krygier, Martin (2011), 'Approaching the rule of law', in W. Mason (ed.), *The Rule of Law in Afghanistan: Missing in Action*, Cambridge: Cambridge University Press.

Kumm, Mattias (2009), 'The cosmopolitan turn in constitutionalism; on the relationship between constitutionalism in and beyond the state', in J.L. Dunoff and J.P. Trachtman (eds), *Ruling the World? Constitutionalism, International Law and Global Governance*, Cambridge: Cambridge University Press.

Kumm, Mattias (2010), 'The best of times and the worst of times: between constitutional triumphalism and nostalgia', in P. Dobner and M. Loughlin (eds), *The Twilight of Constitutionalism?*, Oxford: Oxford University Press.

Kuran, Timur (2011), *The Long Divergence: How Islamic Law Held Back the Middle East*, Princeton, NJ: Princeton University Press.

Kuo, Ming-Sung (2011), 'Taming governance with legality? Critical reflections upon global administrative law as small-c global constitutionalism', *New York University Journal of International Law and Politics*, **55** (1), 55–102.

Lacey, Nicola (2008), 'Out of the "witches' cauldron"? Reinterpreting the context and re-assessing the significance of the Hart-Fuller debate', LSE Law, Society and Economy Working Papers No. 18/2008, London School of Economics Law Department, London.

Lang, Andrew and Joanne Scott (2009), 'The hidden world of WTO governance', *European Journal of International Law*, **20** (3), 575–614.

Law, David and Mila Versteeg (2011), 'The evolution and ideology of global constitutionalism', *California Law Review*, **99** (5), 1163–257.

Lawrence, Jessica C. (2013), 'Contesting constitutionalism: constitutional discourse at the WTO', *Global Constitutionalism*, **2** (3), March, 63–90.

Lawton, James (2011), 'Rule of law is trampled on to protect "spirit of the game"', *Independent*, 1 August, available at http://www.independent.co.uk/sport/cricket/james-lawton-rule-of-law-is-trampled-on-to-protect-spirit-of-the-game-2329584.html (accessed 13 May 2013).

Lee, Jennifer Kristen (2009), 'Legal reform to advance the rights of women in Afghanistan within the framework of Islam', *Santa Clara Law Review*, **49**, 531–64.

Li, Cheng and Chen Guangcheng (2013), 'China's long march toward the rule of law', *New Perspectives Quarterly*, **30** (2), Spring, 20–3.

Lindvall, Johannes (2009), 'The real but limited influence of expert ideas', *World Politics*, **61** (4), October, 703–30.

Lister, Sarah (2007), 'Understanding state building and local government in Afghanistan', Crisis States Research Centre Working Paper No. 14, London School of Economics, London.

Loughlin, Martin (2000), *Swords and Scales: An Introduction to the Relationship Between Law and Politics*, Oxford: Hart Publishing

Loughlin, Martin (2010), *Foundations of Public Law*, Oxford: Oxford University Press.

Loughlin, Martin (2012), 'What is constitutionalisation?', in P. Dobner and M. Loughlin (eds), *The Twilight of Constitutionalism?*, Oxford: Oxford University Press.

Lukes, Steven (2005), *Power: A Radical View* (second edn), Basingstoke: Palgrave Macmillan.

Lyons, Michal (2013), 'Pro-poor business law? On MKURABITA and the legal empowerment of Tanzania's street vendors', *Hague Journal on the Rule of Law*, **5** (1), 74–95.

MacCormick, Neil (2005), *Rhetoric and the Rule of Law: A Theory of Legal Reasoning*, Oxford: Oxford University Press.

MacCormick, Neil (2007), *Institutions of Law: An Essay in Legal Theory*, Oxford: Oxford University Press.

Macdonald, Keith (1995), *The Sociology of the Professions*, London: Sage Publications.

Magen, Amichai (2009), 'The rule of law and its promotion abroad: three problems of scope', *Stanford Journal of International Law*, **45** (1), 51–115.

Magen, Amichai and Leonardo Morlino (eds) (2009), *International Actors, Democratization and the Rule of Law: Anchoring Democracy?*, London: Routledge.

Magnuson, William (2010), 'WTO jurisprudence and its critiques: the Appellate Body's anti-constitutional resistance', *Harvard International Law Journal – Online*, **51**, June, 121–54.

Marks, Susan (2000), *The Riddle of All Constitutions: International Law, Democracy and the Critique of Ideology*, Oxford: Oxford University Press.

Marmor, Andrei (2004), 'The rule of law and its limits', *Law and Philosophy*, **23** (1), January, 1–43.

Marmor, Andrei (2007), *Law in the Age of Pluralism*, New York: Oxford University Press.

Marmor, Andrei (2010), 'The ideal of the rule of law', in D. Patterson (ed.), *Blackwell Companion to Philosophy of Law and Legal Theory* (second edn), Oxford: Blackwell Publishers.

Marsh, Norman S. (1961), 'The rule of law and as a supra-national concept', in A.G. Guest (ed.), *Oxford Essays in Jurisprudence: A Collaborative Work*, Oxford: Oxford University Press.

Mason, Whit (2011), 'Axioms and unknowns', in W. Mason (ed.), *The Rule of Law in Afghanistan: Missing in Inaction*, Cambridge: Cambridge University Press.

Matsushita, Mitsuo (2012), 'The dispute settlement mechanism at the WTO: the Appellate Body – assessment and problems', in A. Narlikar, M. Daunton and R. Stern (eds), *The Oxford Handbook on the World Trade Organization*, Oxford: Oxford University Press.

Mattei, Ugo (1997), 'Three patterns of law: taxonomy and changes in the world's legal systems', *American Journal of Comparative Law*, **45** (1), Winter, 5–44.

Mattei, Ugo and Laura Nader (2008), *Plunder: When the Rule of Law is Illegal*, Oxford: Blackwell Publishing.

May, Christopher (1996), 'Strange fruit: Susan Strange's theory of structural power in the international political economy', *Global Society*, **10** (2), Spring, 167–89.

May, Christopher (2002), *The Information Society: A Sceptical View*, Cambridge: Polity Press.

May, Christopher (2006), 'The denial of history: reification, intellectual property rights and the lessons of the past', *Capital and Class*, **88**, Spring, 33–56.

May, Christopher (2010), *A Global Political Economy of Intellectual Property Rights: The New Enclosures* (second, revised edn), London: Routledge.

May, Christopher (2011), 'The rule of law: what is it and why is it "constantly on people's lips"?', *Political Studies Review*, **9** (3), September, 357–65.

May, Christopher (2012), 'The rule of law: Athenian antecedents to contemporary debates', *Hague Journal on the Rule of Law*, **4** (2), 235–51.

May, Christopher and Susan Sell (2005), *Intellectual Property Rights: A Critical History*, Boulder, CO: Lynne Rienner.

McAdams, James (ed.) (1997), *Transitional Justice and the Rule of Law in New Democracies*, Notre Dame: University of Notre Dame Press.

McAuliffe, Pádraig (2010), 'Transnational justice and the rule of law: the perfect couple or awkward bedfellows?', *Hague Journal on the Rule of Law*, **2** (2), 127–54.

McAuliffe, Pádraig (2011), 'UN peace-building, transnational justice and the rule of law in East Timor: the limits of institutional responses to political questions', *Netherlands International Law Review*, **58**, 103–35.

McCann, Michael (1998), 'How does law matter for social movements', in B.G. Garth and A. Sarat (eds), *How Does Law Matter?*, Evanston, IL: Northwestern University Press and American Bar Foundation.

McCloskey, Deidre N. (2010), *Bourgeois Dignity: Why Economics Can't Explain the Modern World*, Chicago, IL: University of Chicago Press.

McKenna, Christopher (2006), *The World's Newest Profession: Management Consulting in the Twentieth Century*, Cambridge: Cambridge University Press.

Menon, N.R. Madhava (2008), *Rule of Law in a Free Society*, New Delhi: Oxford University Press.

Merkel, Wolfgang (2012), 'Measuring the quality of rule of law: virtues, perils, results', in M. Zürn, A. Nollkaemper and R. Peerenboom (eds), *Rule of Law Dynamics in an Era of International and Transnational Governance*, Cambridge: Cambridge University Press.

Milhaupt, Curtis J. and Katharina Pistor (2008), *Law and Capitalism: What Corporate Crises Reveal About Legal Systems and Economic Development Around the World*, Chicago, IL: University of Chicago Press.

Minzner, Carl (2013), 'China at the tipping point?: the turn against legal reform', *Journal of Democracy*, **24** (1), January, 65–72.

Mlodinow, Leonard (2008), *The Drunkards Walk: How Randomness Rules Our Lives*, London: Allen Lane.

Møller, Jørgen and Svend-Erik Skaaning (2012), 'Systematizing thin and thick conceptions of the rule of law', *Justice System Journal*, **33** (2), 136–53.

Morgan, Mary S. (2006), 'Economic man as model man: ideal types, idealization and caricatures', *Journal of the History of Economic Thought*, **28** (1), March, 1–27.

Morlino Leonardo and Amichai Magen (2009), 'Scope depth and limits of external influence: conclusions', in A. Magen and L. Morlino (eds), *International Actors, Democratization and the Rule of Law: Anchoring Democracy?*, London: Routledge.

Mortensen, Jens L. (2012), 'Seeing like the WTO: numbers, frames and trade law', *New Political Economy*, **17** (1), February, 77–95.

Moyn, Samuel (2010), *The Last Utopia: Human Rights in History*, Cambridge, MA: Belknap/Harvard University Press.

Murphy, Jeffrie G. (ed.) (1971), *Civil Disobedience and Violence*, Belmont: Wadsworth Publishing.

Nalepa, Monica (2010), *Skeletons in the Closet: Transitional Justice in Post-communist Europe*, Cambridge: Cambridge University Press.

Nardin, Terry (2008), 'Theorising the international rule of law', *Review of International Studies*, **34**, 385–401.

Nardulli, Peter F., Buddy Peyton and Joseph Bajjalieh (2013), 'Conceptualising and measuring rule of law constructs 1850–2010', *Journal of Law and Courts*, **1** (1), March, 139–92.

Neate, Francis (2009), 'Introduction: a brief history of the development of the concept of the Rule of Law', in F. Neate (ed.), *The Rule of Law: Perspectives from Around the Globe*, London: LexisNexis and International Bar Association.

Nelken, David (2001), 'Towards a sociology of legal adaptation', in D. Nelken and J. Feest (eds), *Adapting Legal Cultures*, Oñati International Series in Law and Society, Oxford: Hart Publishing.

Neumann, Franz (1937), 'The change in the function of law in a modern society', reprinted in F. Neumann (1957), *The Democratic and Authoritarian State* (edited and with a preface by Herbert Marcuse), Glencoe, IL: The Free Press.

Ngugi, Joel M. (2005), 'Policing neo-liberal reforms: the rule of law as an enabling and restrictive discourse', *University of Pennsylvania Journal of International Economic Law*, **26** (3), 513–99.

Nicholson, Pip and Sally Low (2013), 'Local accounts of rule of law aid: implications for donors', *Hague Journal on the Rule of Law*, **5** (1), 1–43.

North, Douglass C. (1990), *Institutions, Institutional Change and Economic Performance*, Cambridge: Cambridge University Press.

Nye, John (2008), 'Institutions and the institutional environment', in E. Brousseau and J.-M. Glachant (eds), *New Institutional Economics: A Guidebook*, Cambridge: Cambridge University Press.

Oakeshott, Michael (1983), 'The rule of law', in M. Oakeshott, *On History and Other Essays*, Oxford: Basil Blackwell.

Obarrio Juan (2011), 'Traditional justice as rule of law in Africa: an anthropological perspective', in C.L. Sriram, O. Martin-Ortega and J. Herman (eds), *Peacebuilding and Rule of Law in Africa*, London: Routledge.

Obeng-Odoom, Franklin (2013), 'The mystery of capital or the mystification of capital?', *Review of Social Economy* (advance/pre-press e-publication), 1–16.

Oborne, Peter (2012), 'The rule of law in Britain is diminished by the furore over efforts to deport Abu Qatada to Jordan', *Daily Telegraph*, 8 February, available at http://www.telegraph.co.uk/news/worldnews/al-qaeda/9069184/The-rule-of-law-in-Britain-is-diminished-by-the-furore-over-efforts-to-deport-Abu-Qatada-to-Jordan.html (accessed 13 May 2013).

Olson, Andy (2000), 'An empire of the scholars: transnational lawyers and the rule of opinio juris', *Perspectives on Political Science*, **29** (1), Winter, 23–31.

Onuma, Yasuaki (2012), 'International law and power in the multipolar and multicivilisational world of the twenty-first century', in R. Falk, M. Juergensmeyer and V. Popoovoski (eds), *Legality and Legitimacy in Global Affairs*, Oxford: Oxford University Press.

Otto, Jan Michiel (2009), 'Rule of law promotion, land tenure and poverty alleviation: questioning the assumptions of Hernando de Soto', *Hague Journal on the Rule of Law*, **1** (1), 175–95.

Paasivirta, Esa (2010), 'Can external programs influence internal development of the rule of law? Some observations from the European perspective', *University of Pittsburgh Law Review*, **72**, 217–27.

Pahija, Sundhya (2011), *Decolonising International Law: Development, Economic Growth and the Politics of Universality*, Cambridge: Cambridge University Press.

Park, Susan and Antje Vetterlein (2010), *Owning Development: Creating Policy Norms in the IMF and the World Bank*, Cambridge: Cambridge University Press.

Paterson, Alan (2012), *Lawyers and the Public Good: Democracy in Action?*, Cambridge: Cambridge University Press.

Patterson, Dennis (1996), *Law and Truth*, New York: Oxford University Press.

Paulson, Stanley L. and Bonnie Litschewski Paulson (eds) (1998), *Normativity and Norms: Critical Perspectives on Kelsenian Themes*, Oxford: Clarendon Press.

Paulus, Andreas L. (2009), 'The international legal system as a constitution', in J.L. Dunoff and J.P. Trachtman (eds), *Ruling the World? Constitutionalism, International Law and Global Governance*, Cambridge: Cambridge University Press.

Pauwelyn, Joost (2001), 'The role of public international law in the WTO: how far can we go?', *American Journal of International Law*, **95** (3), July, 535–78.

Pauwelyn, Joost (2003), *Conflict of Norms in Public International Law: How WTO Law Relates to Other Rules of International Law*, Cambridge: Cambridge University Press.

Peerenboom, Randall (2002), 'Let one hundred flowers bloom, one hundred schools contend: debating the rule of law in China', *Michigan Journal of International Law*, **23**, Spring, 472–544.

Peerenboom, Randall (ed.) (2004), *Asian Discourses of Rule of Law: Theories and Implementation of Rule of Law in Twelve Asian Countries, France and the U.S.*, London: Routledge.

Pejovich, Svetozar (2008), *Law, Informal Rules and Economic Performance: The Case for Common Law*, Cheltenham, UK and Northampton, MA, USA: Edward Elgar.

Pek, Jane (2008), 'Things better left unwritten?: constitutional text and the rule of law', *New York University Law Journal*, **83** (6), December, 1979–2012.

Perkin, Harold (1990), *The Rise of Professional Society: England since 1880*, London: Routledge.

Peters, Anne (2009a), 'Dual democracy', in J. Klabbers, A. Peters and G. Ulfstein (eds), *The Constitutionalization of International Law*, Oxford: Oxford University Press.

Peters, Anne (2009b), 'The merits of global constitutionalism', *Indiana Journal of Global Legal Studies*, **16** (2), Summer, 397–411.

Petersman, Hans-Ulrich (2002), 'Constitutionalism and WTO law: from a state-centred approach towards a human rights approach in international economic law', in D.L.M. Kennedy and J.D. Southwick (eds), *The Political Economy of International Trade Law: Essays in Honour of Robert E. Hudec*, Cambridge: Cambridge University Press.

Peterson, Jenny H. (2010), '"Rule of law" initiatives and the liberal peace: the impact of politicised reform in post-conflict states', *Disasters*, **34** (1), S15–S39.

Pierson, Paul (2004), *Politics in Time: History, Institutions and Social Analysis*, Princeton, NJ: Princeton University Press.

Pildes, Richard H. (1996), 'The destruction of social capital through law', *University of Pennsylvania Law Review*, **144** (5), May, 2055–77.

Pimentel, David (2010), 'Rule of law reform without cultural imperialism? Reinforcing customary justice through collateral review in Southern Sudan', *Hague Journal on the Rule of Law*, **2** (1), 1–28.

Pistor, Katharina (2002), 'The standardisation of law and its effect on developing economies', *American Journal of Comparative Law*, **50**, 97–130.

Plant, Raymond (2010), *The Neo-liberal State*, Oxford: Oxford University Press.

Posner, Richard A. (1998), 'Creating a legal framework for economic development', *World Bank Research Observer*, **13** (1), February, 1–11.

Postema, Gerald J. (1994), 'Implicit law', *Law and Philosophy*, **13** (3), August, Special Issue on Lon Fuller, 361–87.

Postema, Gerald J. (2010), 'Law's ethos: reflections on a public practice of illegality', *Boston University Law Review*, **90**, August, 1847–68.

Prado, Mariana Mota (2010), 'The paradox of rule of law reforms: how early reforms can create obstacles to future ones', *University of Toronto Law Journal*, **60** (2), 555–78.

Praet, Patrick (2010), 'Prolegomena to the post-sovereign *Rechtstaat*', in H. Kalmo and Q. Skinner (eds), *Sovereignty in Fragments: The Past, Present and Future of a Contested Concept*, Cambridge: Cambridge University Press.

Prandini, Riccardo (2010), 'The morphogenesis of constitutionalism', in P. Dobner and M. Loughlin (eds), *The Twilight of Constitutionalism?*, Oxford: Oxford University Press.

Preuss, Ulrich K. (2010), 'Disconnecting constitutions from statehood: is global constitutionalism a viable concept?', in P. Dobner and M. Loughlin (eds), *The Twilight of Constitutionalism?*, Oxford: Oxford University Press.

Princeton Project (2006), *Forging a World of Liberty Under Law: U.S. National Security in the 21st Century – Final Report of the Princeton Project on National Security*, Princeton, NJ: Woodrow Wilson School of Public and International Affairs, Princeton University.

Quack, Sigrid (2007), 'Legal professionals and transnational law making: a case of distributed agency', *Organization*, **14** (5), 643–66.

Rajagopal, Balakrishnan (2008), 'Invoking the rule of law in post-conflict rebuilding: a critical examination', *William and Mary Law Review*, **49**, 1347–76.

Rajkovic, Nikolas M. (2010), '"Global law" and governmentality: reconceptualising the "rule of law" as rule "through" law', *European Journal of International Relations*, **18** (1), 29–52.

Rausch, Colette and Vivienne O'Connor (2008), 'Model codes: laying the foundations of the rule of law', in A. Hurwitz and R. Huang (eds), *Civil War and the Rule of Law: Security, Development, Human Rights*, Boulder, CO: Lynne Rienner Publishers.

Raustiala, Kal (2013), 'Institutional proliferation and the international legal order', in J.L. Dunoff and M.A. Pollack (eds), *Interdisciplinary Perspectives on International Law and International Relations: The State of the Art*, Cambridge: Cambridge University Press.

Raz, Joseph (1979a), *The Authority of the Law: Essays on Law and Morality*, Oxford: Clarendon Press.

Raz, Joseph (1979b) 'Civil disobedience', reprinted in H.A. Bedau (ed.) (1991), *Civil Disobedience in Focus*, London: Routledge.

Raz, Joseph (1994), *Ethics in the Public Domain: Essays in the Morality of Law and Politics*, Oxford: Clarendon Press.

Reich, Arie (1997), 'From diplomacy to law: the juridicization of international trade relations', *Northwestern Journal of International Law and Business*, **17**, 759–849.

Reitz, John C. (2003) 'Export of the rule of law', *Transnational Law and Contemporary Problems*, **13**, Fall, 429–86.

Richmond, Oliver (2011), 'The rule of law in liberal peacebuilding', in C.L. Sriram, O. Martin-Ortega and J. Herman (eds), *Peacebuilding and the Rule of Law in Africa*, London: Routledge.

Ringer, Thom (2007), 'Development, reform and the rule of law: some prescriptions for a common understanding of the "rule of law" and its place in development theory and practice', *Yale Human Rights and Development Law Journal*, **10**, 178–208.

Risse, Thomas and Stephen C. Ropp (1999), 'International human rights norms and domestic change: conclusions', in T. Risse, S.C. Ropp and K. Sikkink (eds), *The Power of Human Rights: International Norms and Domestic Change*, Cambridge: Cambridge University Press.

Risse, Thomas and Kathryn Sikkink (1999), 'The socialization of international human rights norms into domestic practices: introduction', in T. Risse, S.C. Ropp and K. Sikkink (eds), *The Power of Human Rights: International Norms and Domestic Change*, Cambridge: Cambridge University Press.

Robinson, William I. (1996), *Promoting Polyarchy: Globalisation, US Intervention and Hegemony*, Cambridge: Cambridge University Press.

Rőder, Tilmann J. (2012), 'Civil-military cooperation in building the rule of law', in M. Zürn, A. Nollkaemper and R. Peerenboom (eds), *Rule of*

*Law Dynamics in an Era of International and Transnational Governance*, Cambridge: Cambridge University Press.

Rodriguez, Daniel B., Matthew D. McCubbins and Barry R. Weingast (2010), 'The rule of law unplugged', *Emory Law Journal*, **59** (6), 1455–94.

Rodrik, Dani, Arvind Subramanian and Francesco Trebbi (2002), 'Institutions rule: the primacy of institutions over geography and integration in economic development', National Bureau of Economic Research Working Paper 9305, NBER, Cambridge.

Rose, Jonathan (2004), 'The rule of law in the Western world: an overview', *Journal of Social Philosophy*, **35** (4), Winter, 457–70.

Saito, Natsu Taylor (2010), *Meeting the Enemy: American Exceptionalism and International Law*, New York: New York University Press.

Sampford, Charles (2006), *Retrospectivity and the Rule of Law*, Oxford: Oxford University Press.

Samuels, Kirsti (2006), *Rule of Law Reform in Post-conflict Countries: Operational Initiatives and Lessons Learnt*, Social Development Papers/ Conflict Prevention and Reconstruction, No. 37, October, Washington, DC: Social Development Department, The World Bank.

Sandholtz, Wayne and Kendall Stiles (2009), *International Norms and Cycles of Change*, Oxford: Oxford University Press.

Sands, Phillipe (2008), *Torture Team: Deception, Cruelty and the Compromise of Law*, London: Allen Lane.

Sannerholm, Richard Zajac (2012a), 'Looking back, moving forward: UN peace operations and rule of law assistance in Africa, 1989–2010', *Hague Journal on the Rule of Law*, **4** (2), 359–73.

Sannerholm, Richard Zajac (2012b), 'Rule of law promotion after conflict: experimenting in the Kosovo laboratory', in M. Zürn, A. Nollkaemper and R. Peerenboom (eds), *Rule of Law Dynamics in an Era of International and Transnational Governance*, Cambridge: Cambridge University Press.

Santos, Alvaro (2006), 'The World Bank's uses of the "rule of law" promise in economic development', in D.M. Trubek and A. Santos (eds), *The New Law and Economic Development*, Cambridge: Cambridge University Press.

Sarles, Margaret J. (2001), 'USAID's support of justice reform in Latin America', in P. Domingo and R. Sieder (eds), *Rule of Law in Latin America: The International Promotion of Judicial Reform*, London: Institute of Latin American Studies.

Sayer, Andrew (2000), 'Moral economy and political economy', *Studies in Political Economy*, **61**, Spring, 79–103.

Sayer, Andrew (2007), 'Moral economy as critique', *New Political Economy*, **12** (2), June, 261–70.

Scharf, Michael P. (2009), 'International law in crisis: a qualitative empirical contribution to the compliance debate', *Cardozo Law Review*, **31** (1), 45–97.

Schauer, Frederick (1989), 'Rules, the rule of law, and the constitution', *Constitutional Commentary*, **6**, 69–85.

Schauer, Frederick (1991), *Playing by the Rules: A Philosophical Examination of Rule-based Decision-making in Law and in Life*, Oxford: Clarendon Press.

Scheingold, Stuart A. (2001), 'Cause lawyering and democracy in transnational perspective: a postscript', in A. Sarat and S. Scheingold (eds), *Cause Lawyering and the State in a Global Era*, Oxford: Oxford University Press.

Schmidt, Vivien A. (2010), 'Taking ideas and discourse seriously: explaining change through discursive institutionalism as the fourth "new institutionalism"', *European Political Science Review*, **2** (1), 1–25.

Schneiderman, David (2008), *Constituting Economic Globalisation: Investment Rules and Democratic Promise*, Cambridge: Cambridge University Press.

Schuck, Peter M. (2000), *The Limits of the Law: Essays on Democratic Governance*, Boulder, CO: Westview Press.

Schwöbel, Christine (2012), 'The appeal of the project of global constitutionalism to public international lawyers', *German Law Journal*, **13** (1), 1–22.

Scott, Shirley V. (2007), 'The political life of public international lawyers: granting the imprimatur', *International Relations*, **21** (4), 411–26.

Scott, Shirley V. and Olivia Ambler (2007), 'Does legality *really* matter? Accounting for the decline in US foreign policy legitimacy following the 2003 invasion of Iraq', *European Journal of International Relations*, **13** (1), 67–87.

Scruton, Roger (2013), 'Identity, family, marriage: our values have been betrayed', *Guardian*, 11 May, 43.

Seabrooke, Leonard (2010), 'Everyday legitimacy and institutional change', in A. Gofas and C. Hay (eds), *The Role of Ideas in Political Analysis: A Portrait of Contemporary Debates*, Abingdon: Routledge.

Selznick, Phillip (1999), 'Legal cultures and the rule of law', in M. Krygier and A. Czarnota (eds), *The Rule of Law After Communism: Problems and Prospects in East-Central Europe*, Aldershot: Ashgate and Dartmouth.

Sen, Amartya (2001), *Development as Freedom*, Oxford: Oxford University Press.

Shaffer, Gregory C. (2009), 'How business shapes law: a socio-legal framework', *Connecticut Law Review*, **42** (1), 147–83.

Sharman, Jason C. (2006), *Havens in a Storm: The Struggle for Global Tax Regulation*, Ithaca, NY: Cornell University Press.

Shen, Yuanyuan (2000), 'Conceptions and receptions of legality: understanding the complexity of law reform in modern China', in K.G. Turner, J.V. Feinerman and R.K. Guy (eds), *The Limits of the Rule of Law in China*, Seattle, WA: University of Washington Press.

Shihata, Ibrahim F.I. (1991a), 'The World Bank and "governance" issues in its borrowing members', in I.F.I. Shihata, *The World Bank in a Changing World: Selected Essays* (compiled and edited by F. Tschofen and A.R. Pawa), Dordrecht: Martinus Nijhoff Publishers.

Shihata, Ibrahim F.I. (1991b), 'The World Bank and private sector development – a legal perspective', in I.F.I. Shihata, *The World Bank in a Changing World: Selected Essays* (compiled and edited by F. Tschofen and A.R. Pawa), Dordrecht: Martinus Nijhoff Publishers.

Shihata, Ibrahim F.I. (1997), 'The role of law in business development', *Fordham International Law Journal*, **20**, 1577–88.

Shivji, Issa G. (2006), 'Lawyers in neoliberalism: authority's professional supplicants or society's amateurish conscience?', *Council for the Development of Social Science Research in Africa (CODESRIA) Bulletin*, **3–4**, 16–25.

Sikkink, Kathryn (2002), 'Transnational advocacy networks and the social construction of legal rules', in Y. Dezalay and B.G. Garth (eds), *Global Prescriptions: The Production, Exportation and Importation of a New Legal Orthodoxy*, Ann Arbor, MI: University of Michigan Press.

Sikkink, Kathryn (2011), *The Justice Cascade: How Human Rights Prosecutions are Changing World Politics*, New York: W.W. Norton & Co.

Silbey, Susan S. (1997), '"Let them eat cake": globalization, postmodern colonialism, and the possibilities of justice – 1996 Presidential Address', *Law and Society Review*, **31** (2), 207–35.

Silverstein, Gordon (2003), 'Globalisation and the rule of law: "a machine that runs of itself"?', *International Journal of Constitutional Law*, **1** (3), 427–45.

Simmonds, Nigel (2007), *Law as a Moral Idea*, Oxford: Oxford University Press.

Singer, Peter (1974), *Democracy and Disobedience*, New York: Oxford University Press.

Skinner, Quentin (2002), 'Moral principles and social change', in Q. Skinner, *Visions of Politics, Volume I: Regarding Method*, Cambridge: Cambridge University Press.

Sklar, Martin J. (1988), *The Corporate Reconstruction of American*

*Capitalism, 1890–1916: The Market, the Law and Politics*, Cambridge: Cambridge University Press.

Slaughter, Anne-Marie (2004), *A New World Order*, Princeton, NJ: Princeton University Press.

Smith, Joshua G., Victoria K. Holt and William J. Durch (2007), *Enhancing United Nations Capacity to Support Post-conflict Policing and Rule of Law*, Washington, DC: The Henry L. Stimson Center.

Smith, William (2010), 'Reclaiming the revolutionary spirit: Arendt on civil disobedience', *European Journal of Political Theory*, **9** (2), 149–66.

Solum, Lawrence B. (1999), 'Indeterminacy', in D. Patterson (ed.), *A Companion to the Philosophy of Law and Legal Theory*, Oxford: Blackwell Publishers.

Spaak, Torben (2005), 'Kelsen and Hart on the normativity of the law', in P. Wahlgren (ed.), *Perspectives on Jurisprudence: Essays in Honor of Jes Bjarup*, Scandinavian Studies in Law, Stockholm: Stockholm Institute for Scandinavian Law.

Spence, Mathew (2006), 'The complexity of success in Russia', in T. Carothers (ed.), *Promoting the Rule of Law Abroad: In Search of Knowledge*, Washington, DC: Carnegie Endowment for International Peace.

Spruyt, Hendrik (1994), *The Sovereign State and its Competitors*, Princeton, NJ: Princeton University Press.

Sriram, Chandra Lekha, Olga Martin-Ortega and Johanna Herman (2011), 'Just peace? Lessons learned and policy insights', in C.L. Sriram, O. Martin-Ortega and J. Herman (eds), *Peacebuilding and Rule of Law in Africa*, London: Routledge.

Starr, Martha (2004), 'Reading *The Economist* on globalisation: knowledge, identity and power', *Global Society*, **18** (4), 373–95.

Starr, Martha (2008), 'Globalisation in popular media and through *The Economist*'s lens: knowledge, representations and power', in D.F. Ruccio (ed.), *Economic Representations: Academic and Everyday*, London: Routledge.

Staton, Jeffery K. (2010), 'A comment on *The Rule of Law Unplugged*', *Emory Law Journal*, **59** (6), 1495–513.

Steger, Manfred B. (2008), *The Rise of the Global Imaginary: Political Ideology from the French Revolution to the Global War on Terror*, Oxford: Oxford University Press.

Stern, Nicholas and Francisco Ferreira (1997), 'The World Bank as "intellectual actor"', in D. Kapur, J.P. Lewis and R. Webb (eds), *The World Bank: Its First Half Century, Vol. Two: Perspectives*, Washington, DC: Brookings Institution Press.

Stewart, Ian (2007), 'From the "rule of law" to "legal state": a time of reincarnation', Paper presented at the Public Law Weekend 9–10 November, Australian National University, Canberra, Macquarie Law Working Paper No. 2007-12, available at http://papers.ssrn.com/sol3/papers.cfm?abstract_id=1056401 (accessed 6 February 2013).

Stiglitz, Joseph E. (2013), *The Price of Inequality*, London: Allen Lane.

Stone, Deborah A. (1989), 'Causal stories and the formation of policy agendas', *Political Science Quarterly*, **14** (2), Summer, 281–300.

Strange, Susan (1988), *States and Markets: An Introduction to International Political Economy*, London: Pinter Publishers.

Stromseth, Jane (2011), 'Justice on the ground? International criminal courts and domestic rule of law building in conflict-affected societies', in J. Flemming (ed.), *Getting to the Rule of Law* (NOMOS L), New York: New York University Press.

Stromseth, Jane, David Wippman and Rosa Brooks (2006), *Can Might Make Rights: Building the Rule of Law After Military Interventions*, Cambridge: Cambridge University Press.

Sugarman, David (1993), 'Simple images and complex realities: English lawyers and their relationship to business and politics, 1750–1950', *Law and History Review*, **11** (2), Autumn, 257–301.

Sugarman, David and Ronnie Warrington (1995), 'Land law, citizenship, and the invention of "Englishness": the strange world of the equity of redemption', in J. Brewer and S. Staves (eds), *Early Modern Conceptions of Property*, London: Routledge.

Summers, Robert S. (1993), 'A formal theory of the rule of law', *Ratio Juris*, **6** (2), July, 127–42.

Suter, Keith (2004), 'The success and limitations of international law and the International Court of Justice', *Medicine, Conflict and Survival*, **20** (4), 344–54.

Swenson, Geoffrey and Eli Sugerman (2011), 'Building the rule of law in Afghanistan: the importance of legal education', *Hague Journal on the Rule of Law*, **3** (1), 130–46.

Taiwo, Olufemi (1999), 'The rule of law: the new Leviathan?', *Canadian Journal of Law and Jurisprudence*, **12** (1), January, 151–68.

Taleb, Nassim Nicholas (2007), *Fooled by Randomness: The Hidden Role of Chance in Life and in the Markets*, London: Penguin.

Tamanaha, Brian Z. (2001), *A General Jurisprudence of Law and Society*, Oxford: Oxford University Press.

Tamanaha, Brian Z. (2004), *On the Rule of Law: History, Politics, Theory*, Cambridge: Cambridge University Press.

Tamanaha, Brian Z. (2011), 'The primacy of society and the failures of law and development', *Cornell International Law Journal*, **44**, 209–47.

Tasikas, Vasilios (2007), 'Developing the rule of law in Afghanistan: the need for a new strategic paradigm', *The Army Lawyer*, July, 45–60.

Taylor, Charles (2004), *Modern Social Imaginaries*, Durham, NC: Duke University Press.

Taylor, Charles (2007), *A Secular Age*, Cambridge, MA: Belknap Press/ Harvard University Press.

Teitel, Ruti G. (2000), *Transitional Justice*, Oxford: Oxford University Press.

Teubner, Gunther (2012), *Constitutional Fragments: Societal Constitutionalism and Globalization*, Oxford: Oxford University Press.

Thakur, Ramesh (2012), 'Law, legitimacy and the United Nations', in R. Falk, M. Juergensmeyer and V. Popoovoski (eds), *Legality and Legitimacy in Global Affairs*, Oxford University Press.

Thompson, E.P. (1975), *Whigs and Hunters. The Origin of the Black Act*, London: Allen Lane.

Thompson, Grahame F. (2012), *The Constitutionalization of the Global Corporate Sphere*, Oxford: Oxford University Press.

Tigar, Michael E. (2000), *Law and the Rise of Capitalism* (new edn, with the assistance of Madeleine R. Levy), New York: Monthly Review Press.

Tilly, James (1995), *Strange Multiplicity: Constitutionalism in an Age of Diversity*, Cambridge: Cambridge University Press.

Tolley, Howard B. Jr (1994), *The International Commission of Jurists: Global Advocates for Human Rights*, Philadelphia: University of Pennsylvania.

Tondini, Matteo (2007), 'Rebuilding the system of justice in Afghanistan: a preliminary assessment', *Journal of Intervention and Statebuilding*, **1** (3), November, 333–54.

Toope, Stephen J. (2003), 'Legal and judicial reform through development assistance: some lessons', *McGill Law Journal*, **48**, 357–413.

Torke, James W. (2001), 'What is this thing called the rule of law', *Indiana Law Review*, **34** (4), 1445–56.

Trebilcock, Michael J. and Ronald J. Daniels (2008), *Rule of Law Reform and Development: Charting the Fragile Path of Progress*, Cheltenham, UK and Northampton, MA, USA: Edward Elgar.

Trebilcock, Michael J. and Marianna Mota Prado (2011), *What Makes Poor Countries Poor? Institutional Determinants of Development*, Cheltenham, UK and Northampton, MA, USA: Edward Elgar.

Troper, Michel (2003), 'The limits of the rule of law', in C. Saunders and K. Le Roy (eds), *The Rule of Law*, Annandale, NSW: The Federation Press.

Trubek, David M. (1972), 'Max Weber on law and the rise of capitalism', *Wisconsin Law Review*, **3**, 720–53.

Trubek, David M. (2006), 'The "rule of law" in development assistance: past, present and future', in D.M. Trubek and A. Santos (eds), *The New Law and Economic Development*, Cambridge: Cambridge University Press.

Tshuma, Lawrence (1999), 'The political economy of the World Bank's legal framework for economic development', *Social and Legal Studies*, **8** (1), March, 75–96.

Tully, James (1995), *Strange Multiplicity: Constitutionalism in an Age of Diversity*, Cambridge: Cambridge University Press.

Turner, Karen (1992), 'Rule of law ideals in early China?', *Journal of Chinese Law*, **6** (1), Spring, 1–44.

Turner, Rachel S. (2008), 'Neo-liberal constitutionalism: ideology, government and the rule of law', *CCSE Journal of Politics and Law*, **1** (2), 47–55.

Twining, William (2009), *Human Rights, Southern Voices – Francis Deng, Abdullahi An-Na'im, Yash Ghai and Upendra Baxi*, Cambridge: Cambridge University Press.

UNGA (United Nation General Assembly) (2012), *Declaration of the High-level Meeting of the General Assembly on the Rule of Law at the National and International Levels*, Document A/67/L1, New York: United Nations.

Unger, Roberto Mangabeira (1976), *Law in Modern Society: Towards a Criticism of Social Theory*, New York: The Free Press.

Upham, Frank (2004), 'The illusory promise of the rule of law', in A. Sajó (ed.), *Human Rights with Modesty: The Problem of Universalism*, Leiden: Martinus Nijhoff Publishers.

Upham, Frank (2009), 'From Demsetz to Deng: speculations on the implications of Chinese growth for law and development theory', *New York University Journal of International Law and Politics*, **41**, Spring, 551–602.

Valcke, Catherine (1994), 'Civil disobedience and the rule of law – a Lockean insight', in I. Shapiro (ed.), *The Rule of Law NOMOS*, Yearbook of the American Society for Political and Legal Philosophy, Vol. XXXVI, New York: New York University Press.

van Caenegem, R.C. (1991), *Legal History: A European Perspective*, London: Hambledon Press.

van Harten, Gus (2007), *Investment Treaty Arbitration and Public Law*, Oxford: Oxford University Press.

van Rooij, Benjamin (2012), 'Bringing justice to the poor, bottom-up legal development cooperation', *Hague Journal on the Rule of Law*, **4** (2), 286–318.

van Waarden, Frans (2009), 'Power to the legal professionals: is there an

Americanisation of European Law?', *Regulation and Governance*, **3**, 197–216.

van Waarden, Frans and Youri Hildebrand (2009), 'From corporatism to lawyocracy? On liberalisation and juridification', *Regulation and Governance*, **3**, 259–86.

van Waeyenberge, Elisa and Ben Fine (2011), 'A knowledge bank?', in K. Bayliss, B. Fine and E. van Waeyenberge (eds), *The Political Economy of Development: The World Bank, Neoliberalism and Development Research*, London: Pluto Press.

Vanberg, Viktor J. (2005), 'Market and state: the perspective of constitutional political economy', *Journal of Institutional Economics*, **1** (1), 23–49.

Vauchez, Antione (2012), 'The force of a weak field: law and lawyers in the government of Europe', in Y. Dezalay and B.G. Garth (eds), *Lawyers and the Construction of Transitional Justice*, Abingdon: Routledge and GlassHouse.

Viola, Francesco (2007), 'The rule of law in legal pluralism', in T. Gizbert-Studnicki and J. Stelmach (eds), *Law and Legal Cultures in the 21st Century: Diversity and Unity*, Warsaw: Oficyna.

Voigt, Stefan (2012), 'How to measure the rule of law', *Kyklos*, **65** (2), May, 262–84.

von Benda-Beckmann, Franz (1989), 'Scape-goat and magic charm: law in development theory and practice', *Journal of Legal Pluralism and Unofficial Law*, **28**, 129–48.

von Benda-Beckmann, Franz (2001), 'Legal pluralism and social justice in economic and political development', *IDS Bulletin*, **32** (1), 46–56.

Wade, Robert (1996), 'Japan, the World Bank and the art of paradigm maintenance: the East Asian miracle in political perspective', *New Left Review*, **1** (217), May–June, 3–36.

Waldron, Jeremy (2002), 'Is the rule of law an essentially contested concept (in Florida)?', *Law and Philosophy*, **21**, 137–64.

Waldron, Jeremy (2004), 'The rule of law as a theater of debate', in J. Burley (ed.), *Dworkin and His Critics with Replies by Dworkin*, Malden, MA: Blackwell Publishing.

Waldron, Jeremy (2008), 'The concept and the rule of law', *Georgia Law Review*, **43** (1), Fall, 1–61.

Waldron, Jeremy (2011), 'Thoughtfulness and the rule of law', *British Academy Review*, **18**, Summer, 1–11.

Walker, Neil (2007), 'Post-constituent constitutionalism? The case of the European Union', in M. Loughlin and N. Walker (eds), *The Paradox of Constitutionalism: Constituent Power and Constitutional Form*, Oxford: Oxford University Press.

Walker, Neil (2009), 'The rule of law and the EU: necessity's mixed virtue', in G. Palombella and N. Walker (eds), *Relocating the Rule of Law*, Oxford: Hart Publishing.

Watson, Alan (1983), 'Legal change: sources of law and legal culture', *University of Pennsylvania Law Review*, **131** (5), April, 1121–57.

Watts, Sir Arthur (1993), 'The international rule of law', *German Yearbook of International Law*, **36**, 15–45.

Weaver, Catherine (2008), *Hypocrisy Trap: The World Bank and the Poverty of Reform*, Princeton, NJ: Princeton University Press.

Weaver, Catherine (2010), 'The meaning of development: constructing the World Bank's good governance agenda', in R. Abdelal, M. Blyth and C. Parsons (eds), *Constructing the International Economy*, Ithaca, NY: Cornell University Press.

Weber, Max (1970), *From Max Weber: Essays in Sociology* (trans., edited and with an introduction by H.H. Gerth and C. Wright Mills), London: Routledge & Kegan Paul.

Weber, Max (1978), *Economy and Society: An Outline of Interpretive Sociology* (edited by G. Roth and C. Wittich), Berkeley, CA: University of California Press.

Weeramantry, Lucian G. (2000), *The International Commission of Jurists: The Pioneering Years*, The Hague: Kluwer Law International.

Weidong, Ji (2008), 'Redefining relations between the rule of law and market clues drawn from four basic issues found in China today', in S. Kashimura and A. Saito (eds), *Horizontal Legal Order: Law and Transaction in Economy and Society*, Singapore: Centre for Legal Dynamics of Advanced Market Societies, Kobe University and LexisNexis.

Weiler, J.H.H. (2000), 'The rule of lawyers and the ethos of diplomats: reflections on the internal and external legitimacy of WTO dispute settlement', Harvard Jean Monnet Working Paper 9/00, Harvard Law School, Cambridge, MA.

West, Robin L. (2003), *Re-imagining Justice: Progressive Interpretations of Formal Equality, Rights and the Rule of Law*, Aldershot: Ashgate Publishing.

Westmoreland, Robert (1998), 'Hayek: the rule of law or the law of rules (book review)', *Law and Philosophy*, **17** (1), 77–109.

Williamson, Oliver E. (1985), *The Economic Institutions of Capitalism*, New York: The Free Press.

Woo-Cummings, Meredith (2003), 'Diverse paths towards "the right institutions": law, the state, and economic reform in East Asia', in L. Weiss (ed.), *State in the Global Economy: Bringing Domestic Institutions Back In*, Cambridge: Cambridge University Press.

World Bank (1996), *From Plan to Market* (World Development Report 1996), Oxford: Oxford University Press and World Bank.

World Bank (1997), *The State in a Changing World* (World Development Report 1997), Oxford: Oxford University Press and World Bank.

World Bank (2002), *Building Institutions for Markets* (World Development Report 2002), Oxford: Oxford University Press and World Bank.

*World Policy Journal* (2011), 'This land is your land: a conversation with Hernando de Soto', *World Policy Journal*, **28** (2), 35–40.

Wüstermann Jens and Sonja Kierzek (2007), 'Transnational legalization of accounting: the case of international financial reporting standards', in C. Brütsch and D. Lehmkhul (eds), *Law and Legalization in Transnational Relations*, Abingdon: Routledge.

Zakaria, Fareed (2003), *The Future of Freedom: Illiberal Democracy at Home and Abroad*, New York: W.W. Norton & Co.

Zangel, Bernhard (2005), 'Is there an emerging international rule of law?', *European Review*, **13**, Supplementary Issue, The Rule of Law: Internationalisation and Privatization, 73–91.

Zywicki, Todd J. (2003), 'The rule of law, freedom and prosperity', *Supreme Court Economic Review*, **10**, 1–26.

# Name index

# Subject index